OPENING
TO INNER LIGHT

Also by Ralph Metzner

Maps of Consciousness
Know Your Type: Maps of Identity
The Ecstatic Adventure, editor
The Psychedelic Experience, with Timothy Leary and Richard Alpert

Opening to Inner Light

THE TRANSFORMATION OF HUMAN NATURE AND CONSCIOUSNESS

Ralph Metzner

JEREMY P. TARCHER, INC.
Los Angeles
Distributed by St. Martin's Press
New York

Library of Congress Cataloging-in-Publication Data
Metzner, Ralph.
    Opening to inner light.
    Bibliography: p.
    Includes index.
    1. Spiritual life.   I. Title.
BL624.M47 1986   155.2'5   85-9757
ISBN 0-87477-353-9
ISBN 0-87477-354-7 (pbk.)

    Jeremy P. Tarcher, Inc.
    9110 Sunset Blvd.
    Los Angeles, CA 90069

Design by Mike Yazzolino

Manufactured in the United States of America
10 9 8 7 6 5 4 3 2 1

First Edition

I dedicate this book to my son Ari Krishna Metzner, who was born in 1966 and died of an accident in 1974. During its most intensely transformative phase, he graced my life with his joyous and exuberant spirit.

Contents

Preface

This book will describe the processes of human evolutionary transformation as they are actually experienced by individuals. I hope that these descriptions might prove useful to those who are just beginning a transformational phase in their lives and also to those who find themselves in the midst of one and are, perhaps, searching for signposts and conceptual tools. It is said that human transformation was the only miracle the Buddha recognized as such.

A central thesis of this work is that metaphors, symbols, and analogies are essential in describing the process. Further, they function to stimulate and catalyze these inner transformations. I suggest—and hope—that the reading of this book could, in itself, facilitate the kinds of changes it describes. It would please me greatly if the reader were to find the images and metaphors as personally helpful as I have found them.

My experience in writing this book was itself transformative, as each of the metaphors I was writing about triggered corresponding inner experiences. For example, when first writing about the progression from fragmentation to wholeness, I felt extremely scattered; describing the imprisonment-to-liberation metaphor, I frequently experienced being "stuck" or "caught."

Several years ago I first began to realize that whereas there are literally hundreds of specific methods of bringing about psychospiritual transformation (methods of yoga and psychotherapy in particular), there appear to be only about a dozen or so key metaphors describing the process itself that occur over and over in the world's literature. I first presented this idea at the annual conference of the International Transpersonal Association in Boston in 1979. I wanted to demonstrate that, with some variations in language and in emphasis, the essential human process of evolutionary growth is described in similar terms in all major cultures and sacred traditions all over the world.

If it were possible to demonstrate this, it seems to me that this would be a small contribution to the unification of the consciousness of humanity. By elucidating these underlying structures, which have been variously referred to as archetypes, or deep structures, or primordial images, we are uncovering something of humanity's common language. The language of symbols is the universal common language, the language that we all understood before there was the "confusion of tongues." It is the language we still use and understand: in dreams, in poetry and art, in the visions and voices that tell us of nonordinary realities, of the sacred, of the mystery.

To bring out this common underlying language, the book draws on the writings of Eastern and Western mysticism, comparative mythology, literature and poetry, the writings of philosophers and teachers in the esoteric, shamanic, yogic, and hermetic traditions, and the formulations of modern depth psychotherapy, anthropology, and transpersonal psychology. I am reaching beyond psychology, the field in which I was formally trained, in order to illustrate and understand the patterns and metaphors of transformation, and I have probably made mistakes, omissions, and questionable assumptions in the process. I beg the indulgence of scholars and experts in these areas for my transdisciplinary temerity, and would appreciate having my errors corrected.

The experience of self-transformation apparently has similar basic features, regardless of historical period or cultural background. Thus, personal accounts of such experiences, drawn from published anthologies and from my own files of patients, clients, and students, are also cited as examples. They often reveal the same metaphoric deep structures as are found in the ancient texts. Based on this admittedly nonstatistical research, I feel confident in saying that very many transformation experiences do in fact occur as the metaphors of this book suggest. A number of the experiential accounts given are my own, and the aptness of the metaphors has been validated personally, as well as through the testimony of many individuals known to me.

It is probably neither necessary nor desirable to read this book in sequence. Instead, I recommend reading the introduction for a theoretical overview, then choosing a chapter on a metaphor that resonates strongly with you—letting that resonance be amplified through attention and imagination. As R. M. Rilke said, "Within us alone can this intimate and constant transformation of the visible into the invisible take place."

Two disclaimers and their associated assumptions are appropriate here. First, this book does not deal with social or collective transformation, although this is a vast and complex question of burning interest to many. My own feeling is that individual transformation is an essential aspect of—even a prerequisite to —changes at the familial, organizational, societal, and global levels. While it is important to work on all of these levels simultaneously, preliminary observation suggests to me that positive transformation in groups, organizations, societies, and on the whole planet, is a function of the number of individuals who are consciously attempting to evolve and transform themselves. It appears natural for individuals, after having liberated their own minds to some degree, to want to share their insights with others, and apply them in social relationships.

The second self-imposed limitation of this work is that it does not delineate linear developmental models showing sequences of stages of evolution. This is not to say that development does not proceed in stages—only that agreement on mapping these stages seems quite elusive. Much of the literature on evolutionary stages seems to me to be overly abstract, highly subjective, and sometimes indicative of a kind of premature conceptual crystallization. Subtle judgments of spiritual superiority seem to slip too easily into discussions of levels and stages.

Perhaps it is only a matter of personality type, or cognitive style. That I prefer a pluralistic model, of the transformation experience, with emphasis on the fluid processes of change, in their manifold variety and individual uniqueness. Others lean to a more uniform model, with emphasis on hierarchical structures, with levels and stages clearly defined and outlined. Each approach certainly has its value.

There are so many people to whom I wish to acknowledge my indebtedness, that I will list them in three groups. First, there are those (twentieth-century) individuals whose writings or art have inspired me and taught me a great deal: C. G. Jung, Sigmund Freud, Wilhelm Reich, Mircea Eliade, Sri Aurobindo, Joseph Campbell, A. K. Coomaraswamy, Aldous Huxley, Buckminster Fuller, G. I. Gurdjieff, P. D. Ouspensky, Alice Bailey, William James, Evelyn Underhill, Pierre Teilhard de Chardin, Erich Neumann, Gregory Bateson, Marie-Louise von Franz, Edward Edinger, Carlos Castaneda, Jane Roberts, Walter Russell, R. Gordon Wasson, Rudolf Steiner, William Irwin Thompson, Robert Bly, Herman Hesse, W. B. Yeats, T. S. Eliot—as well as the many writers and philosophers of previous centuries whose words and ideas are cited in these pages.

The second group consists of those individuals whose writings or artwork have influenced me and whom I have also had the honor and good fortune to interact with and count as friends: Alan Watts, Huston Smith, Stanislav and Christina Grof, Arthur Young, Frank Barr, Marilyn Ferguson, Andrew Weil, June Singer, Timothy Leary, Richard Alpert (Ram Dass), Michael Harner, R. D. Laing, Rolf von Eckartsberg, Jill Purce, Ken Wilber, Susan Boulet, Rowena Pattee, Charles Tart, Stanley Krippner, John Perry, John and Toni Lilly, Rupert Sheldrake, Lama Govinda, Terence McKenna, Frances Vaughan, Roger Walsh, Charles Muses, Alexander Shulgin, Michael Murphy, Willis Harman, Will Schutz, Frank Barron, Claudio Naranjo, Paul Winter, and my teacher of Agni yoga, Russell Schofield.

The third group I wish to acknowledge are colleagues and friends whose counsel and assistance in the exploration and communication of these ideas has been most valuable. They are: Salvador Arrien, Angeles Arrien, Shyam Bhatnagar, Hugh Redmond, Ann Armstrong, Patricia Thurber, Elias and Isa Velonis, Jeremy Tarcher, James and Dorothy Fadiman, Bob Boyll, Padma Catell, Gunther Weil, Paul Lee, Cecil Burney, Marilee Stark, Elizabeth Campbell, Jack Downing, Leo Zeff, Michael Flanagin, Alan Levin, John Enright, George Greer, Robert Fuller, Michael and Justine Toms, Sandra Lewis, John Prendergast, Michael Kahn, David Surrenda, Ray Vespe, Dominie Cappadonna, Richard Baker, and Seymour and Sylvia Boorstein. In addition, there are many others— teachers, colleagues, and students at the California Institute of Integral Studies —from whom I have learned a great deal over the past ten years.

PREFACE

To all of these and to many unnamed others—students, clients, friends, and colleagues—Aquarian conspirators, coevolutionists, travelers, seekers all—I express my gratitude for their help and my appreciation for the uniquely beautiful contribution each one is making to the miraculously unfolding destiny of twentieth-century humankind.

Introduction: From Caterpillar to Butterfly

What the caterpillar calls the end of the world, the rest of the world calls butterfly.

—RICHARD BACH

Our experience confirms what the elders and wise ones of all times have said —that we live in a constant state of change. Modern science tells us the world consists of patterns of unceasing transformation of energy and matter. We observe these changes in ourselves and in those we know and care for: changes of physical growth, the learning of muscular skills, emotional development, acquisition of knowledge, conformance to the changing expectations of our culture, becoming ill, becoming healed. We grow up . . . we grow old . . . but we always grow. Our lives appear to unfold in multiple interweavings of cycles of change at many levels, punctuated by discontinuous transitions. We see certain of these basic transitions—marriage and divorce, illness and accidents, births and deaths—as "life-changing" events.

In addition to such changes, which are natural and ordinary, in the sense that they are an accepted part of life, there exists in human experience another kind of transformation, a radical restructuring of the entire psyche that has been variously referred to as *mystical experience, ecstasy, cosmic consciousness, oceanic feeling, oneness, transcendence, union with God, nirvana, satori, liberation, peak experience,* and other names. Such experiences may occur in some people without their recognizing much of what is really happening and just how extraordinary this process is.

We have evidence that the prevalence of this kind of experience may be greatly underestimated. Andrew Greeley and William McCready reported in the *New York Times* on a survey they made with a sample of fifteen hundred "normal," middle-class Americans.[1] Forty percent of the respondents answered affirmatively to the question "Have you ever had the feeling of being very close to a powerful spiritual force that seemed to lift you out of yourself?" This finding prompted the researchers to title their article, "Are We a Nation of Mystics?" People who have these kinds of experiences may not know what they are or how

1

to talk about them, but they agree that the experience is powerful, sometimes devastating, and invariably life transforming.

There are many thoughtful people who believe that our time is one of accelerated social and individual transformation. Fundamental world views, paradigms of reality, conceptions of human nature are being questioned and challenged.[2] There are even suggestions from some observers that humanity as a whole species is undergoing a collective transformation. We have no precedent in our experience for this kind of evolutionary change. We are being challenged to examine our understanding of evolution itself.[3]

And that is not all. Albert Einstein remarked, "The atomic bomb has changed everything except our way of thinking." In a world teetering on the brink of nuclear holocaust, economic collapse, and ecological catastrophe, we are being challenged to examine ourselves. We feel we have to ask ourselves, "What are we?" after all, to have arrived at such an insanely dangerous impasse. It seems to me that two important conclusions are emerging with increasing certainty: (1) that the evolutionary transformation of society and of humanity must take place first in the individual, and (2) that the transformation of the individual requires a turning inward, toward self—not in narcissistic self-absorption but in aware self-confrontation.

What can we say, in psychological terms, about this kind of profound transformation in which so many find themselves involved with varying degrees of urgency and intensity? I would agree with those who speak of this transformation in terms of "consciousness." *Consciousness*—defined as the context, or field, in which thoughts, feelings, perceptions, sensations, images, impulses, intentions, and the like, exist and occur—is transformed when any of the following occur: changes in thinking, worldview, beliefs; feelings, motives, impulses, values; as well as altered perceptions, such as heightened seeing *(clairvoyance)* and sensing *(clairsentience)*.

A further characteristic of this transformation of consciousness is the alteration of perception of time and space. When time seems to pass at a different rate and when the space around us seems different and unfamiliar, we sometimes experience a giddy or fearful recognition that we are in a process of change, with an unpredictable outcome: we know we are going to be different, but we don't know how.

When our very concept of reality and our self-concept change, we speak of personal, or self, transformation. This kind of experience changes the way we feel about the world—our emotional attitude of basic trust or mistrust, faith or doubt, acceptance or rejection—and changes our feelings about ourselves, our self-acceptance, self-esteem, self-love.

Whatever our definition of personality or of self may be, it is clear that as self-concepts, self-feelings, and self-images change, the personality changes, too. We feel and sense ourselves to be different persons. Without entering at this point into the debates over whether the ego should be annihilated (as in many spiritual traditions) or strengthened (as in Western psychotherapy), we can agree, I believe, that the ego or its function, role, and place is changed.

This book explores the meanings of human self-transformation. Other expressions signifying this realm of human experience agree in their assignment of a pivotal role to the self-concept. *Self-actualization,* a term used in humanistic and existential psychology, implies a bringing into actuality of something that had been a latent potentiality. The term *self-realization* suggests a making real, or a seeing as real, something that had been until then only a dream or a vague intuition. Jung's term *individuation* means (a) becoming an individual distinct from the mass consciousness, and (b) becoming "indivisible," or whole.

Although the self-concept, or self-image, plays a pivotal role in most accounts of psychospiritual transformation, it is not a necessary one. Buddhist psychology, which does not recognize the existence of any self or ego, explains the transformation simply as an altered mode of functioning of the five "complex aggregates" *(skandhas)* of consciousness. These aggregates, or systems—memory, perception, feeling/valuing, form awareness, conscious comprehension—together constitute what we think of as personality. In the process of transformation, their functions and aims are radically changed.[4]

There are two other aspects of individual identity, of persona or selfhood, that may be affected in the kind of core transformation we have been discussing; they are behavior and appearance. Whether a person's actual *behavior* changes as a result of a deep transformative experience is an open question; obviously, it depends on the individual's prior behavior. We know of extreme cases, such as that of Saul, who became Paul and changed from an enemy to a defender of the faith. Criminals have been known to become saints. Others may, after a transcendent vision, simply find themselves confirmed in their life path and their spiritual practice, with no outwardly observable change in behavior. After enlightenment, the Zen masters said, you may go back to cutting wood and drawing water.

Bodily appearance also may or may not be altered when consciousness and self are transformed. The traditions of yoga, alchemy, and shamanism contain numerous examples of *psychophysical* transformation. In illness and healing recovery, physical form and appearance may change drastically. Anyone who has undergone the "remission" of a malignant tumor, spontaneously or as a result of psychic healing, has brought about a kind of alchemical transformation of the physical elements of the body. Michael Murphy and his associates have accumulated a large body of documentation and evidence of unusual psychophysical changes occuring in sports and other situations involving extreme physical challenge.[5]

Attempts at describing the process of transformation of consciousness and personality in abstract, psychological language are comparatively recent. In prior periods—in the religious and mystical literature of East and West, in the traditions of shamanism, alchemy, and yoga, and in the allegorical language of mythology—symbols and metaphors are used to convey essential information and guidelines for those who find themselves plunged into the midst of a transformative crisis, and those who are pursuing a disciplined path of development. People have often found that it is helpful to turn to the old texts and stories for guidance and insight into the process they are undergoing. Historical accounts and images from other cultures often evoke a kind of echo or resonance in us. Maybe this is a recognition of our common humanity; or some feel that we may be experiencing traces of "another life."

Through the work of Freud, Jung, and the other depth psychologists and students of comparative mythology and religion, it has become apparent that myths still function as they did in the eras before psychological theories were invented: myths seem to articulate certain deep, archetypal patterns of growth. While Freud proposed that all men live out the Oedipus myth, modern psychologists agree that there are many different myths that men and women have found themselves living, without realizing it. From the discovery of such deep, mythic undertones in one's life, and the unsuspected level of meaning that is revealed, comes support for healing and the self-reflection that leads to understanding.

Symbols and Metaphors of Transformation

In virtually all the traditional systems of human transformation, symbols, metaphors, analogies, parables, myths, and allegories play a central role. This is true of the modern psychological, especially transpersonal, approaches, as well as the traditional religious, mystical, and esoteric ways. In shamanism, for example, the altered state of consciousness, or trance, which the shaman healer undergoes, is symbolized as a journey or a flight through the air. And modern explorers of consciousness, whether using psychedelic drugs or not, have created the language of "the trip" or of "being high." Similarly, alchemy uses the description of chemical processes going on in a retort, as analogies or metaphors for experimental processes going on in the psychophysical (body-mind) system of the practitioner. Psychotherapists, especially those of a Jungian persuasion, frequently hear dreams with alchemical themes, such as purification or sublimation, from their patients who are in the midst of a transformation. We need only recall the yogic images of energy centers as flowers that unfold, or the idea of the *kundalini* serpent that rises, to realize how extensive is the use of analogy and symbolism in these traditions. Some modern psychiatrists suggest the existence of a "kundalini syndrome," occurring in some yoga practitioners, in which serpentine energy currents surge uncontrollably through the body, and bring about a major transformation of consciousness.

We might usefully compare the central transformative metaphors used by three of the pioneers of modern depth psychology, Sigmund Freud, Wilhelm

Reich, and C. G. Jung. For Freud, the unconscious was a deep and dangerous unknown, like the ocean; and psychoanalysis—making the unconscious conscious —was like reclaiming land from the sea, as practiced in Holland. In Reich's theory, repressed unconscious factors have become assembled into a kind of invisible armor, impacted into the tissues of the body, especially the musculature; bioenergetic therapy aims at the melting, or dissolving, of this armor. In Jung's view, the unconscious, both personal and collective, is like the night sky, an infinite unknown, studded with myriads of tiny sparks of light that can become the sources of illumination, insight, and creativity for the person in the process of individuation.[6]

Consciousness itself has been thought of in terms of two analogies. One is as a kind of space, as in Buddhist notions of "emptiness," or in such expressions as "state of consciousness," or context, or field. The other analogy is that of a river, as in the expressions "stream of consciousness" and "stream of thought." We have, then, a geographical metaphor and a historical one, which correspond to the two main dimensions of our experience of reality—space and time.

In literature and mythology, which may be regarded as the repositories of psychological teachings before there was a separate discipline of psychology (i.e., prior to the late nineteenth century), we find two widely used analogies for the human life cycle: the cycle of the day and that of the year. In the diurnal analogy, we think of birth and youth as the sunrise and morning, adulthood as midday, maturity as the afternoon, and aging as the evening of our days. In the seasonal metaphor, we speak of the springtime of our youth, the summer of full adult power and expression, the autumnal maturity of our capacities through midlife, and the "winter of our discontent," of aging and dying.

As these examples make clear, the use of metaphor and symbolism spreads far beyond the realm of literature and the arts. It appears to be such a pervasive characteristic of human language that it may even be regarded as a built-in feature of all human thinking. George Lakoff and Mark Johnson, in a book entitled *Metaphors We Live By,* have made just this point.[7] Adducing evidence from linguistics and philosophy, they show how our ordinary conceptual system— which governs how we think, how we talk, and how we act, both consciously and unconsciously—is fundamentally metaphorical in nature. For example, an unconsciously held, or implicit, metaphor in our culture is the idea that money is liquid, as expressed by "cash flow" and "liquid assets."

Lakoff and Johnson argue that surely the implicit metaphors of ordinary language have an experiential basis. There is, among others, an interesting group of metaphors they call orientational, which are based on our experience of the up/down dimension of space. We relate this dimension to feelings of happiness ("my spirits rose," "I feel down"), consciousness ("waking up," "falling asleep"), health and life ("he's at the peak of health," "he dropped dead"), control and power ("the height of power," "being under control"), status ("high society"), time ("upcoming events") and moral and other kinds of evaluation ("high-quality work," "high-mindedness," "low character," "the depths of depravity"). Some of these metaphors we shall encounter again as we discuss the processes of consciousness transformation. Most models of psychospiritual development, for instance, use metaphors of an upward progression—"raising one's level of consciousness," "bringing an unconscious complex up into awareness," "climbing to the top of the holy, or mystical, mountain," "ascending the ladder of evolution, or the ladder of perfection"—and many more.

A useful distinction can be drawn between symbol and metaphor. In this book *symbol* is more likely to be an object or thing; whereas *metaphor* stands for a process that extends through time. Thus, the tree is a symbol of the human being, standing vertically between heaven and earth, linking the upper world of Spirit and the lower worlds of Nature. On the other hand, the growth of a tree from seed to flowering maturity is a metaphor for the growth of the individual, the unfolding of a human's life from seed-conception to full creative expression. The path, or road, is a symbol of development of consciousness; traveling on the road is a metaphor for the process of expanding the horizons of awareness.

The word *symbol* comes from the Greek roots *sym* ("together") and *ballein* ("to throw"). Thus, a symbol is a throwing together, a linkage, connecting two disparate elements in our psyche. The word *metaphor* comes from the Greek roots *meta* ("beyond") and *pherein* ("to carry"). Thus, it is a carrying beyond, a transferring of meaning from one domain into another. *Analogy* comes from the Greek *analogos* ("proportionate"), which in turn is based on *ana* ("according to") and *legein* ("to collect" and "to speak"). Thus, by analogy we can gather (understand) and speak of, a similarity in proportion. A clock is a good example of an analog device: it shows the same proportions and relationships as the passage of the sun in relationship to the horizon.

In the writings of the mystics we find detailed and comprehensive descriptions of experiences of transformation, couched in the metaphors and symbols of the particular religion that the mystic adhered to. Transcending the boundaries of culture and religion in their visions and their writings, mystics are pioneers of evolution, reporting back to the rest of humanity on what lies ahead for all of us. As Evelyn Underhill writes in her masterful book *Mysticism,* "The mystic cannot wholly do without symbol and image, inadequate to his vision though they must always be: for his experience must be expressed if it is to be communicated, and its actuality is inexpressible except in some hint or parallel which will stimulate the dormant intuition of the reader."[8] The Jesus of the New Testament used parables constantly, as we know. The phrase "The Kingdom of Heaven is like . . . ," which runs like a golden thread through the gospel narrative, is considered by some to tell the story of a transformation of consciousness from human to divine, from personal to transpersonal.

Likewise, myths, legends, and folktales are important sources of transformational metaphors and symbols. They often contain metaphoric accounts of transformative experiences. They are like the stories told by explorers to future, would-be voyagers, describing in symbolic form major features of the interior landscapes traversed by the consciousness voyager. Sometimes in a cautionary mode, sometimes in an inspirational mode, they allude metaphorically to the interior conflicts to be resolved, hardships to be endured, obstacles to be overcome, rewards to be won, tools to be used, allies to be found, visions to be seen.[9]

Symbols and metaphors, then, function in the psyche as connecting links between states and levels of consciousness, bridging between domains of reality. They serve to elucidate the structures and functions of consciousness while we are undergoing both ordinary and extraordinary transformations. Many of the deepest, most powerful archetypal symbols are not necessarily articulated verbally. They may be numbers, shapes, colors, natural phenomena, plants, or animals, and they may be expressed in a great variety of cultural forms, including painting, sculpture, architecture, song, dance, ritual, movement, gesture. These primordial, or archetypal, images are found in virtually all cultures and during all ages, thus representing a kind of universal language.[10]

Another, most important function of symbols is their ability to induce or catalyze changes in our perception, feeling, or thinking. For example, a Buddhist monk meditating on a symbolic figure will experience specific definite changes in his consciousness, intentionally induced or facilitated by that symbolic image. In Jungian psychotherapy the patient is often encouraged, in a process known as "active imagination," to extend and develop the meaning associations of the image encountered in a dream. Jung repeatedly emphasized the active, dynamic nature of symbols and their ability to work within us—even on us—without our conscious recognition.

While Freud postulated that the symbols in the unconscious functioned primarily to conceal the impulses and conflicts that they symbolized, for Jung the symbol was a bridge between conscious and unconscious, an element that "points beyond itself to a meaning that is darkly divined yet still beyond our grasp." Religious symbols in particular, according to Jung, have a distinctly revelatory and transformative character. "Even today we can see in individuals the spontaneous genesis of genuine and valid religious symbols, springing from the unconscious like flowers of a strange species, while consciousness stands by perplexed."[11] Jung is referring here to the dynamic, spontaneous activity of symbols in the psyche, an activity that brings symbolic visions to people in dreams, meditations, and other such states of consciousness. Such visions always "just come," they are not "made up," and they may surprise the individual in whom they arise.

The following chapters present ten key metaphors that are found in most of the world's great spiritual and philosophical traditions. Mystics, hermits, monks, yogis, saints, sages, magicians, shamans, physicians, wizards, teachers, warriors, scholars, artists, poets, philosophers, scientists, psychologists—all of those who have functioned as way-showers on the evolutionary path—have found these metaphors and symbols indispensable for describing their experience, for awakening intuition and for catalyzing transformation.

I invite the reader then to explore these central metaphors. A particular metaphor may trigger a memory of a deeply moving transformative experience the reader has had. Another may point dimly to some totally new, as yet unknown yet subtly sensed dimension of experience. There is no preestablished sequence, no predetermined goal. Each one finds his own path, each works out her own destiny. The myth of each life is a unique configuration of elements.

While it is widely believed and asserted that "all roads lead to the same mountaintop," I find this to be an oversimplified and misleading analogy. I prefer the ancient symbolism of humans as radiating sources of light, as "walking stars" treading the Earth path; or the image of giant trees rooted in the Earth, with crown and branches reaching to the heavens; or that of caterpillars dimly sensing their potential as scintillating, liberated butterflies. The exploration of the psyche, of inner space, seems to me very analogous to the exploration of outer space: one can go in all directions for an infinite distance and length of time. As Buckminster Fuller pointed out, each individual exists at the center of a movable sphere of omnidirectional awareness, that moves, like a shadow, everywhere we move.[12]

The process of sharing these inexpressible experiences of transformation may bring us to a greater awareness of our interdependent, common humanity: whether we speak of union with God, or with the Tao, or of cosmic consciousness, or of wholeness, there is a common core here in all of us; we are one in this—and further, we are interconnected with the natural world and the cosmos in which we live. Everything is then seen as metaphor: reality itself throws symbols at us with abundance of meaning. We seem to be designed for comprehension and communication of meaning.

The phenomenal world is a mirror reflection of a basic ground reality unknowable by us, according to the ancient Indian sages. "All phenomena," said Goethe, "are merely metaphorical" ("Alles Vergaengliche ist nur ein Gleichnis"). Or, as Gregory Bateson stated it, mind is metaphorical, and mind is "the pattern that connects." In this kind of vision, we are "carried across" metaphorically, across boundaries of culture, of historical era, of race and language. We find linkages, from self to world, from world to world, and from self to other selves.

Theories of Human Transformation

It may be useful to take a brief look at some of the theoretical approaches to the understanding of transformation that have been proposed by historians of religion, philosophers, evolutionary theorists, and psychologists. These theories, as we shall see, have often resorted to the same symbols, metaphors, and images we find in the accounts of the mystics and in the myths of ancient peoples, to explain their perspectives on transformation. Each of these theories and each of the metaphors contribute a valuable thread to the tapestry of our understanding.

William James, in his work on religious experience, used the classic concept of *conversion,* literally a "turning around," to describe not only a person's change from one religion to another, but also the process of attaining a sense of the religious dimension of life, a sense of the sacred. "To be converted, to be regenerated, to receive grace, to experience religion, to gain an assurance, are so many phrases which denote the process, gradual or sudden, by which a self hitherto divided, and consciously wrong, inferior and unhappy, becomes unified and consciously right, superior and happy, in consequence of its firmer hold upon religious realities."[13] Religious conversion then is one form that a transformative experience might take for contemporary men and women. The metaphors of awakening and of progressing from fragmentation to wholeness are related to this conversion model of transformation.

The historian of religion Mircea Eliade has emphasized the importance of the *discovery of the sacred.* This does not necessarily imply belief in God or gods or spirits; rather, awareness of the sacred is inherent in man's mode of being in the world. "Through experience of the sacred the mind grasps the difference between what is revealed as real, potent, rich, and meaningful and that which is deficient in those qualities—in other words, the chaotic and perilous flux of things, their fortuitous and meaningless appearances and disappearances."[14] This kind of experience of a sacred quality of the world, of all life, and of our life in particular is often a significant element in the transformative experience of modern individuals, even those of an atheistic or agnostic orientation. The metaphor of uncovering the veils of illusion to discover the real is felt to be a particularly appropriate one for this kind of experience. A person may echo the words of that wonderful spiritual "Amazing Grace," "I was blind and now I see."

The language of *mysticism* speaks of the human transformation most directly; and in a way that is not particularly bound to a specific set of religious beliefs concerning the nature of God or divinity. Mysticism refers to an experience of which one cannot speak (it comes from the Greek *muein,* "to keep silent"). As William James wrote: "We pass into mystical states out of ordinary consciousness as from a lesser into a more, as from a smallness into a vastness, and at the same time as from an unrest to a rest. We feel them as reconciling, unifying states." And Evelyn Underhill speaks of mysticism as "an organic process which . . . involves the achievement here and now of the immortal heritage of man . . . the art of establishing his conscious relation with the Absolute."[15] The mystical literature of East and West provides lucid and detailed accounts of the phenomenology of transformative experiences. Mystics try to show us the ineffable, to point to visions of reality inexpressible in ordinary terms. They are the butterflies who try to awaken the human larval caterpillars to the "immortal heritage" that awaits them.

Many writers have outlined *stages of the mystic path.* Underhill states that in Christian mysticism the stages are (1) awakening or conversion to divine reality; (2) purgation and purification; (3) illumination, visions, ecstatic states; (4) death, "the dark night of the soul"; and (5) union with the divine. The teachings of the Gnostics distinguished three stages: (1) awakening, (2) revelation, and (3) anamnesis, or recollection. There are also many other models that outline a developmental sequence of stages in transformation. Each of these stages is associated with a metaphor, and without prejudging whether these experiences always occur exactly in this order, we will examine these metaphors.

Another concept that recurs again and again in this literature is *rebirth* and regeneration. The so-called mystery religions of ancient times preserved secret teachings of rebirth and expressed them by staging them in ceremonies and rituals. Some native cultures in various parts of the Earth still practice ancient rituals of rebirth and regeneration. As Jung pointed out in his essay "Concerning Rebirth," much of this literature is concerned with beliefs about reincarnation and resurrection into life after death. Rebirth *(renovatio)* within one lifetime, however, is "an essential transformation, that implies a change of essential nature."[16]

Those who went through the "mysteries" in these religions were provided an experience they were not allowed to speak about. Through hearing the mythic story recited and seeing it enacted, they were initiated, or entered into the process, the way, as prescribed in that particular culture. In some instances, hallucinogenic plant derivatives may have been used, as has been suggested recently for the Eleusinian mysteries by Wasson, Ruck, and Hofmann.[17] This kind of initiation, clearly involving an altered state of consciousness, could be regarded as a preview or rehearsal for those who were preparing to experience the dying and regeneration in the domain of their own psyches.

From a merging of Hellenistic philosophy and early Christian thought, we have the concept of *metanoia,* which literally means "beyond [*meta*] the mind [*nous*]," a transcending of the rational mind. *Metanoia* was usually translated in the Christian writings as "repentance," which means "to feel sorry again"; it is more accurately rendered, as A. K. Coomaraswamy has said, by "change of mind," or intellectual metamorphosis. "Metanoia is a transformation of one's whole being, from human thinking to divine understanding."[18]

In modern psychology, the terminology of development, personal development, or *spiritual development* has been used to describe this central human process. The work of developmental psychologists, such as Freud, Erikson, Piaget, Loevinger, Kohlberg, and others, has delineated sequences of human development from infancy to adulthood (and more recently into maturity and old age) in such areas as sexuality, social relationships, cognition, and moral values.

Eastern philosophies on the other hand, focus on development beyond the stage of normal, well-adjusted maturity into transpersonal, transrational levels of consciousness, variously called subtle, causal, mystical, spiritual, or unitive. Some work has been done, for example, by Ken Wilber,[19] to formulate an integration of these two traditions: in this approach, human development proceeds along a linear sequence of "levels," each of which transcends and includes the previous one. The details of these linear models will not concern us in this work. It is my belief that the processes described by the metaphors occur at all levels or, one might say, at each transition from one level to another.

Other theorists of human development have suggested the concept of *transition:* William Bridges, for instance, has pointed to a basic formal pattern that underlies all kinds of transitions, whether they are those of adolescence, midlife, illness, career change, marriage, separation, aging, or others.[20] There is always an ending, then a neutral, or intermediate, zone, then a new beginning. When something ends, we tend to feel afraid of loss—and of death. In the intermediate zone, we feel confused, ungrounded. At the times of new beginnings we feel uncertain, anxious about choice and commitment. We shall see, in the subsequent chapters of this book, that this three-phase pattern is pervasive in the literature. We are probably always involved in some endings, some in-between zones, and some new beginnings.

Scientifically oriented thinkers have used biological *evolution,* the development of species, as an analogy for individual human transformation. On the assumption that ontogeny, individual development, parallels and repeats phylogeny, the development of the species, humans are seen at the growing edge of a new evolutionary phase. This phase involves not physical organic changes but changes in mind, in consciousness; not the physical environment, the ecosphere, but the mental field of the planet, what Pierre Teilhard de Chardin called the "noosphere." For Sri Aurobindo, in man a definite new step is possible, a kind of reversal, "for it is through his consciousness, through its transmutation and no longer through a new bodily organism, that evolution can and must be affected."[21]

Another biological analogy for human transformation is the notion of *metamorphosis.* In this process, seen primarily in insects, crabs, mollusks, and the like (rarely in vertebrates, and never in mammals), the juvenile form of the animal is unrecognizably different from the mature form.[22] The caterpillar that metamorphoses into a butterfly has been one of the most enduring symbols of human transformation. This implies that human beings are in a kind of larval stage, and that a change is possible that would make us as different from the way we are now as butterflies are from caterpillars. The caterpillar lives in a different world than the butterfly. Can it know anything about this "higher" world, which includes more dimensions of movement? Can we humans know anything about the world of the ultrahuman, the transformed human? This question challenges us to explore and understand the sometimes tantalizingly obscure symbols and metaphors. Perhaps those who have made it to "butterfly" are trying to tell us "larvae" something.

In the alchemical tradition, which can be regarded as an early attempt to formulate a science of consciousness, there occurs the idea of the *transmutation of elements.* Psychologically, the elements symbolize the elemental aspects of our nature, which are to be transmuted from a disorderly state of chaos and impurity to a state of harmony and balance. This alchemical principle is recast into psychological terms in Jung's theory of individuation, according to which the four functions (thinking, feeling, sensing, and intuition), which are normally in a state of imbalance and disorder, are integrated until the psyche reaches a state of undividedness, or indivisibility. The alchemists and practitioners of the humoral theory of illness and medicine believed that physical and psychic processes involved multiple interactions and transmutations of the elemental energies and substances ("humors") within the total organism.

Modern biology and medicine have the concept of metabolism, which refers to the transformations of solid, liquid, and gaseous substances into characteristic biochemical structures and physiological activities. There is an analogy here to the functions of mind, or awareness, which Sir Julian Huxley pointed out in proposing the concept of *psychometabolism:* this is the brain's transformation of the raw material of subjective experience into characteristic patterns of awareness, which canalize and help to direct behavior. The primary problem of psychometabolism, according to Huxley, is "how the developing human being can integrate his interior life, whether by reconciling emotional or intellectual conflict in a higher synthesis, or by reconciling diversity in a more embracing unity."[23]

Variations on the theme of self-transformation

1. The transformation may be abrupt or gradual. Ecstasy, peak experience, inspired revelation, the flash of inventive insight, the poet's vision—all these are sudden experiences that may bring about profound changes in a person's life. Likewise, a conversion experience may be abrupt and total, as William James has described in many cases in his book. Zen Buddhism speaks of the moment of satori, the moment filled with paradox, which changes everything and nothing. On the other hand, there is much teaching, and much evidence that this moment is the result of gradual, step-by-step changes, whether in healing, in psychotherapy, in meditation, or in learning of any kind. Evelyn Underhill is one of many students of mysticism who argue that all conversions are gradual: "the apparently abrupt conversion is really, as a rule, the sequel and result of a long period of restlessness, uncertainty, and mental stress."[24]

2. The transformation may be temporary or lasting. We call a temporary transformation an "altered state of consciousness," the lasting transformation,

"personality change." Altered states include sleep, dreaming, hypnotic trance, meditation, psychedelic states, absorption in creative activity, illness, depression, elation, and madness. The psychiatrist and health researcher Andrew Weil has suggested that altering consciousness may be an inherent need of the human brain, the "natural mind." Here the reader may raise the question: So what? Does the altered state experience lead to lasting trait or behavior changes? What kind of long-term changes occur in people who experience such states? Are the changes all good? We need to ask ourselves what is the persistent quality of consciousness that we are expressing.[25] It is the outcome of action that tells us how enlightened someone is. As Jesus said, "Ye shall know them by their fruits."

3. The transformation may be externally or internally induced. We have all encountered examples of profound transformations of consciousness triggered by some external event, such as an accident, the sight of a spectacular natural wonder, or contact with another. The "love at first sight" phenomenon can certainly be regarded as an externally induced change of state. In a more mystical vein, the external person is typically a guru or spiritual teacher. The rite of baptism in Christianity, the "power transmission" *(shaktipat)* in Tantric Hinduism, the hypnotic induction in modern psychology, are ritualized forms of such externally induced alteration. On the other hand, there are equally numerous examples of changes of state and character occurring apparently without any external influence at all. The concept of self-actualization definitely implies that something unfolds gradually and slowly from within, emerging from the inner depths of the psyche. The opening of a flower (compared to the opening of a yogic chakra) and the growth of a tree or butterfly (compared to the psychic growth of a person) are analogies that suggest self-induced, intrinsic transformation.

4. The transformation may occur through grace or intention. Experiences of heightened consciousness, of mystical oneness or rapture, may be accompanied by a sense of their having been given freely and unexpectedly through God's grace. Aldous Huxley called his ecstatic mescaline visions a "gratuitous grace." Religious devotees are often exhorted to rely completely and only on the grace of the guru, or saint, or deity for the transformation of their lives. Then there are the esoteric traditions of spiritual practice, which emphasize the role of meticulous training in and practice of various meditative and yogic disciplines, and conscious efforts to bring about desired changes. The transmutational work *(opus)* of the alchemists and depth psychologists, the healing "journeys" (altered states) undertaken by the shamanic healer, the ritual sacralizing of sexuality in the Tantras, and Gurdjieff's process—"conscious labor and intentional suffering"— all fall within this category.

5. The transformation may be invisible to others or openly manifest. The healings and miracles performed by Jesus were the "signs" that were needed by the common people of his time, to persuade them of his nature and mission. Yet the history of religion is filled with unrecognized saints who labored in selfless

love and service, motivated by an inner vision or experience that transformed their being. Eastern texts describe the special physical and psychological features of an enlightened Buddha or the various psychic capacities *(siddhis)* that yogis acquire in the course of their practice, which serve as signposts along the way. On the other hand, there is the Taoist tradition of the self-effacing sage, "tentative, as if fording a river in winter; hesitant, as if in fear of his neighbors; formal, like a guest." The mind of this Taoist sage is described as being like muddy water, which if it is left to settle gradually becomes clear.[26]

6. The transformation may be progressive, regressive, or digressive. This is probably the most important question about the nature and value of a transformative experience. Progressive transformation leads from limitation to freedom, from darkness to light, from fragmentation to wholeness, from separation to oneness, from sleeplike inertia to awakened awareness, from personality to Spirit, from ego to Self, from mortality to immortality, from illusion to realization. It is, in its myriad variations, the single goal of the classic mystical quest and of all spiritual disciplines. Regressive transformations are those that take the opposite direction, from limited "normal" consciousness to even greater limitation or imprisonment, to deeper darkness, more extreme fragmentation and separation, into the chaotic depths of madness, despair, and the states of consciousness associated with violence, injury, and disease. Jung referred to these regressive changes as "diminutions of personality," citing such examples as the primitives' "loss of soul," the hysteric's loss of function, the listlessness of depression.[27]

By digressive transformations, I mean those changes in consciousness that are neither progressive nor regressive but simply different. Some kinds of hypnotic or trance states might be cited as "state" examples as well as possession by spirits, as reported in primitive cultures. Other instances of this kind of transformation discussed by Jung include those brought about by identification with a group, whether a mob, race, nation, or political party, and those brought about by identification with a cult hero. To these, a modern observer might add the transformations wrought by identification (plus idealization and imitation) with a popular star of the sports or entertainment world; and the changes in individuals subjected to various programs of "thought reform," brainwashing, behavior modification, aversion therapy, programming, reprogramming, or deprogramming.

The subject of this book is primarily progressive transformation, although discussions of regressive transformations are included for comparison and elucidation. The focus of attention on these progressive transformations—otherwise known as "evolutionary," "psychospiritual," or "mystical" transformations—carries with it the implicit judgment that these are better, more worthwhile, and more important to study. Indeed, I would go so far as to state that humanity is truly at an evolutionary choice point: we know in our hearts that we are either going to have to grow up very fast, change ourselves in radical ways, or we will destroy ourselves and perhaps the entire planetary ecosystem as well. We have a desperate need for greater awareness of our own inner dynamics and processes if we are going to survive the twentieth-century global crisis.

Finally, there is a variation on the theme of transformation that is often overlooked and yet that is very important: the distinction between *transcendence* and *transformation*.[28] To put it simply: to *transcend* is to go beyond; to *transform* is to make different. We transcend a given state of consciousness or a personality characteristic by rising above it (note the spatial metaphor) or by moving beyond it. For example, we may transcend a state of fear or anxiety by moving into an attitude of love and trust, or we may transcend a sense of separateness by meditating on the perception of oneness. The thought patterns of fear or separateness remain in our minds and may be reactivated at another time. It is as if we were stopping the music by lifting the tone arm off the recording. In psychological alchemy, transcendence is associated with the element air, with its upward motion; and with the process of sublimation, where an impulse is channeled into a "higher" expression (for example, sexual energy channeled into creativity).

Transformation in the stronger sense (sometimes also called transmutation), however, implies that the patterns of thought or perception are actually changed. The structures and functioning of our psyche become different. Some writers speak of this as a transformation of energy: the energy of fear or anger is transmuted into a different form of expression. If, as a result of unitive experiences and spiritual practices, a person no longer has the sense of separateness, even in ordinary, everyday consciousness, then the personality structure itself has been transformed. In the sound-recording analogy, the engraved patterns on the record have literally been erased or remade. Transformation is symbolized by the element fire; and is associated with the notion of purification and with *solutio,* the dissolving of problems or barriers.

I will let the old Chinese master Chuang Tsu, have the last word here: "When one is changing, how does one know that a change is taking place? When one is not changing, how does one know that a change hasn't already occurred? Maybe you and I are still in a dream and have not yet awakened. . . . Be content with what is happening and forget about change; then you can enter into the oneness of the mystery of heaven."[29]

1

Awakening from the Dream of Reality

My inside, listen to me, the greatest spirit, the Teacher, is near. Wake up, wake up!

—KABIR

This is a startling metaphor, and the experience it alludes to is equally startling: the transformation of consciousness is like the change from dreaming to waking. We all know those too-rare moments of insight, when we find ourselves contemplating some aspect of our lives as a dream that just ended: a particular career that we have been pursuing, a relationship that has burst like a beautiful bubble, dashing our dreams and fantasies of love. We find ourselves thinking, "I have been asleep, I have been dreaming; now I am awake, and things are very different." There is often a great feeling of freedom in those moments, as well as panic at times—and laughter, if we can manage it. We look back on the state of consciousness from which we just emerged as resembling sleep, dreaming, hypnosis, or a trance, and we find ourselves with an expanded awareness, a more objective perception, and a greater sense of being in the here-now.

The metaphor of awakening is an ancient one, found in Hinduism, Buddhism, and Sufism, as well as Christianity, Judaism, Gnosticism; and a great deal of folklore, mythology, and literature; and the personal accounts of modern mystics and consciousness explorers. It is probably such a widely used metaphor because so many have had the experience. And yet some readers may wonder what this metaphor could possibly mean. Surely, one may say, "Am I not conscious and awake, now as I am reading this?" Perhaps yes—and perhaps not. This transformation metaphor teaches us that we only think we are awake, but in fact, we are asleep, dreaming that we are awake. Some people feel insulted by the suggestion they might be asleep, when they think they are awake. But those who experience an awakening, even if only momentarily, are usually delighted at the revelation.

The metaphor of awakening implies an important philosophical world view: the view that our perception of reality, our ordinary awareness of the world, is a kind of dream, illusory and transient; and that it benefits our life to try to awaken from this sleep. This notion is akin to what is usually referred to as the idealist philosophy, which holds that reality is subjective, illusory, a creation of ideas or images. As we shall see, there are some very compelling reasons for such a worldview, and there is much in our experience that makes sense when looked at from this perspective.

A typical account of an awakening is the following, from a student in one of my classes on altered states of consciousness. The student, a man in his thirties, was meditating when he became aware of an immense energy field that passes through, encompasses, and unites everything.

> I had the sensation that the energy field was both palpable and impalpable, both moving and not moving. . . . I felt I had awakened to another level of consciousness. What I usually experienced as reality, phenomenal reality, seemed in the process of merging with or dissolving into this energy, which was a greater reality. When my normal consciousness returned, the veil fell. I could not "see" the energy field anymore. I must have fallen asleep again.[1]

Our Ordinary Awareness Is Dreamlike

The idea that our ordinary consciousness, our world, our life, is dreamlike has found expression in the writings of many spiritual traditions, as well as in poetry and philosophy. According to this metaphor, living is a kind of sleeping; dying is a kind of waking up. Shakespeare's Prospero, in *The Tempest,* declared that "we are such stuff as dreams are made on; and our little life is rounded with a sleep." In many folk belief systems, death is regarded as akin to sleep. We speak euphemistically about "putting an animal to sleep," and in Greek mythology *Hypnos* (Sleep) and *Thanatos* (Death) were brother gods. Moreover, spiritual teachers counsel us that a close encounter with death can produce an experience of "awakening," which can be a valuable shock propelling us to another level of awareness.

If the end of life is compared to awakening from a sleep, the beginning of life—birth—is often compared to falling into a sleep. In Wordsworth's ode "Intimations of Immortality" we read: "Our birth is but a sleep and a forgetting: / The Soul that rises with us, our life's Star,/Hath had elsewhere its setting,/And cometh from afar." This parallels Gnostic doctrines of incarnation as a fall into matter, a descent into form; and parallels the notion, propounded by many philosophers and psychologists, that childhood conditioning produces a state of amnesia, a shutting down or reduction of the free and open, fluid awareness of the infant. Some Gnostics used the myth of Endymion as an image of our condition: he was a Greek youth who had been put into a permanent sleep by Zeus. Thus, according to these teachings, we live a kind of passive, static existence, in which vitality is minimized: and we are fascinated by the dreamlike images and fantasies of our inner worlds.

The old Germanic legend of Sleeping Beauty is an enchanting parable on this theme. The princess Beauty symbolizes the human psyche, and the wicked witch who curses the infant at birth represents the process of early conditioning, which brings about oblivious, unawakened consciousness. According to the story, the adolescent princess Beauty pricks her finger on the poisoned spindle, becoming subject to the sleep-producing spell. "Spinner" is also a German colloquial expression for someone with crazy ideas. Metaphorically speaking, this represents the notion that the developmental crises of adolescence trigger confused thinking that cause the personality to seek escape and relief in deep, forgetful "sleep." The castle and its residents symbolize the body and its functions. The castle is lifeless: all the people in it, including Sleeping Beauty's parents, the servants and cooks, are asleep. Personality and body consciousness are steeped in narcotic oblivion and remain that way until the Prince, who is the awakener, arrives, and everything comes alive. The Prince is the royal self, the higher self, the one whose kiss or touch awakens us.

In the Gnostic text known as The Gospel of Truth, in a passage referred to as "the nightmare parable," we find existence described as nightmare; "and everyone has acted as though asleep at the time when he was ignorant. And this is the way he has come to knowledge, as if he had awakened." Those who remain unawakened are described as "creatures of oblivion." Jacques Lacarrière, a modern writer on the Gnostics, states that for them, "sleep is to consciousness what weight is to the body: a state of death, inertia, a petrification of psychic forces. . . . to awaken, to be alert, to keep vigil, these are the recurring themes in Gnostic texts."[2]

The modern Russian magus and teacher G. I. Gurdjieff, who was strongly influenced by Sufi and Gnostic ideas, constantly emphasized the mechanical, somnambulistic quality of our everyday consciousness: we do not think, or do; it thinks, it does. We have no awareness of our mental processes, they simply flow along, following the automated lines of habit conditioning. We think we are awake, but in fact we are asleep, dreaming that we are awake. According to Gurdjieff, objective consciousness, which is brought about by sustained, systematic effort at self-observation and self-remembering, is a state that compares to ordinary consciousness as the latter compares to dream sleep.

It becomes clear that when the ancient philosophers and seers described life or the world as dreamlike, they were uttering suggestions: their statements are prescriptive as well as descriptive. We must realize we are asleep before we can hope to wake up; even then, it is hard enough! They are saying, in effect: look at your experience *as if* it were a dream/sleep, and then perhaps you will have a chance to awaken from it. In a famous verse, the Buddhist Diamond Sutra says, "The phenomena of life may be likened unto a dream, a phantasm, a bubble, a shadow, the glistening dew, or lightning flash, and thus they ought to be contemplated."[3] By recommending that we regard reality as a dream, the Buddha is pushing or challenging us to awaken, even if only a little.

The second-century Buddhist philosopher Nagarjuna, in a commentary on this sutra, says:

> There is no reality in a dream, and yet, while one dreams, one believes in the
> reality of the things one sees in the dream. After one wakes up one recognizes
> the falseness of the dream and laughs at oneself. Just so, in the dream state
> of fettered existence a man has a belief in things which do not exist. But when
> he has found the Path, then, at the moment of enlightenment he understands
> that there is no reality in them and he laughs at himself. . . . Man, by the force
> of the dream state resulting from ignorance, believes in the existence of all
> sorts of things which do not exist, such as I and mine, male and female, etc.[4]

In other words, our ideas and feelings around self, around possessions, and
around male-female relationships are, from an enlightened perspective, seen to be
dreamlike and unreal. The objects and people of the world we know, which we
hold to be "real," are seen by one on the path of transformation as exactly
analogous to the images of dreams and fantasies.

A parallel description of the human condition is given by the fourth-century
Christian theologian Gregory of Nyssa in a passage on the theme of "Angelic
Vigilance":

> All who are seriously concerned with the life of heaven must conquer sleep;
> they must be constantly awake in spirit, driving off, like a kind of drowsiness,
> the deceiver of souls and the destroyer of truth. By drowsiness and sleep here
> I am referring to those dream-like fantasies which are shaped by those sub-
> merged in the deceptions of this life: I mean public office, money, influence,
> external show, the seduction of pleasure, love of reputation and enjoyment,
> honor, and all the other things which, by some sort of illusion, are sought after
> vainly by those who live without reflection. For all these things will pass away
> with the flux of time; their existence is mere seeming; they are not what we
> think they are.[5]

Thus, the teachings of transformation from many cultures and religions
agree in pointing out the sleeplike nature of our ordinary consciousness, and they
share the popular belief that all of us are pursuing dreams—of honor, wealth,
pleasure, happiness; but they take the analogy one step further and say, it is possible
and desirable—even necessary—to awaken from these dreams. For regardless of
whether they are nightmares or pleasant fantasies, these "dreams" that we seek or
avoid are essentially illusions, the transient creations of the imagination.

In the sleep state of consciousness, we each are aware only of our personal,
subjective world; each one's dream is different and separate, and they do not
usually interact with one another. When we awaken we realize that we live in one
great world, that we share its unity. The transition from sleeping to waking is
often seen as a transition from subjectivity to objectivity. However, as Gurdjieff
and other philosophers of transformation argue, ordinary waking consciousness
is just as subjective as sleep. As Herakleitos said: "Those who are asleep live each
in a private world; those who are awake live in the one Great World."

Dreaming, Sleeping, and Waking in Everyday Life

Since the discovery, in the 1950s, that rapid eye movements (REMs) usually accompany dreaming and that different kinds of EEG brain waves, as well as respiratory and muscle-tone patterns, distinguish dreaming and nondreaming sleep, Western psychology has acknowledged three normal states: sleeping, dreaming, and waking (not considering, for now, the altered states induced by certain drugs or special procedures, such as hypnosis).

The ancient Indian philosophers of the Upanishads long ago formulated a notion that there were four basic states: the three just mentioned, plus the fourth state *(turiya),* which is a state of relaxed, quiet yet alert unitive awareness, a state usually brought about through meditation. Thus we find Western psychology, through its objective methods, is reaching conclusions similar to those reached by the Eastern seers through experiential, intuitive means.

The characteristic cyclic changes in these different states, and the accompanying brain changes, have been carefully studied and measured in sleep laboratories. Generally, when falling asleep, we start in light sleep, descend down through several "levels," and reach the deepest sleep around 30 to 40 minutes later. Then we reascend through the stages, returning to the lightest stage, where we almost wake up (sometimes do, in fact), and then enter the rapid-eye movement (REM) dreaming stage around 90 to 110 minutes after first entering sleep. This cycle is usually repeated several more times a night, with variations in the lengths of different stages. Thus, several times during a night's sleep we approach waking, like an underwater swimmer coming up close to the water's surface; then we dream, and then redescend to the lower depths of dreamless oblivion. The level of arousal, or wakefulness, varies continually, in regular cycles as well as in smaller, random fluctuations.

From the waking side a similar situation holds. Using remote measuring devices, sleep researchers have recorded EEG brain waves from subjects going about their daily routine. Thus they have discovered that most people frequently and repeatedly enter into short microsleep periods, lasting from thirty seconds to three minutes, which are clearly indicated by their brain waves, but of which they themselves are totally unaware. In other words, we continually fall into sleep while apparently awake, just as we regularly almost awaken while apparently asleep.[6] These findings regarding periodic, unaware, brain sleep states provide interesting support to the Buddhist, Sufi, and Gnostic ideas concerning the unawakened consciousness of normal human existence.

It appears, then, that our awareness fluctuates constantly, with varying levels of alertness or wakefulness within any state, as well as regular, cyclic changes between states. There are definite thresholds between each state, and the in-between transition phases appear to be particularly rich in imagery and fantasy activity. We are all familiar with the reveries at the time of falling asleep, and the dreams just preceding awakening are usually most vividly remembered.

The subjective experience of crossing that threshold between waking and sleeping is apparently associated in our minds with the up-down spatial orientation: we always wake "up," and "fall" asleep. Sleep, like gravity, seems to pull us downward; on the other hand, the dreams preceding waking often involve climbing or rising up in some way. Waking up is often experienced as a kind of struggle upward against the downward drag of inertia.[7]

Within the dream state, a particularly interesting and rare kind of dream is the lucid dream, in which the dreamer comes to realize that he or she is dreaming. Suddenly, a heightened awareness is added to dream experience: besides the flow of subjective dream images, there is now an objective witness, or observer. In lucid dreams, the dreamer not only observes the dream with awareness that it is a dream, he or she can also intervene in it, alter it, or terminate it by deliberately waking up. Some dream researchers believe that flying dreams are particularly associated with, and may lead to, lucid dreaming. In flying dreams we again notice the metaphor of upward motion associated with "heightened" (!) awareness.[8]

The state of lucid dreaming may provide the basis for the exploration of interior regions of the psyche. In some shamanic traditions, such as those recounted in Castaneda's Don Juan books and in the Australian aboriginal myths of the "Dream Time," this is precisely what is going on. To the aboriginal shamans, Dream Time is a much vaster realm than waking reality: it is the primordial time in which the great ancestor spirits created the world, and it is a world that can still be accessed now, through lucid, conscious dreaming.[9]

In Tibetan Buddhism, there are practices of "dream yoga," which are designed to help the practitioner maintain lucid awareness while falling asleep, as well as to attain lucidity from the dream state. Castaneda describes Mexican Indian practices with a similar purpose. In such lucid, or objective, dreams—or "big dreams," as the American Indians call them—dreamers may obtain information for healing or problem solving; they may "see" future events (in precognitive dreams), or they may interact with other individuals, known or unknown to them in waking reality. "Mutual dreams," in which two or more people simultaneously have the same dream, may be much more common than the rareness of report would suggest.[10]

In groups and cultures that practice "dreaming" the domain of consciousness we are in when dreaming is regarded as equally real as the domain of everyday waking reality. This view, that the dream is a reality, is the mirror image of the view—discussed above—that the world, the supposed "reality," is a dream. At the least, the message emerging from the ancient teachings and from frontiers of modern scientific research is that waking and dreaming consciousness are in several important ways more alike than they are different. Their status as reality is quite similar in many respects.

I take this to be the meaning of the famous story of Chuang Tzu, the Taoist sage, who reported that on awakening from a dream one day, he could not remember whether he was a man who dreamed he was a butterfly, or a butterfly dreaming he was an old philosopher. We might say he had equated dream consciousness and ordinary waking consciousness so well, that he could not then distinguish between them.

The Transformation as an Awakening

The shift in awareness from ordinary, subjective dreaming to lucid, objective dreaming seems an appropriate metaphor for transformative awakening. Just as it is possible to awaken, to become lucid, in a dream, so it is possible to attain moments or periods of heightened awareness—"wakefulness"—in waking life. Such experiences involve a radical alteration in the range and scope of awareness and thus clearly qualify as transformative experiences.

The experience of awakening to lucid awareness, in the psychological sense, can occur in a variety of different ways. These varieties of awakening are parallel to the varieties of transformation experience discussed in the Introduction.

The awakening may be sudden or gradual. Triggered by a sound, a word, a touch, a flash of insight, it may feel like an abrupt and dramatic discontinuity in the flow of our normal, somnolent consciousness. Or it may instead be a progressive series of gradual and partial awakenings, of mini-satoris: periods of heightened awareness followed by periods of sinking back into inertia, into the habitual dream fantasies of conditioned consciousness.

The awakening may be momentary or lasting. Some psychedelic drug states are experienced as brief previews, as it were, of the more awakened consciousness possible for human beings. Other methods, involving consistently applied discipline and psychospiritual practice, such as meditation, would be necessary to convert the preview into a permanent aspect of the individual's awareness.

The awakening may be ecstatic or traumatic, and it may involve a reversal of the feeling state that one inhabits during the dream that precedes it. Just as the awakening from a terrifying nightmare is marked by a sense of relief, even an ecstatic feeling of liberation, so the transition from ordinary, conditioned consciousness to awakened consciousness is often exhilarating and joyous, marked by a sense of healing taking place, a peaceful resolution of inner conflicts, and an upsurge of creative inspiration. Yet just as awakening from a beautiful happy dream can be disappointing or shocking, so we may experience a "rude awakening" when sudden pain, emotional shock, the threat of death to oneself or a loved one, traumatic illness, or disappointments bring about what is appropriately referred to as an "eye-opening" experience. When we awaken from a pleasant, though illusory, "dream," we are "dis-illusioned." This kind of disillusionment can produce growth and positive transformation if we accept it as a challenge to recognize the deeper dimensions of our life.

The awakening may be involuntary, induced perhaps by the compassionate gesture or incisive word of a wise teacher or friend or perhaps by an unexpected, "accidental" coincidence of circumstances that serves to break our trance and make us "come to our senses." In systems of yoga, meditation, or other kinds of spiritual practice, such as the Gurdjieffian self-remembering, however, the awakening is intentional and purposive, even planned.

The desirability of planned wakefulness is vividly illustrated in Christ's parable about the master away from home. The "master of the house" symbolizes the inner Self, and the "servants" represent the various subpersonalities, or egos. "Be alert, be wakeful. You do not know when the moment comes. It is like a man away from home: he has left his house and put his servants in charge, each with his own work to do, and he has ordered the doorkeeper to stay awake. Keep awake, then, for you do not know when the master of the house is coming" (Mark 13:33–36).

In the tradition of Indian yoga, we find the metaphor of awakening in the teachings concerning *kundalini,* which is said to be, in ordinary consciousness, a serpent coiled asleep in the "root center" *(muladhara),* at the base of the spine. This *kundalini* is a kind of energy, which, as a result of yogic practices, may begin to flow in sinuous, serpentine motions through the body, rising up toward the "crown center" *(sahasrara),* at the top of the head. While it has been long been assumed that these kinds of psychophysical energy transformations occur only in practitioners of yoga, it is now recognized that "kundalini" phenomena (swirling, hot currents of energy coursing through the body, accompanied by hyperalert and energized feeling states) can and do occur in anybody. I have experienced them myself, and so have numbers of my acquaintances and psychotherapy clients.[11]

Meditation can also be seen as a planned effort at awakening. Modern consciousness researchers conceive of meditation as the intentional rechanneling or refocusing of attention. One very widespread form of meditation, exemplified in the Buddhist *Vipassana* system, involves continuous impartial observation of one's breath, feelings, and thoughts. This activity would naturally develop an observing attitude, very similar to the attentive witness stance of lucid dreaming. While it is often believed that meditation is a passive and tranquil state, producing relaxation akin to sleep, this is not, in fact, the goal of meditation. While there is outward immobility, the meditator is inwardly moving through progressive levels of concentration with increasing degrees of awareness and insight. In Daniel Goleman's words, "Virtually every system of meditation recognizes the awakened state as the ultimate goal of meditation."[12] The name Buddha itself means "the Awakened One."

In Gurdjieff's system, "self-remembering" is the key process. "Only by beginning to remember himself does a man really awaken. And then all surrounding life acquires for him a different aspect and a different meaning." Gurdjieff goes to great lengths to describe the kinds of obstacles that prevent human beings from waking up—the principal obstacle being that humans do not realize they are asleep. Even if they do, however, it is necessary to plan and organize the effort of awakening, providing for oneself the equivalent of alarm clocks—external devices to help one awaken; and one has to work cooperatively with others, especially with teachers or leaders who have awakened somewhat more.[13]

In these approaches of yoga, of meditation, and other spiritual disciplines, conscious, intentional transformative awakening is regarded as a kind of *initiation:* a teacher, guru, or master provides the impetus that initiates the student's acquaintance with other realms and levels of consciousness. This is often the first step on someone's spiritual journey. Evelyn Underhill, in her books on mysticism, writes that "awakening" is the first step on the mystical path. However, since awakenings can occur in progressive series, it is clearly possible that there be later, additional awakenings. Indeed, some believe that the change of state that occurs at death is a kind of final awakening, a time when we at last become detached from our body-bound consciousness and see our life objectively, as a dream or film that just ended.

In Greek mythology, the master initiator, the awakener and teacher is the god Hermes, the Roman Mercurius: he touches people's eyes with his staff to summon them to the awakening of death; he initiates them into the mysteries, including the Egyptian alchemical teachings later referred to as Hermetic; he gives Odysseus a magical herb that will allow that courageous hero to withstand the bewitchment of Circe. The witch-goddess had turned Odysseus' men into swine, symbolically inducing in them an animallike sleep state, where they were conscious only of their "swinish" nature. Hermes the god is the herald who carries messages from the gods to mankind; Hermes-Mercurius as the archetype is that part of our psyche through which insight and knowledge come from the "higher" realms (the divine, transpersonal realms) to the human, personal realms. He is the Prince who awakens Sleeping Beauty; he is the archetype of the Awakener.

The transformation of consciousness described metaphorically as an awakening can take two different forms: rising beyond or detaching from body consciousness (transcendence), or changing and sensitizing body consciousness itself (transmutation). In the former process, associated more with ascetic and monastic devotional traditions of East and West, there is a withdrawal of attention from the outer, physical world and a heightened awareness of the inner psychic and spiritual realms. Saint Teresa wrote, "In the orison of union, the soul is fully awake as regards God, but wholly asleep as regards things of this world." And Ramakrishna, the great Indian yogi and saint, stated: "One is aware of pleasure and pain, birth and death, disease and grief, as long as one is identified with the body. All these belong to the body alone and not to the Self. . . . Attaining self-knowledge, one looks on pleasure and pain, birth and death, as a dream."[14]

The latter process, transmutational awakening, occurs when the body itself is regarded as the temple of Spirit, as the microcosmic counterpart to the material universe. This implies then that the physical elements of the body itself become transformed also: organs, tissues, cells, minerals, molecules, atoms are to become awakened to the presence of Spirit or Self within. The only way to describe this experience is as a feeling of being "present" within the body and the personality: one has sensitized awareness of both external and internal realities, the physical and the metaphysical realms. This kind of approach is associated more with the alchemical tradition, Tantric and Taoist teachings in the East, as well as with Zen Buddhism in certain respects. Transmutational awakening experiences are also common with the use of psychedelics, in which people report feeling every cell of their body charged with aliveness and sensitized to an exquisite degree.[15]

The question may be raised whether the awakening experience is necessarily always benign or progressive, or whether it might, in fact, be dangerous. Could not the shock of an unexpected opening of the mind or the trauma of a painful realization plunge an individual into depression or attract an injury or accident? There are situations in which we seem to be functioning perfectly and fluidly in some difficult, even dangerous, activity and in which our experience is dreamlike; if we were to awaken from this state, we might well bring about disruptive or disastrous behavior. In traditional thought, the somnambulists walking on roof-tops should not be awakened lest they lose their footing on changing states of consciousness. The Sioux medicine man Black Elk reports a striking incident of this sort: In a battle with white soldiers he repeatedly charged into a barrage of gunfire without being hurt. He felt himself to be in a dream, protected by an invisible shield. At a certain moment he suddenly "woke up" and immediately felt the hot stabbing of a bullet wound in his abdomen.[16]

Moreover, the *kundalini* yoga experience has been reported to manifest in some individuals an extremely painful, psychotic-like "kundalini syndrome." Gopi Krishna, an Indian scholar who practiced kundalini yoga without benefit of a teacher's guidance, has given vivid descriptions of the uncontrollable flaming, searing, roaring energies that surged through his body for months, threatening to literally burn him up. Such experiences underscore the need to practice *kundalini* techniques under a competent teacher; otherwise, the intensity of the awakened kundalini energy can be too great for a nervous system insufficiently prepared for the much higher "voltages" coursing through the body.[17]

In a wider sense, it is certainly true that an awakening experience, especially a traumatic one, could, in fact, have undesirable consequences. A man suddenly confronted by the imminence of his own death *could* have the kind of transcendental experience that has been reported in the literature—leading to self-examination and renewed interest in spiritual development—*or* he could plunge into chronic fear, resignation and depression, perhaps attempting to mask these through escapist behavior, such as alcoholism.

While this kind of situation does undoubtedly occur, one could well argue that the opposite danger is much greater: most of us are asleep most of the time, and we bring about physical, emotional, and social "accidents" and injuries—through lack of awareness, blind inattention—to a far greater extent than we probably realize. To take only a few minor examples: would we spill food, cut a finger, speak a hurtful word, bang up our car, if we were really awake at the time? The mindless violence, senseless confusion, and meaningless trivialities which characterize so much of unconscious human life surely cause huge amounts of frustration, despair, and suffering. Or consider war: Gurdjieff calls it a "mass psychosis" in which millions of sleeping men fight and kill millions of other sleepers. To awaken from the permanent nightmare of ordinary existence certainly seems like a worthwhile idea, even though the awakening may cause momentary shock, confusion, insecurity, or panic; in the long run, if we trust our true, inner nature, it is bound to lead to a life of greater vitality and a deepening sense of the preciousness of existence.

When we awaken we become aware of something, a central core being, that is always unchangingly present and fully pervasive throughout our psyche. This is essence, the Self that is immortal and omnipresent. As the Katha Upanishad states: "That person who is awake in those that sleep, . . . that indeed is the pure. That is Brahman, that is called the Immortal." When awake, we are more aware of our inner Self and of the external world; we are more in touch with past history and future possibilities as well.

We are urged to *awaken from* the dream of "reality," in which we have been enmeshed for ages, and we are urged to *awaken to* the divine nature, inherent within, the Teacher, the Friend, the Self. This notion parallels the idea of life after death as a resurrection, a kind of revivifying of the dead. In the words of Saint Paul: "I tell you a mystery. We shall not all sleep, but we shall all be changed, in the twinkling of an eye, at the last trumpet."[18] The "last trumpet" is the wake-up call for the final transition, to a new and higher level of consciousness.

Thus, the metaphor of awakening relates to the idea of coming alive from a deathlike "sleep" consciousness to a unitive, nonjudgmental awareness of the true inner Spirit. Awakening also relates to the metaphor of returning to one's source, or primordial "home," to the "higher realms" of consciousness from which we descended at birth and which we have forgotten, until helped to remember.

The Zen philosopher D. T. Suzuki wrote: "What is awakened in the Zen experience is not a 'new' experience but an 'old' one, which has been dormant since our loss of 'innocence'. . . . The awakening is really the rediscovery or the excavation of a long-lost treasure . . . the finding ourselves back in our original abode where we lived even before our birth."[19]

2

Uncovering the Veils of Illusion

If the doors of perception were cleansed every thing would appear to man as it is—infinite.

—WILLIAM BLAKE

It is an ancient notion that the world perceived in our everyday consciousness is a shadow play of appearances, illusory and evanescent, and that the transformation of consciousness involves transcending or dissolving this web of images. In chapter 1, on the metaphor of awakening, we saw how in Buddhism and other wisdom teachings, the world of appearances is said to be like a dream. We also find this world described in terms of several other similes or analogies: it is like stars, we are told, because faint and unreachable; and like dewdrops, bubbles, clouds, or lightning, because short-lived and shape shifting; like dreams and magic shows, because unreal and illusory; and like cataracts or coverings, because true perception is somehow blocked or distorted.

The themes of illusion, evanescence, and obstruction occur again in the following beautiful verse attributed to the eleventh-century Buddhist scholar-mystic Naropa:

> A magic spell, a dream, a gleam before the eyes,
> A reflection, lightning, an echo, a rainbow,
> Moonlight upon water, cloud-lands,
> Dimness before the eyes, fog and apparations,
> These are the twelve similes of the phenomenal.[1]

Several additional analogies are mentioned here. Reflections, echoes, rainbows, moonlight on water—these are also fleeting, insubstantial phenomena; and dimness and fog, like clouds and cataracts, obscure and distort our vision of reality.

The aspect of transformation symbolized in these images is related to the idea and the experience of *discovery,* which is "un-covering"; and to *disillusionment,* which is "abandoning of illusions"; and to *revelation,* which is, from the Latin *revelare,* "pulling back the veil" or "unveiling"; and, of course, to awakening from a dream. It is also related to the experience of *insight,* as "inner sight," or seeing that sees beneath the surface appearance; and to *enlightenment,* as an experience of more light, produced by the removal of obscuring veils or coverings. And it is, finally, related to the transformation of the personality, because there are coverings, masks, or sheaths enveloping the central Self—which, as they are removed or dissolved, provide an experience appropriately described as "self-disclosure" or "unmasking the self."

An example of a profoundly transformative conversion experience, described in the same imagery, is given by William James in his *Varieties of Religious Experience.* He cites the account of Alphonse Ratisbonne, a Jew who had a conversion experience in a Catholic church in Rome in 1842:

> I did not know where I was: I did not know whether I was Alphonse or another. I only felt myself changed and believed myself another me. . . . In the bottom of my soul I felt an explosion of the most ardent joy. . . . All that I can say is that in an instant the bandage had fallen from my eyes; and not one bandage only, but the whole manifold of bandages with which I had been brought up. One after another they rapidly disappeared, even as the mud and ice disappear under the rays of the burning sun. I came out as from a sepulchre, from an abyss of darkness; and I was living, perfectly living. . . . I can explain the change no better than by the simile of a profound sleep or the analogy of a man born blind who should suddenly open his eyes to the day.[2]

The experience of having coverings or blinders removed is frequently reported in psychedelic states and is associated with a sensitized perception of luminosity and vibrancy in vision and the other senses. Aldous Huxley's account of his mescaline experiences in *The Doors of Perception,* published in 1954, first suggested the relevance of this metaphor for these visionary states. The feeling of the self being "uncovered," analogous to the peeling of the layers of an onion, is also extremely common.

The *origin* of these obstructions is described in the Eastern teachings by reference to the concept of *avidya.* This term is commonly translated "ignorance," but may more appropriately be regarded as "unconsciousness." It is a consequence of being born into this world, an inherent feature of human life. One text states: "*Avidya* overpowers beings through the lack of vision, or through false vision, just as a cataract overpowers the eyes."[3] In other words, ordinary human consciousness is obstructed, blind, unconscious, a play of illusions *(maya).*

In some of the writings of transformational philosophers, we find the analogy of our perception and our thinking being obscured by fog or clouds. There is a famous fourteenth-century English text of mystical literature, "The Cloud of Unknowing," which states: "Anything that you do not know or have forgotten may be said to be 'dark' to you, for you cannot see it with the inward eye. For this reason it is called a 'cloud,' not of the sky, of course, but of 'unknowing,' a cloud of unknowing between you and your God."[4] This is the cloud of ignorance *(avidya),* of unconsciousness; the cloud that blocks the light of the inner sun, the light of Spirit.

If ordinary, unawakened consciousness is clouded or obstructed, then transformed consciousness is comparable to seeing in the clear, unobscured light of the
sun. William James writes: "in conversion or religious regeneration, . . . a not
infrequent consequence of the change operated in the subject is a transfiguration
of the face of nature in his eyes. A new heaven seems to shine upon a new earth."[5]
Everything we look at in such states seems illuminated with a kind of pristine,
luminous beauty, comparable to the light of a new day dawning.

In Buddhism we find the fascinating idea that not only vision, but thought
also is obstructed, with "thought coverings" *(citta-avarana)*. These thought coverings are the result of emotional cravings and aversions, which cause us to have
mental blocks, or conceptual blind spots, in certain areas. Transformed consciousness is a state in which the individual is freed from the suffering, the
emotional ups and downs, that stem from these unconscious mental blocks. In
the words of the Heart Sutra, "A bodhisattva, through having relied on the
perfection of wisdom, dwells without thought-coverings [*citta-avarana*]. In the
absence of thought-coverings he has not been made to tremble, he has overcome
what can upset, and in the end he attains to enlightenment [*nirvana*]."[6] In this
state one is no longer attached, either through craving or through aversion, to
the world of sense objects, of phenomenal appearances. One sees, and lives in,
what one modern seer-writer, Stewart Edward White, called "the unobstructed
universe."

The symbolism of clouds points not only to the occluding and darkening
of our thought and perception but also to its transitory, illusory nature. Clouds,
like bubbles, dewdrops, dreams, fog, echoes, and rainbows arise and fade on the
screen of our awareness, and do not appear to us as things, or objects. They are
intangible, and hence they do not seem very real. Yet the sages and teachers tell
us that we should look at things and sense-objects, as no more real or substantial.
When we do, we experience a kind of detachment, a bemused acceptance of the
inevitability of change, a lessened desire to possess and to hold.

The individual is then aware of, awakened to, the presence of the inner Self,
the true Buddha nature. Just as when we recognize the dream we can awaken,
so when we see the phenomenal world as the play of appearances it is, we can
realize our true nature, we can attain "self-realization." The Indian philosophers
called this the realization of *Atman-Brahman:* the Self *(Atman)* as identical with
Absolute Beingness *(Braham)*. In the words of Shankara: "*Brahman* is not the
universe of the senses. Everything is a manifestation of *Brahman.* The appearance
of the world as other than *Brahman* is unreal, like a mirage in the desert."[7]

The World Perceived as Maya

This is the view of the Vedanta philosophy: only *Brahman,* Absolute Beingness, is real; all else is illusion, mirage, flickering shadows, dreams. The Indian

philosopher-seers used the concept of maya to refer to the illusory, evanescent quality of the phenomenal world. *Maya* is usually translated as "illusion," because of the Vedantists' insistence that only Absolute Beingness, *Brahman,* is real. Originally, however, *maya* relates to word roots meaning "show" and "measure"; but *maya* came later to mean "power," particularly creative and magical power. On the individual human scale, *maya* is the power that deludes us into taking the phenomenal world for real, the power we have to project outward the created images of our own mind. Our thoughts create our reality. Shankara tells us we "superimpose" our concepts of space, time, and material objects on to the external world, when actually there is only unchanging, infinite Being. He says this is as delusional as the man who mistakes a rope for a snake in the dark, who superimposes his image of a snake on what is only a rope.[8]

An eloquent description of this realization of the world as a projected play of illusory images, is found in Gopi Krishna's account of his experiences with the awakening of *kundalini.*

> The phenomenal world, ceaselessly in motion, characterized by creation, incessant change and dissolution, receded into the background and assumed the appearance of an extremely thin, rapidly melting layer of foam upon a substantial rolling ocean of life, a veil of exceedingly fine vapor before an infinitely large conscious Sun, constituting a complete reversal of the relationship between the world and the limited human consciousness. It showed the previously all-dominating cosmos reduced to the subordinate position of an evanescent and illusory appendage.[9]

This is the perspective that may be attained in a transformative experience, regardless of where it occurs or in what cultural context. It is also the perspective that transformational thinkers recommend, as preparing the way for such a transformative breakthrough.

Maya, then, is the magic picture show of the mind, which is projected with such power and vividness that we are deluded into taking it for something real "out there." There are fascinating parallels between this view and the emerging worldview of modern physics, particularly in relation to quantum theory, with its notion of the interdependence of the observer and observed reality. As physicist Fritjof Capra states:

> As we penetrate into matter, nature does not show us any isolated building blocks, but rather appears as a complicated web of relations between the various parts of the whole. These relations always include the observer in an essential way. . . . The properties of any atomic object can only be understood in terms of the objects's interaction with the observer. . . . In atomic physics, we can never speak about nature without, at the same time, speaking about ourselves.[10]

The Buddhists take this notion of the world as created, imagined illusions one step further: To them the ultimate reality is void, or emptiness (*sunyata*). And since all outwardly perceived objects are themselves illusory, only the infinite emptiness within them is real. This kind of awareness—of the world as having characteristics of "no-thing-ness"—has also been called a state of "consciousness without an object." In a famous verse from the Heart Sutra, we read, "Form is emptiness, and emptiness is not different from form, nor is form different from emptiness: indeed, emptiness is form."[11]

This, also, is not just a concept but may be an actual perception. A woman describing her experience in meditation reported that "my perception of everything around me and of my own body and personality was exactly balanced between awareness of 'form' as one aspect and of 'emptiness' as open space. It was like a double perspective, the inside and the outside of a sphere simultaneously, convex and concave, form as surface and space as container. I felt myself moving in awareness just exactly along the 'edge' between form and formlessness. The latter was like a kind of cliff, or abyss, of infinite depth."[12]

The paradoxical equivalence of form and emptiness formulated by Buddhist philosophers also has its parallel in modern quantum-relativistic physics. To quote Capra again:

> The field theories of modern physics force us to abandon the classical distinction between material particles and the void. Einstein's field theory of gravity and quantum field theory both show that particles cannot be separated from the space surrounding them. . . . They have to be seen as condensations of a continuous field which is present throughout space. . . . Here, then, is the closest parallel to the Void of Eastern mysticism in modern physics. Like the Eastern Void, the "physical vacuum"—as it is called in field theory—is not a state of mere nothingness, but contains the potentiality for all forms of the particle world.[13]

Another formulation that is strikingly similar to the form-and-emptiness notion is Niels Bohr's principle of complementarity, according to which reality necessarily has two complementary aspects, the wave aspect and the particle aspect, each of these giving only half the picture.

A well-known variant of the theme of illusion and reality is Plato's parable of the cave: we human beings, Socrates tells us, are like prisoners chained to the wall of a dark cave, in which fires cast flickering shadows on the walls—and we identify these shadows as the events and phenomena of the real world. Outside the cave, there is the lighted world illumined by the daytime sun, but when one of us prisoners manages to break free from our chains, he or she is dazzled by the great radiance and only then realizes that what has ordinarily been taken for real is a play of shadows. Here, as always, the transformation of consciousness involves a radical restructuring of our mode of perception: as we awaken, we recognize we have been asleep; as we see clearly, we realize that we have been fascinated by illusory images.[14]

According to these ideas, there are no "real" things out there that can be identified or described separately from how we as observers see them. Matter and the perception of matter are interdependently interrelated, modern physics tell us. In its ultimate ground, there is only a kind of emptiness, like space, that is filled with potentialities. Our perception, our consciousness, somehow contains veils, coverings, or screens, through which, or onto which, we project these visions that we call phenomenal reality. William James, in describing the insights he obtained from his experiments with the psychedelic nitrous oxide, stated:

> Our normal waking consciousness, rational consciousness as we call it, is but one special type of consciousness, whilst all about it, *parted from it by the filmiest of screens* [emphasis mine], there lie potential forms of consciousness entirely different. . . . No account of the universe in its totality can be final which leaves these other forms of consciousness quite disregarded.[15]

The Transformation of Vision

Teachers of psychospiritual transformation often speak of a dual aspect of vision; we are "blind" or "seeing"; our sight is clouded or clear, veiled or unveiled. Transformation, then, involves the shift referred to in the hymn "Amazing Grace"—"I was blind and now I see." The experience is described as an emerging out of darkness into light, becoming un-blinded, and as the removal of multiple coverings from our eyes. The "cleansing of the doors of perception" that occurs in some psychedelic states, and as a consequence of some meditations, has also been amply described and documented in the literature of consciousness research.

A striking and well-known instance is the conversion of Saul to Paul on the road to Damascus. After the flash of illumination that knocked him off his horse, Saul was blinded for three days. A healer named Ananias came to him and told him he would help him with his sight by laying on of hands. "And immediately it seemed that scales fell from his eyes, and he regained his sight. Thereupon he was baptized" (Acts 9:1–19). In this case, the impact of the conversion vision was so strong that he was first blinded (perhaps as a kind of lesson) and *then* his eyes were opened.

Such transformation of vision—in these cases, from cloudy to clear—can also occur in the opposite direction, in what I call "regressive" transformation in chapter 1. Psychiatrists speak of the "clouded sensorium" of the psychotic; a depressed or grief-stricken person may feel a cloud hovering over her or his head; and with sensitized perception (clairvoyance), one can "see" the gray, brown, or dark veils and coverings that seem to surround the face and body of a person in an emotionally distraught or despondent state. William James quotes an asylum patient who said, "I see, I touch, but the things do not come near me, a thick veil alters the hue and look of everything."[16]

The closed mind is often accompanied by relatively closed narrow eyes, and we have all encountered the pinpoint gaze of the people who distrust or dislike what they see. Conversely, when a person has an "eye-opening" inner break-through in consciousness, this can well be manifested in a more open facial expression and wider, more radiant eyes. And the notion that our pupils dilate when we take delight in what we are seeing has been a part of folklore for a long time and even temporarily entered the field of advertising and market-survey techniques.

There are other, subtler dualities of vision that can be involved in this kind of experience: outer versus inner sight, or perception of the material world versus perception of spiritual visions, or the perspective of time versus the perspective of eternity. Such transformation involves the reorientation of vision inward, to the inner realms of spirit and eternity. Blake wanted "to open the immortal eyes of Man inwards, into the Worlds of Thought, into Eternity."

Many writers suggest that inner, spiritual vision and outer, physical vision are somehow in competition with each other, that we cannot focus in both orientations at once. Jung seems to believe this also, since in his view, the intuitive function (inner) and the sensation function (outer) are always opposite.[17] There is an alternate view, which I personally favor, that says that transformation requires the balancing of the two perspectives. This is more akin to the shamanic concept that we must learn to master both ordinary and nonordinary reality, that we must be able to see and to "see," to perceive both the obstructed and the unobstructed reality.

This inward vision, the eye of wisdom, is related to the function of *clairvoyance,* which literally means "clear seeing," seeing without obstructions, without coverings or veils. This kind of vision sees the subtle auric energy fields that surround and interpenetrate all living things; it sees into the essences of things, into what the seer-mystic Jacob Boehme called their "signatures," their interior lineaments or designs. Students of psychic abilities also recognize *clairaudience,* or "clear hearing," and *clairsentience,* or "clear sensing." Here, too, the implication is that there are aspects of reality that exist but are normally not perceived by us because of some kind of obstruction or limitation. For certain individuals and in certain states of consciousness, it is possible to perceive these other, more subtle energetic phenomena. Some have used the analogy of a color photograph compared to a black-and-white photograph of the same scene: the color photo "sees" and shows more aspects of the same reality than the black-and-white one does.

The transformed vision we are speaking of here can also involve greater depth and dimensionality: ordinary, unawakened perception tends to have a flat, two-dimensional field, whereas heightened, sensitized perception has a depth and almost spherical feel to it. In experiments with hypnotic suggestion, Bernard Aaronson demonstrated that an individual under the hypnotic set to "see greater depth" does, in fact, do so, and feels euphoric, with expanded psychedelic aware-ness. An individual with the opposite mental set—to see less depth—feels alienated, tense, and tends to withdraw. Ecstatic experiences, with or without drugs, are often accompanied by a kind of spherical expansion of visual space.[18]

The notion of two kinds of eyes, or two kinds of vision, was sometimes extended to three eyes, to fourfold vision, and to multiple eyes all over one's body. The symbolism of three eyes was developed by the medieval Scholastic philosophers and by Indian yoga as well. The medieval theologians taught that we have (a) the eye of the flesh, which sees worldly things, (b) the eye of reason, by which we know mind and concepts, and (c) the eye of contemplation, by which we know transcendent, spiritual realities. The way of true wisdom, involved the ability to consciously function with and differentiate these three sources of knowledge.

In the Indian yoga teachings, we find a different meaning given to the notion of three eyes. Here the left eye is lunar, related to night, the feminine, the receptive; the right eye is solar, related to daytime, the masculine, and the dynamic-expressive. The vision of these two must balance and alternate rhythmically. The third eye, in the center of the forehead, was regarded as the eye of inner vision, intuition, and clairvoyant perception, when awakened through meditational, yogic practices.

One of our greatest visionary artists, William Blake, began to speak, in the later part of his life, of the "fourfold vision" that he was given:

> 'Tis fourfold in my supreme delight
> And threefold in soft Beulah's night
> And twofold always. May God us keep
> From single vision and Newton's sleep.

"Newton's sleep" is Blake's sarcastic term for the unawakened attitude that sees only the external world, the material universe of Newtonian physics. Twofold vision is the complementary inner/outer, subtle/physical polarity. "Soft Beulah's night" refers to the poet's muse or anima, hence to an inspirational or prophetic vision. And fourfold vision is complete, whole, all-inclusive vision: this could refer to the four functions (thinking, feeling, sensation, intuition) or to the four cosmic directions or to any number of fourfold schemata of understanding.

The fourfold pattern is always related to the mandala, the central symbol of individuation, or wholeness. One could say that a key component of the transformation of vision in psychospiritual development is the perceiving of the visual field as a kind of mandala. American Indian vision seekers saw the "circle of the Sky" touch the "circle of the Earth," forming one great hoop. This mandala, perceived in visionary states, has depth as well; in other words, it is a sphere with a six-armed cross inside. It is Buckminster Fuller's sphere of "omnidirectional awareness," moving always with us. And in Indian Tantric yoga, the practitioners meditate with a mandala until they have succeeded in projecting and integrating their mental contents into this circular diagram. In this way the meditator comes to realize that our ordinary perception of the world is also a projected image.

Beyond threefold and fourfold vision, there exists the symbolism of multiple eyes: in Hindu and Buddhist art one finds statues and paintings of divine or enlightened beings that have eyes all over the body, in the arms, legs, torso, palms, etc. This image symbolizes an awakened state in which awareness or light or presence has entered into every part and aspect of a being: the image signals aware action, movement, gesture, expression, as well as heightened perception.

Such symbolic expressions in religious or yogic art can be, and have been, readily transferred to practical application in the growth processes of modern individuals. For instance, a student in an art-therapy class spontaneously drew a self-portrait and then drew a large eye around the figure. Drawing this, which one could call a metaphor for giving herself a context of awareness or insight, had the effect of lifting her out of a prolonged depressive mood.

Another experience illustrates the relationship between changing vision and changing emotional state: in an LSD experience, a man saw the branches of a tree moving and sparkling with vivid, glistening colors. A feeling of anxiety arose in him as a result of conversation with his companion. He noticed that the tree branches stopped moving and the colors drained out, until the branches were blackish grey. As he observed these changes and succeeded in relaxing his anxious tension, the branches fluttered again, and the colors flowed back in. Visual appearances and emotional mood changed in synchrony.

I suggest that many people have had similar experiences in a variety of different situations. When we are afraid of or annoyed at something, the visual aspect tends to be fearful or threatening. When we regard someone with the eyes of love or attraction, they begin to look lovely and attractive. Beauty, it has often been said, is in the eye of the beholder—and so, of course, are ugliness, aggression, greed, and threat.

The transformation of vision is a metaphorical "cleansing of the doors of perception," to use Blake's phrase. It is a purifying of the perceptual channels, so that we are no longer limited to seeing in the darkness of the cave of our own illusions. Blake spoke of "melting apparent surfaces away, and displaying the infinite which was hid." When the surface appearances are dissolved, when we can "see through" someone or something, we become aware of how our own emotional states affect the appearances we perceive. We can then own and withdraw our projections and recognize the "transference" from past relationships to present ones. Finally, then, "everything would appear to man as it is—infinite."[19]

Unmasking the Self

Veils cover our eyes, obstructing and distorting our view of reality. Similar veils obstruct our perception of ourselves, our self-image, thus distorting and darkening awareness of our true nature or identity. Carl Jung's psychology speaks of this artificial, illusory self-concept as the *persona:* this is the mask we manufacture for the sake of appearances, a kind of "cover" identity that hides our actual Self. The persona was actually the mask used by Roman actors to speak through as they acted their roles, and *persona* is the basis of our word *personality.* This suggests that personality, or ego, is a kind of cover, or mask, and that the "real" individual is hidden beneath.

Wilhelm Reich's genius was to see and point out that this self-image cover is actually embodied in the muscular tension patterns that he called the "armor." Reich and his followers, as well as other body/mind practitioners, such as Rolf, Alexander, and Feldenkrais, have amply demonstrated that profound changes in personality and feeling can occur as the muscular armor is directly altered or dissolved. We are not conscious of the armoring, but it is manifested in our behavior and thinking. We express ourselves with it or through it; we are therefore limited in our expressive range by the emotional defensive patterns woven into the muscles and tissues of our bodies. Meister Eckhart said it seven hundred years ago when he wrote: "A man has many skins in himself, covering the depths of his heart. Man knows so many things, but he does not know himself. Why, thirty or forty skins or hides, just like an ox's or bear's, so thick and hard, cover the soul."[20]

Clothes also symbolically represent the personality or character, the front with which we face the world, our habits of expression and behavior. The English word *habit* still has meanings connected to clothing, as in the term *riding habit.* And perhaps most intimately, the skin itself is symbolically perceived as equivalent to or related to the persona. Alan Watts spoke of the "skin-encapsulated ego," the typical self-image whose perceived boundaries are the skin. Under the sway of this skin-ego image, I think, "I am being touched" when somebody touches my skin. If, on the other hand, "I feel touched" emotionally by someone's word or gesture, then my self-boundary is expanded well beyond the skin.

The *mask,* the *armor,* the *clothes,* the *skin*—are all symbols for personality or character. Corresponding to each of these symbols of personality are metaphors for the transformative experience. In an experience of conversion, insight, or revelation (unveiling), the individual may experience a mask being removed or a rigid character armor being dissolved or clothes being taken off, so that he or she feels naked (and then has to deal with all the emotional charge and shame surrounding nakedness); the person may also experience the feeling of his or her skin boundary dissolving, the inside and outside becoming continuous and flowing together. Each of these metaphors has clear structural similarity to the idea of removing veils or coverings from perception.

A person who experiences the dissolving of body boundaries will interpret it differently according to his or her prior beliefs and expectations. For someone totally identified with their body image, the experience of its dissolution could be catastrophic. And this phenomenon would be interpreted by most psychiatrists as a symptom of weak ego boundaries, or "depersonalization." On the other hand, for someone familiar with Buddhist or other mystical literature who anticipates this kind of experience and has a sense of identity that includes the body but is not limited to it, such an experience could be sought-after ecstatic release into an expanded state of consciousness. In the words of Shunryu Suzuki, "When you become you, Zen becomes Zen. When you are you, you see things as they are, and you become one with your surroundings."[21]

Many other related metaphors of self-transformation that appear to encompass the same theme exist in the world's literature. In older, primal cultures, many of these come from observations of the animal world. For instance, the snake's shedding of its skin was often regarded as a teaching concerning regeneration and transformation of self. The bird that breaks the shell and emerges from the "crack in the cosmic egg" is another image. People frequently feel themselves to exist within a hardened "shell," analogous to Reich's "armor," which they find difficult to break out of. The insect in its larval stage, completely enfolded in its cocoon and unaware of its latent capacities, is yet another metaphor for the undeveloped, unactualized self. Adolf Portmann has pointed out that the larva "masks" the insect's mature, developed form. Similarly, the persona acquired in childhood masks the adult self.

The idea that in the process of growing up, of becoming mature or adult, there is a kind of unmasking, a more direct seeing of oneself, is also implicit in the famous passage of Saint Paul: "When I was a child, my speech, my outlook, and my thoughts were all childish. When I grew up, I finished with childish things. Now we see only puzzling reflections in a mirror [through a glass, darkly]; but then face to face. Now my knowledge [of myself] is partial; then it will be complete, even as God's knowledge of me" (1 Corinthians 13:11–12). When the personality confronts the Self, there is no hiding, no puzzling darkness, but only direct and complete self-knowledge.

A vivid account of such a radical and complete unmasking and self-confrontation is given by William James, quoting the experience related by J. A. Symonds:

> . . . time, sensation, and the multitudinous factors of experience which seem to qualify what we are pleased to call our Self. . . . At last nothing remained but a pure, absolute, abstract Self. The universe became without form and void of content. But Self persisted, formidable in its vivid keenness, feeling the most poignant doubts about reality . . . the sense that I had followed the thread of being to the verge of the abyss, and had arrived at demonstration of eternal maya or illusion. Often have I asked myself, on waking from that formless state of denuded, keenly sentient being, which is the unreality? The trance of fiery, vacant, apprehensive, skeptical Self from which I issue, or

these surrounding phenomena and habits which veil that inner Self and build a sort of flesh-and-blood conventionality?[22]

A powerful mythological expression of this theme is the story, from the ancient Near East, of the descent of the Mother Goddess, Inanna or Ishtar, into the underworld, to revive her son-lover, who has been lost to Death. This is symbolically an initiation mystery tale, which describes the tests one must pass on the way to self-knowledge and inner unification. As the goddess descends into the underworld of the dead, she passes through seven thresholds, and at each one she has to remove one ornament or covering: at the first, her crown; the next, her earrings and facial jewelry; then her necklace, her breast shields, her bracelets, her jeweled belt, and finally her pelvic garment. Clearly these seven stages of descent relate to the uncovering, or opening, of seven energy centers. The "ornaments" symbolize the conventional, conditioned self-images that obstruct and cover the natural expression of life energy through the centers.

Undefended, unadorned, and without any of the usual social disguises, with her centers opened, she has to confront the ancient, terrible Goddess of Death and the Underworld. She has to endure horrible sickness and torment and be as dead for three days before she can recover the other half of her psyche, her animus-lover, from whom she has become separated.[23]

Beyond the obvious and widespread symbolic identification of veils with the clothes, masks, and armor that express character, there is also another, deeper meaning to these symbols. The perceptual experience of piercing or removing a veil is like traversing a kind of threshold or boundary region between planes of consciousness. Ancient teachings held that each human being has many bodies, or forms, separated from one another by "veils," "curtains," or "skins." Birth, or incarnation, involves taking on bodies, clothes, or skins—the Self or Spirit becomes embodied. The phrase in the Book of Genesis about the "coats of skins" the Lord made for Adam and Eve may be a reference to this idea.

Indian yoga psychology speaks of the series of "sheaths" (koshas) with which the Self-Spirit (Atman) is clothed, the outermost and densest one being the physical body. This physical body is referred to as anna-maya-kosha, the "sheath form made of food"; "higher" forms are made of "breath," of "feeling," of "mind," of "bliss."

During the incarnational descent into form, we take on one after another of these veils. In an extraordinary passage written by an Islamic Rifa'i dervish, quoted in R. A. Nicholson's The Mystics of Islam, we find the incarnational descent described as a passage through seventy thousand veils:

Seventy thousand veils separate Allah, the One Reality, from the world of matter and sense. And every soul passes before his birth through these seventy thousand. The inner half of these are veils of light; the outer half veils of darkness.... Thus the child is born weeping, for the soul knows its separation

from Allah, the One Reality. . . . The passage through the veils has brought
with it forgetfulness. . . . He is now, as it were, in prison in his body, separated
by these thick curtains from Allah.[24]

Regardless of whether we count seven or seventy thousand, the descent into
bodily form is always seen as a taking on of veils, clothes, or sheaths; or a falling
into sleep, a forgetting.

On the other hand, the journey to God, or to the Self, is always experienced
as an uncovering, a removal of veils. Meister Eckhart refers to this ascending,
evolutionary transformation in the following passage: "In being lifted up, the soul
is made naked before the idea of God, for God's begetting; the image of God is
unveiled and free in the open soul."[25] Ignorance and lack of understanding are
always symbolized by blindness, deafness, or clouded or covered thinking; insight,
true perception, and spiritual awareness are experienced as unveiling, "re-veal-
ing", dis-covering, dis-illusionment.

Saint Paul writes:

"To this very day, every time the Law of Moses is read, a veil lies over the
minds of the hearers. However, as Scripture says, "when one turns to the
Lord, the veil is removed." Now the Lord of whom this passage speaks is the
Spirit; and where the Spirit of the Lord is, there is liberty. And because there
is for us no veil over the face, we all reflect as in a mirror the splendor of the
Lord; thus we are transfigured into his likeness, from splendor to splendor;
such is the influence of the Lord who is Spirit. (2 Corinthians 3:15–18)

Turning inward, toward the Lord, Spirit, Atman, brings about the ascent
through the dimensions, the experience of transcendent reality, with clairvoyant
vision of the inner domains and subtle body sheaths. It also brings about the
unmasking of the persona, the dissolving of conditioned self-images.

As the eye is unveiled, the I is transformed.

3

From Captivity to Liberation

To know consists in opening out a way whence the imprisoned splendor may escape.

—ROBERT BROWNING

Escape from prison has been one of the most consistent metaphors for the process of human transformation, both in the myths and texts of the ancients and in the psychological writings of modern thinkers. Liberation from the bonds of karma, escape from the ceaseless round of *samsara* (existence), freedom from the snares of illusion, deliverance from the clutches of sin—these are but some of the traditional expressions that allude to this aspect of transformation. The confined and bounded quality of ordinary human consciousness is evident to all of us: we may feel trapped in a relationship, tied down by obligations, bound by job demands, attached to possessions, fixated on someone we desire, or generally "hung up." The pattern of psychological defenses can and does become a rigid bodily armor. Psychoanalysts tell us we are the "prisoners of childhood" or write about "man in the trap."[1]

In Plato's cave parable, humans are compared to prisoners chained to the wall of a dark cave, watching with fascination the illusory flickering shadows cast by fires on the walls of the cave. This metaphor tells us that our illusory perception of the world is based on our being attached, tied to the rock wall, which is the material world. "The soul [psyche] . . . has been captured, it is in chains. . . . It is said to be in a tomb, and in a cave; yet by turning again towards ideas, it frees itself from its bonds."[2] Turning toward ideas means turning inward, toward self-knowledge, self-realization: the *Atman,* Spirit, Self is unbounded, unconditioned, unlimited. According to the Vedanta philosopher Shankara, "A liberated being, endowed with knowledge of Atman, abandons attachments to the limitations of form, and becomes pure being-consciousness-joy, like *Brahman.* "[3] Spirit/soul is bound and imprisoned in matter/body. Liberation *(moksha)* is both possible and desirable—indeed, necessary.

The myth of Prometheus powerfully expresses the archetype of imprisonment and liberating transformation. Prometheus, whose name means "Foresight," was one of the race of titans, who were the biblical "giants on the Earth," offspring of an older generation of chthonic deities, less than a god but more than human. Prometheus was the bringer of fire, the culture hero who in the early stages of humanity's development helped develop the arts of civilization. Psychologically he represents the heroic principle of individualization, becoming an individual. He is the Spirit in every human being that brings the fire of life down to Earth. Bringing fire to earth symbolizes bringing life into body and form: it is embodiment, incarnation.

The price we pay for the Promethean project of incarnation is imprisonment. Prometheus, the heroic human Spirit, is as in Plato's parable, chained to the rock, trapped in material form. Every day vultures rip and tear at his liver, which every night is restored and regenerated. The liver may be regarded as the organ of "living," expressing vitality and life force. The vultures are the harbingers of entropic decay and degeneration. Prometheus, then, is every one of us, as we are trapped in the limitations of material form and ravaged by the inevitable forces of old age, decay, and disease.

This imagery of the world as a prison appears also in the Neoplatonists and very emphatically in the Gnostic texts. For these philosophers, the world in general and the body in particular constitute a fortress, a dungeon, a tomb, a garment of chains—a condition marked by weight, cold, and immobility.[4] Mystics such as Saint John of the Cross regard the body as a prison for the soul, which longs to be freed from it, to transcend it. Such imagery is perhaps an intensification of the more common notion and more common sensation of the body as a sheath, shell, vehicle, or house, for spirit. In the dreams of psychotherapy patients, such events as explorations of a house or damages or repairs to a house often represent actions and experiences involving the body. If I become acutely conscious of limitations and obstructions my body presents to me, images of prisons, traps, nets, or labyrinths come to mind very naturally.

In an extraordinary passage from a Buddhist text, the world of sense objects, *samsara,* is compared to an unusual variety of metaphorical prisons and traps:

> *Samsara* is . . . a dungeon dark, a deep swamp of three poisons, . . . 'Tis being caught in a spider's web, or a bird entangled in a fowler's net; 'Tis like being bound hand to neck by Mara, or immersed in a pond of beastliness. . . . It is the net of fate . . . and living neath the floating shadows of old age and birth, entanglement in bondage. It is a flame flickering in the wind, untruth, a dream, bewilderment.[5]

I take these images to mean the emotional reactivity to sense experience, the endless grasping for and avoiding of the objects of our sensory world, which exposes us to being immersed in or ensnared by contradictory sensations of pleasure and pain, craving and suffering, delusion, illusion, false ideals, and ideas.

Among modern philosophers and writers, the existentialists in particular have identified and described the prison-like and angst-producing aspects of worldly existence. Søren Kierkegaard, the melancholy Dane, in his books *Fear and Trembling* and *Sickness unto Death,* wrote of the "demonic shut-upness" that results from the conflicts in our being and of the "dread" that results as we accept the "absurdity" of these oppositions. One senses that most of the existentialists never found a way to escape from the prison of existence: they only developed detailed and elaborate descriptions of its dimensions. The French philosopher Albert Camus, in his book *The Myth of Sisyphus,* adopted a posture of poetic rebellion, struggling forever, like his titanic hero, to roll a boulder up the mountain, or trying to find meaning in "the whirlpool's shrieking face." Jean-Paul Sartre's play *No Exit,* about four people locked hellishly and inescapably in one room, is another powerful statement of this theme.

A personal experience may be relevant here, that provided me with a very different perspective and understanding of the psychological meaning of imprisonment. In 1961 and 1962 I and several other graduate students at Harvard University worked with Timothy Leary on a psychedelic drug research project involving convicts in a maximum security prison. The purpose of the research was to attempt to produce insight and change through the judicious use of psilocybin (the active ingredient of the sacred mushrooms of ancient Mexico) in a supportive group environment. To minimize the prisoners' feeling of being experimental guinea pigs, we adopted a policy of research staff also partaking of the drug with the prisoners on an alternating basis.[6]

So I had the first six or so psychedelic experiences of my life behind the bars of a maximum security prison. I remember vividly, to this day, the extraordinary experience of having my visual field expanded until it became a 360-degree circle or sphere, within which sphere the prison walls, the bars on the windows, and the locks on the doors, had become meaningless. Though still visible and "real," they seemed ineffectual in imprisoning the human spirit, which soared unconstrained that day.

These experiences taught me that we can have inner freedom, even while in an outer prison. And in many other experiences before and since that time, I have learned that we can have inner bondage even while outwardly apparently free. The inner prisons, the bars and locks of the mind, are more subtle and less obvious—yet perhaps for that reason more insidious. Since we do not ordinarily see them, we have no incentive to try to escape. As Gurdjieff says, if we do not realize we are in prison, we have no chance of escaping at all.

A widespread variation of the imprisonment theme is the idea of a treadmill, a wheel, the ceaseless round of existence. Here we find symbolic expressions of the frustrations of repetitive routine work; the futility of the daily "grind." A man or woman tied to a meaningless repetitive job might very well feel like a prisoner, with awareness contracted, perception numbed or blinded. He or she might feel condemned or punished somehow or trapped by bad past karma, if belief in reincarnation is accepted. The story of Samson is relevant here: this hero of the

Israelites, a liberator, a slayer of enemies, was finally caught (through the well-known ruse of the faithless Delilah) and put to work grinding corn on a treadmill in prison. Like Samson, we might sense that our life purpose has to do with liberation, but instead we find ourselves imprisoned. "Ask for this great deliverer now," wrote John Milton, "and find him eyeless in Gaza at the mill with the slaves."[7]

Other images portray life as a repetitive wheel or round. People involved in hellish psychotic experiences might find themselves identifying with the Greek myth of Ixion, who was bound to a fiery wheel and condemned to roll forever through the heavens. Obsessive workaholics might identify with Sisyphus, who was condemned to forever push a huge stone up a mountain, only to have it always roll down again. The fourth-century Byzantine mystic Gregory of Nyssa wrote that our journey through life can often be likened to a man walking on a sand dune or treadmill.

> Like the beasts who turn a mill wheel we turn round and round, our eyes blindfolded, in the mill of this life. I will tell you what this cycle is: hunger, satiety, sleep, waking; one follows the other, the other follows the one, and never does the round come to an end until we escape from this mill. . . . Those who climb a dune take long strides; all their trouble is in vain, for the sliding sand keeps bringing them back down. There is expenditure of movement, but no progress.[8]

Gregory tells us what we must do to escape from the treadmill: "If a man has withdrawn his feet from the bottom of the abyss and given them a firm hold in the rock, the firmer he is in the good and the more rapid becomes his progress. His stability is for him like a wing in his journey toward the height; his flight is winged by virtue of his stability in the good." Here is a paradoxical image: The stability of the seeker, his persistence in growth and in virtue, generate their own momentum, which can provide the motivation necessary to carry on with the transformation. It gives the seeker the wings for his "flight," which is both fleeing and flying.

"Flying toward the heights" is an ascensional metaphor, analogous to climbing the tree or the mountain. It symbolizes the freedom of rising up into higher dimensions of consciousness, to the higher, spiritual worlds, where we gain a transcendent perspective on the patterns of our fate. Inner flying, or what modern researchers call out-of-body experience, is one of the ways an initiate uses to transcend or escape from the prison of the material world. Another relevant myth is that of Daedalus escaping from the labyrinth of King Minos by fashioning wings and flying over the walls. We shall return, in the last section of this chapter, to a discussion of this and other methods of escaping from "prison."

The cave, the armor, the dungeon, the treadmill, the labyrinth—have thus all been used as images for the bound, trapped, imprisoned, repetitive, closed-in nature of human consciousness. The labyrinth, or maze, is a particularly apt symbol for the conditioned mind, bound up in anxiety and defensiveness. In a maze, as in this kind of thinking, we can't see where we're going; we take numerous blind alleys, go backwards, sideways, and around in circles, usually without knowing it; we have to backtrack, double over, analyze, figure, review, project, and so on—and we may still never find our way out. The monstrous Minotaur that sits in the center of the labyrinth is a symbol of the unacceptable shadow part of our nature, that which we try to hide and deny: the enemy within.

Body and Form as Prison

So we have seen that many mythic and religious writings contain the metaphor of bodily form as inherently a cave, dungeon, trap, or labyrinth. To many people such a notion might seem like the life-negating delusion of melancholy existentialists or masochistic ascetics. We might prefer to think of the body as an instrument for work, creativity, and play in the "real world," or we might think of it as our medium for the experience of hedonistic delight and pleasure, or conceive of it as a temple for divine Spirit. Indeed, this last image is often given in various mystical and sacred texts as a state or attitude to which we should aspire.

Yet when we are in the "grip" of a disease, or "racked" with pain, the imagery of the body as captivity or a crippling limitation seems only too real. Our awareness is contracted, reduced to the area of pain or illness; we can't move or breathe properly; we feel weak, debilitated, and frustrated, and perhaps imagine that we are being punished for some transgression. The writings and teachings of Buddhists and Gnostics, and those of other mystical traditions, are quite explicit on this subject: bodily life itself is equivalent to imprisonment. From this point of view, illness and paralysis only intensify and exacerbate an already existing, "normal" captivity.

This metaphor tells us that because of the law of karma, we are the prisoners of our own past actions. We cannot avoid or escape reaping the consequences of what we have sown before. Our thinking is bound and conditioned, fixated on fears and painful past experiences. Likewise, our behavior is limited and restricted. We are as though addicted, that is, "hooked," in relation to sense stimuli and pleasures. We are *fascinated* (which means "bound") by glamour and idealisms, such as wealth, fame, power, and beauty. We are *attached* to the objects of our desires—and to our aversions. A middle-aged married woman, for instance, said in therapy that she "felt nailed down by petty concerns."

In modern times this metaphor of imprisonment has reemerged in several interesting variants, which are remarkable chiefly for their distinctive somatic, even anatomic specificity. Reich's theory of armoring, for instance, says that "the muscular armor is functionally equivalent to the character armor."

In thus loosening the character incrustations, we set free the affects (feelings) which had previously undergone inhibition and fixation. . . . Part of the work shifts from the psychological and characterological to the immediate dissolution of the muscular armor. . . . I could not avoid the impression that the physical rigidity, actually, represents the most essential part of the process of repression. . . . The character-analytic work on the layers of the character incrustations is the more effective, the more completely it brings about a dissolution of the corresponding muscular attitudes. . . . This muscular attitude is identical with what we call "bodily expression."[9]

Alexander Lowen, a psychiatrist who was a student of Reich and who further developed Reich's ideas, states that "all unresolved emotional conflicts become structured in the body in the form of chronic muscular tensions." Lowen has some interesting observations about the expression "being hung-up" and how this is manifested in somatic reality. "A person is said to be 'hung up' when he is caught in an emotional conflict that immobilizes him and prevents any effective action to change the situation."

In an individual who has the "hung-up syndrome," according to Lowen, the upper torso may actually be held up, as if suspended by an invisible coat hanger, with the shoulders pulled up and back in fear.[10] Being "hung up" is a form of captivity with both psychological and somatic aspects. In medieval times, this state of consciousness was expressed in symbols such as The Hanged Man of the Tarot.

Another highly relevant and innovative approach to body structure is the "structural integration" work of Ida Rolf. This involves deep, often painful, massaging of the body in order to bring it into better alignment with the axis of gravity. In Rolf's system, the key connecting structures of the body are the fascia, the connective tissue that covers muscles and links them with bones. These fascia become rigid and distorted in the course of life, and they are actually loosened and lengthened in the structural integration work. Don Johnson, a philosopher and practitioner of Rolfing, as it is also known, describes how the fascia function as a kind of internal physical armor, as rigid walls that actually limit and constrict the free motion of our bodies.

Fascia is the forgotten organ of the body. It starts just below the skin to form an inner covering for the entire body. . . . Fascia is the primary vehicle for change in the body—for good as well as ill. A severe leg fracture, for example, will cause the fascia in that area to become like gristle. This knot inhibits the free movement of the neighboring muscles. In other places, lack of use or poor posture will give rise to shortening of fascial planes and adhesions of these planes to bones and muscles, also limiting body movement and the flow of fluids through the flesh. . . . Fascia is the unifying organ of the body. It is the matrix for the flow of metabolites, for circulation, and for nervous flow. Shortening and thickening of fascia distorts the whole body. By loosening and moving the fascia, you can readily alter the body.[11]

Thus, from this modern research on the integrated totality of psychological and physical structures and functions, a whole new picture of the body-mind complex is emerging, which confirms in striking anatomical detail, some of the ancient metaphorical and symbolic themes of the body as constricting, binding, prison-like structure. T. S. Eliot wrote that "the enchainment of the past and future (is) woven in the weakness of the changing body."[12] These structural formations and deformations constitute the "prison" of the body, limiting its mobility and restricting the free flow of somatic and emotional energy.

Those who have personally experienced Reichian bioenergetic therapy, Rolf's structural integration, or the work of other such pioneers as Alexander, Feldenkreis, or Trager can testify to the striking liberating changes that can occur with these approaches; and they become aware of the binding limitations they have been unconsciously living under.

Other kinds of inner transformation process work, particularly those forms of meditation and yoga that emphasize close attention to bodily structures and functions, can also lead to this realization. The individual may become aware of internal images, feelings, and sensations that represent the body in terms of the prison metaphors. Typical is this account, from a student of Agni Yoga:

> In working to release loads and tensions from my body, I frequently experience the obstruction as an armor plating locked on or around the muscle or organ; and as this is unlocked, sheaths of metallic-like stuff fly off and disintegrate. Sometimes these obstructions literally have the form of hasps and locks and chains. As these are unlocked and the systems freed, the experience is of greater ability to breathe, to flex, to move and to relate.[13]

Yet another kind of experiential validation of the metaphor of body as prison comes from what are known in parapsychology as "out-of-body experiences." Such experiences, which I believe are much more common than is generally assumed, have been described in detail by Robert Monroe in a book entitled *Journeys Out of the Body,* and they have been fairly extensively studied by parapsychologists.[14] The consensus from people experiencing this phenemenon is that leaving the body is always experienced as a kind of flying or floating, a release and freedom from the usual physical limitations. Similarly, the consensus about the experience of returning to the body is that it always feels like coming into a more limited, bound, heavy, immobile state. Shirley MacLaine, in her autobiographical account of her psychic and out-of-body experiences, writes, "I melded back into my body. My body felt comfortable, familiar, but it also felt restricting and cumbersome and limiting."[15] Regardless of what kind of scientific or psychological interpretation we give to this kind of experience, the universal agreement on the subjective, experiential characteristics is quite remarkable.

If we accept the notion that experiencing the body as prison and restrictive armor is fairly common, both in illness and in certain kinds of therapy, yoga and psychic experiences, the question still arises as to why some individuals might be more predisposed to this kind of experience than others. Clearly, some people do feel very free, agile, and expressive in their bodies, and may not resonate to the prison metaphor very much. A possible answer to this question is given in the research with LSD psychotherapy conducted by Stanislav Grof. Grof found that subjects in this kind of deep exploration (and this has since been verified with other kinds of nondrug experiential therapies) can relive aspects of their birth trauma.

He observed that there is a profound connection between feelings of being trapped, bound, shut in, imprisoned, and the apparent memory of the second stage of the four-phase birth process. In his model, this is the stage in which powerful uterine contractions are impinging on the fetus but the cervix is closed, and there is as yet no passage out. Grof has proposed that each stage of the birth process functions as a kind of matrix ("basic perinatal matrix"), around which later physical and psychological experiences *that have the same form and feelings* are organized. He describes the typical stage two experiences as follows:

> The activation of this matrix results in a rather characteristic experience of "no exit" or "hell." The subject feels encaged in a claustrophobic world and experiences incredible physical and psychological tortures. This experience is characterized by a striking darkness of the visual field and by ominous colors. Typically, the situation is absolutely unbearable, and at the same time appears to be endless and hopeless; no escape can be seen. . . . Agonizing feelings of separation, alienation, metaphysical loneliness, helplessness, hopelessness, inferiority, and guilt are standard components of [this phase]. The individual trapped in the "no exit" situation clearly sees that human existence is meaningless, yet feels a desperate need to find meaning in life. This struggle often coincides with what is experienced as the attempts of the fetus to escape from the closed uterine system and save its life.[16]

We can see that this kind of experience could be the actual, personal, sensory, and perceptual memory that underlies the metaphysical worldview of existentialism, with its focus on anxiety, alienation, helplessness, and its despairing and desperate search for meaning. We can also see that these kinds of perceptions, if somehow activated spontaneously, instead of in a controlled, purposive psychotherapy situation, could readily precipitate an individual into a hellish psychotic state. As Aldous Huxley pointed out, such experiences under psychedelics are quite comparable to the visions and hallucinations of schizophrenia—and, he might have added, to the initiatory experiences of apprentice shamans.

Some of the more dramatic kinds of experiences associated with this birth stage and metaphor include images and feelings of being trapped in metallic cages or huge impersonal machinery; of being sucked into a gigantic whirlpool or cosmic maelstrom; of being swallowed and devoured by a ferocious monster, dragon, python, or whale; of being tied, bound, gagged, and immobilized; or being caught in the sticky web of some monstrous spider. And there are the mythic counterparts to all these experiences—Jonah being swallowed by the whale; Theseus battling the Minotaur; Inanna hanging on the peg in the Underworld; the devouring Kronos, Kali, or Typhon; and the sinners in Dante's *Inferno* who are encased in tree trunks or frozen in lakes of ice.

When, in the course of a transformation process, someone is going through this kind of hellish imprisonment experience, it can be of great value to see that the experience has been known and described for ages and that many people have had similar experiences in other eras and countries. We are not alone, and we are not the first to go through this. Such recognition contributes in no small way to the individual's ability to continue and complete the process of transformation.

Probably the best-known mythic "prisoner," besides Prometheus, is Osiris. This most beloved deity of the Egyptian pantheon goes through a number of symbolic transformations that illustrate the theme of embodiment as imprisonment; his story is the archetypal pattern of incarnation as captivity, followed by liberation. Osiris, like Prometheus for the Greeks, Christ for the Christians, and Odin for the Nordic peoples, represents the immortal Spirit in the mortal human. Each of these figures is trapped, chained, hung, or fixed, a condition that represents the limited, contracted condition of human, earthly, bodily existence.

Each human being is an immortal god in mortal bodily form. As god, each one is light and splendor; as incarnated human being, each one is trapped, bound, imprisoned. The spiritual essence, or beingness, within each human being, is the "imprisoned splendor" that the mystics experience and describe.[17] Odin hanging on the world tree, Christ on the cross, Prometheus bound to the rock, and Osiris trapped in the coffer are all images of the archetype of imprisoned splendor, which each one of us is destined to liberate.

In the story of Osiris, as told by the historian Plutarch, the god is tricked into lying down in a beautiful coffer or chest that has been carved exactly to his dimensions, which is then locked and thrown into a river; floating down the river to the sea, the chest then lands and is incorporated into a tree trunk; the tree, with the god still within it, becomes the wooden framework of a house. Subsequent parts of the myth relate how Osiris is liberated from his imprisonment by the divine stratagems of his consort Isis.

I offer the following interpretation of this myth:[18] the four stages—chest, river, tree, house—represent the four major "inner bodies" or levels on the incarnational descent into bodily form on Earth. The chest or coffer, with its beautifully carved designs, represents the mental body; the river is the flowing astral dimension, also known as the emotional body; the tree symbolizes the etheric, or perceptual, dimension, associated with the treelike sensory nervous system; and the house frame represents the physical body, the most material, utilitarian form. Each of the forms that the god-man comes into represents a kind of imprisonment, contraction, or limitation.

Like Osiris, each one of us has "come down" into progressively more and more limited forms, more and more constricted, denser bodies, to the ultimate density of the physical. In this last and densest form, we usually have most of our awareness. And in this physical house/body form, we may become aware of the most intimate details of our imprisonment: the armored muscles, rigid fascia, hardened flesh of our somatic dungeon. And like Osiris, each one of us has the potential to transform captivity into freedom, to break through, to transcend or dissolve the limitations imposed on us by personal karma and by the process of incarnation itself.

Knots, Ties, Nets, and Bonds in Relationships

Obstructions to the free flow of awareness and energy in the body that give rise to the imagery of imprisonment are frequently experienced and described as "knots." These knots may actually be tensed and contracted muscles; or they may be congealed and congested connective or vascular tissue. We all know the knot in the stomach of anxiety, and the lump in the throat of inhibited sadness. These kinds of knots may make us feel tight, tense, or tongue-tied, unable to express our feelings through words or gestures.

In the subtle body, with its energy channels *(nadis)* and centers *(chakras)*, there may be corresponding knots and ties. In the Indian Upanishads, there are references to "knots in the heart" *(granthi)* that must surely refer to obstructions in the heart center. "When all the knots that fetter the heart are cut asunder, then a mortal becomes immortal," says the Katho Upanishad. The heart center, like the other centers, is a gateway to the higher realms, the transpersonal dimensions; thus when the blocks in that gateway are removed, the full splendor of the immortal being of light can be experienced and known. The Mundaka Upanishad states, "When the knot of the heart is unloosened, and all doubts are cut off, then man's work is finished, then is seen That which is above and below."[19]

In our personal experience, the area of human life that probably gives rise to the most complex and difficult "knots in the heart" is the area of emotional and sexual relationships. We may be fascinated (literally "bound") by the charm of a loved one. There are the ties of dependency, as in being tied to a mother's apron strings. When we solemnize the relationship in marriage (a state referred to as "the tender trap"), we speak of "getting hitched" and "tying the knot." People often feel trapped in a marriage or relationship that has become fixed, rigid, or routine. And when a love relationship ends, there may be a painful feeling of a tie being cut, or an agonizing, constricting knot in the heart. The psychiatrist R. D. Laing has written a whole book of poems, *Knots,* on the convoluted entanglements of both normal and disturbed relationships.

The Huichol Indians of Mexico have an interesting custom: before setting out on their annual sacred tribal pilgrimage, they make knots in a piece of string for every intimate relationship they've had in the past year. They then burn the knotted string to symbolize the burning away of attachments. This is a metaphor for the purification of emotional knots and ties by inner fire, the alchemical *calcinatio,* as we shall see in chapter 4. In psychedelic or other kinds of deep experiential psychotherapy, a person may experience the dissolving or loosening of a knot or lump in the heart center and may experience difficult, tense, anxious, angry, or sad feelings toward a loved one releasing at the same time. As the personal and interpersonal knots are untied, then the heart and mind become more open to receiving and perceiving the light-fire of Spirit, "that which is above and below."

The symbolic meaning of knots is not all bad. As Mircea Eliade points out, "knots have opposite meaning: they can bring about illness, or cure it or drive it away; protect against bewitchment or bewitch; hinder childbirth or facilitate it; preserve newborns or make them ill; bring death or prevent it."[20] There is, for example, the "endless knot," which is one of the eight emblems of good fortune in Chinese and Tibetan Buddhism. And the figure-of-eight knot is, of course, our symbol for infinity. Some see the two loops of this figure as representing the intertwined connection between Spirit and Matter, between inner and outer worlds of life.

Another, related kind of symbolism is that of nets. We have already noted that the feeling of immobilizing netting in the body may be based on such structures as rigid fascia, hardened and congested connective tissue, or tense nerve networks. In relationships we may get the feeling of being somehow entangled or trapped in a web or net of expectations, obligations, illusions, and perhaps deceptions. If we find someone attractive, we may be captivated, bewitched, spellbound, or enthralled.

This theme was given a perceptively humorous rendering in the Greek myth of the liaison between Ares and Aphrodite. When the god of war and the goddess of love engaged in amorous dalliance, Aphrodite's husband, the lame smith Hephaistos, was informed of this by Helios, the sun god. The jealous Hephaistos then fashioned a gossamer-thin, yet extraordinarily strong, net of golden threads; and, in a surprise move, he threw it over the couple as they lay in their bed of passion. Thereupon he invited the other gods to come and view the plight of the lovers. At the sight of the undignified entanglement of the impulsive Ares and the affectionate Aphrodite, the heavens echoed with the resounding, good-natured laughter of the Olympians. Just so, we may often feel ridiculous to the point of embarrassment at the indignities to which our romantic passions expose us.

Family relationships that involve ties of dependency and love can become so entangled and confused that one or several individuals may feel "caught in a bind," suffering anguish and conflict. One important theory of schizophrenia holds that this condition is at least partly caused by "double binds," contradictory patterns of communication.[21] The child may get conflicting messages (e.g., the voice speaks love; the eyes show hate)—this is a bind; what makes it a *double* bind is that the child cannot leave the situation. Adult patterns of communication are often equally contradictory, confused, and entangled, resisting the efforts of even the most skillful therapists or counselors to unravel.

Nets, like knots, have paradoxical meanings and values. The opposite feelings we have about them are reflected in etymology, for language contains and reveals psychological truths. For example, the words *net* and *noose* come from the Latin *nectere*, "to bind, fasten, or tie." But this is also the root word for *node*, *nexus*, and *connection*. Our ties bind us but also link and connect us. We may be imprisoned, in "bondage," but we desire close emotional "bonding" with family and friends as well. While we may get trapped and entangled in nets, we also use them to catch fish. And we have "networks" of relationships among people, which serve the purposes of communication and mutual support. The same Latin word *ligare*, "to tie or connect," underlies *ligaments*, which connect bones; *obligations*, which tie us to our fellow man; and *religion*, which supposedly should "reconnect" us with the Divine.

A net, tie, or bind is experienced as limiting or immobilizing if we are caught or trapped in it involuntarily: then we are the victims. If, on the other hand, we use it consciously and intentionally, then the tie, network, or connection provides the channels through which communication and exchange of energy can flow.

In ancient civilizations there were deities that used a rope, net, or noose to bind and immobilize demons and to bring illness and death to human beings. These were the gods of fate, the lords of karma. They included Indra in Vedic India, Uranus in Greece, Odin in Scandinavia, and Jehovah, of whom all-suffering Job said, "He hath put his net around me." This theme of "the god who binds" is related to the similar idea, found in other cultures, of the Fates. These are often three ancient goddesses who spin out a thread for each individual: one goddess starts the thread, one continues it, and one cuts it at death.[22] Fate is that pattern of events we cannot escape from; we are trapped or bound in it, we are its victims.

The dual meanings of these symbols hint at the process of liberation. The net is not only something in which we are trapped and entangled, it is also the network for communication and energy exchange. The entire world is seen, especially in the traditions of *Tantra* (a word related to words for weaving and texture), as a vast, interconnecting web or woven fabric. Modern scientists have similarly concluded that all phenomena are interrelated in complex interrelating networks of energy transformation. Teilhard de Chardin's concept of the noosphere, a network of thought encompassing the planet, is one such idea. The notion of networks of individuals who share a common interest and provide information and support to one another through the network is one that has enormous potential for furthering individual and social transformation.

The transition from the state of consciousness where we feel trapped or entangled in a net to the state of consciousness where we are consciously and intentionally participating in a network is one aspect of the process of liberation through transformation. The question is, how does one escape from prison; how can the knots be untied or loosened; how can the limiting net be changed into a liberating network?

Strategies of Escape and Liberation

This transformative process, like the others discussed in this book, can vary in a number of ways: it can be abrupt or gradual, it can be temporary or lasting, it can be a spontaneous discovery or one aided by an outer teacher or liberator, and it could come through grace or conscious effort and intention. While my values favor the second possibility in each pair—a progressive, permanent, guided, and intentional approach—this does not rule out that liberating experiences can and do occur in the other modes mentioned—sudden, temporary, spontaneously, effortlessly.

I follow Gurdjieff's view that the single most important prerequisite for escaping from prison is awakening.

> You do not realize your own situation. You are in prison. All you can wish
> for, if you are a sensible man, is to escape. But how to escape? . . . If a man
> is at any time to have a chance of escape, then he must first of all realize that
> he is in prison. So long as he fails to realize this, so long as he thinks he is
> free, he has no chance whatsoever.[23]

We must realize we are in the trap or the labyrinth; that our character and body are armored and constricted; that there are knots and nets in various areas of our consciousness and our life. If I don't perceive my imprisonment, my boundedness and limitations, there is really no motivation for change.

Closely related to the need for awakening to one's situation is the factor of intention: we must want to escape, will it, desire it, long for it. In any kind of psychological work or exploration of altered states of consciousness (with drugs, hypnosis, meditation, or other methods), the importance of mental set—intention —has long been recognized. While intention by itself may not be sufficient (since the road to hell is proverbially paved with good intentions), techniques and methods practiced without clear and strong intention are probably going to be ineffective, in my view. To quote Gurdjieff again, "If liberation is possible, it is possible only as a result of great efforts, and above all, of conscious efforts toward a definite aim."

Transcendence, symbolized by flight, is one of the traditional ways of escape, and it applies at all levels. We can transcend the painful armoring that blocks the expression of passionate feelings by giving up, or "rising above," those passions. We can transcend the entangling knot or net of a confused relationship by giving up the relationship, taking the well-known flight from commitment. And as the traditional texts have it, we can, through transcendence, attain release from the bondage of material existence. Using techniques of consciousness alteration as advocated in shamanism, yoga, meditation, and mystical literature, we can rise up out of the "vale of tears," the dungeon of *samsara.*

Transcendence is a "going beyond," an alteration of consciousness state, that leaves the existing system in place. For example, an out-of-body experience, or an LSD experience, may release us from the body's armoring temporarily, but we return to it afterwards. There is a difference between escaping from the prison, and actually transforming the prison (i.e., dissolving the armor). The value of transcendent experiences lies in the fact that they afford us a kind of pre-view as it were, a vision of the freedom that is possible, that can serve as inspiration and motivation for the intentional work of liberation.

Direct healing work on the body-mind complex can be very effective in the process of unloosening the knots, thus freeing our awareness. This can range from the physical alteration of fascial structures, as in Rolfing, and various ways of dissolving muscular rigidities through breathing or movement, to subtle inner techniques of psychophysical yoga.

Yogic methods involving inner "fire" (discussed in chapter 4, on purification) may also be used. The inner fire, the "flame of attention," can burn up the knots, melt the metallic armorings, or open up the constricting walls of emotional defensiveness. The alchemical process of *solutio,* which refers to something dissolving in "water," is also appropriate. Alchemical "water" is the realm of feeling, so *solutio* is a metaphor for the dissolving of rigid thought patterns, ideas, or images in the warm, nurturing flow of feeling forgiveness.

Another approach to escape-liberation is the analytical tracing back to find the origins of a defensive armored posture, emotional knot, or relationship entanglement. Theseus found his way out of the labyrinth by means of the golden thread of Ariadne. This might be seen as a metaphor for the process of depth psychological analysis: following the thread of meaning, reversing and retracing every step that we have taken in the tortuous twists and turns of the defensive, rational ego-mind. In his famous "Knot Sermon," the Buddha also demonstrated that "if you wish to untie a knot, you must first find out how the knot was tied. For he who knows the origin of things, knows also their dissolution."

Several different animal figures have traditionally been associated with the theme of liberating the prisoner or escaping from the dungeon of earthly existence. Chief among them are probably birds: from the ingenious Daedalus to the Birdman of Alcatraz, we have had prisoner heroes who have passionately studied the flying of birds. *Flight* is "escape," "winged motion in air," and also, metaphorically, the ascent and traverse of higher dimensions. To people who are undergoing transformative processes, birds often appear in dreams, visions, and other kinds of altered states—indicating that the transcendent power of the bird is operative within their psyches.

In some Asiatic, as well as Native American, cultures, demons, like birds, are regarded as allies in the quest for liberation. In Tibetan and Indonesian shamanic folklore, the demons, or "wrathful deities," are representative of the dynamic forces of "breaking through": they are the guardians of internal borders and thresholds, the boundaries between states of consciousness. With their bulging eyes and ferocious mien and gesture, they provoke attention and awakening; they startle the initiate yogi or shamanic practitioner into fierce hyperalertness.

Guidance is certainly helpful, if not essential for liberation: one can best escape from prison with the help of those who have escaped before. Osiris is freed from the tree/house through the wise skill of his female consort Isis; Thesus finds his way out of the labyrinth with the golden thread provided by his anima-guide Ariadne. Human beings have ever prayed to their gods and goddesses, their teachers and guides, for help in delivering them from the snares and traps of the enemies of life. And the liberating guidance, the deliverance into peace, the release of the imprisoned splendor, has been most generously aided and facilitated.

The transformation from a state of captivity to a liberated state is, I believe, reflected in the difference between our concepts of fate and destiny. Fate, which corresponds to what the Indian tradition calls *karma,* is unavoidable, fixed, and based on the past, either on what has been decreed (fate) or on our past actions (karma). We feel ourselves to be the passive victims of fate, caught in its web or net. Destiny, on the other hand, which corresponds loosely with the Indian notion of *dharma,* is future oriented, free, and flexible: it is our purpose or destination, what we choose to be and do—our intention. We fulfill our destiny by exercising our free will. But until our will is, in fact, freed from the fateful, binding consequences of our past karmic actions and tendencies, we cannot really exercise that freedom. We have free will in theory, potentially, but not in practice or actuality —until we are liberated. When, through the process and practice of transformation, we no longer experience ourselves as victims of our fate, we can become masters of our destiny.

4

Purification by Inner Fire

Will transformation. O be inspired with flame.

—R. M. RILKE

Fire is the transformative element par excellence. From the earliest times men and women have been in awe of the power of the fires of nature—the sun, lightning, volcanoes, wildfires—and perceived or imagined great fire deities that lived in the flames. Since the sun was experienced as the power that originated and maintained life, so God, as the spiritual source and basis of our existence, was often conceived of as Sun or Fire. Many are moved to echo the words of Herakleitos, "Everything becomes fire, and from fire everything is born."

The concept of *energy* plays a similarly central role in the modern scientific worldview. We have learned that we live in a sea of energies and radiations, a vast spectrum of vibratory frequencies, only a minute portion of which is perceived by the unaided senses. The fundamental law of the conservation of energy tells us that energy is neither created nor destroyed, only transformed. And Einstein's formula $E = mc^2$ tells us that mass and energy are equivalent, that things and objects are basically packets of energy bound into matter.

In the evolution of mankind and of social life, the domestification of fire was an epochal event celebrated in numerous myths of a fire bringer, such as Prometheus. Mankind's creative ingenuity exploited the transformative power of fire for human use—in cooking, smithing, metallurgy, technological invention, industrial applications, and, most of all, in warfare and weaponry (e.g., firearms). The inviting warmth and comfort of the fireplace, where we share visions and stories, has contributed to familial and tribal bonding for hundreds of thousands of years. In his studies of primitive religion, Sir James Frazer listed many rites in which torches, bonfires, burning embers, and even ashes were considered capable of stimulating the growth and well-being of vegetation, animals, and humans.

As humans observed the qualities of fire in these processes, it was natural to draw analogies between external fires and internal processes in the body and psyche. Fire and flames became symbolically associated with ardor, sexual passion, anger, excitement, vitality, inspiration, and vision, because of the feelings of heat and energy that we experience coursing through the body during such emotional states. The dramatic power of fire to bring about total destruction or transformation of matter led to its becoming associated with inner and outer processes of purification, purgation, destructuring, and the dissolving of limitations and obstructions.

However, it is clear that much religious and psychological literature speaks of fire as more than a symbol: fire and heat are spoken of as actual inner experiences. We are all familiar with the intense feelings of heat and fiery energy that occur in the body during fever. According to age-old medical traditions, a fever is not so much a symptom of illness as it is the body's way of eliminating toxins and bacteria and accelerating the healing process. There is an analogous process, a psychic fever perhaps, when a person feels that he or she is being purged or purified of something alien and harmful. As we shall see, such feelings of inner heat and fire will be interpreted by individuals according to their personal and cultural backgrounds.

Spiritually or religiously inclined people may see them as heavenly or spiritual fire energy, the mystical fire of union with the Divine. Others may experience them as painful, feeling as if plunged into hellish torment. Or they may be felt to be the forces of purgatory, cleansing and purifying. Such experiences can occur unexpectedly and spontaneously, in mystical ecstasies or in chaotic psychoses. However, there are also ancient and still-active traditions of yoga, psychological alchemy, and spiritual disciplines in which methods of arousing or utilizing inner fire or heat are intentionally and consciously practiced for psychophysical transformation and purification.

Fire Deities and Spirit-Fire

Significantly, the association of fire with divine spirit is widespread and ancient. Many people are afraid of fire and hence do not resonate to the idea of fire as a positive, transformative energy within themselves. I once shared this feeling to a degree, but found, through my studies of Agni Yoga (Yoga of Fire), and of alchemy, that my perspective changed completely and became much more positive. I was fascinated to discover that so many ancient peoples and contemporary native cultures value fire and regard it as sacred.[1]

Fire deities abound in every ancient culture. Among the Greeks, Helios, the sun god, drew his chariots of fire across the sky each day; Hephaistos was the crippled master-smith, who, aided by subterranean fire genii, fashioned invincible weapons and shields for gods and men; and Prometheus was the hero who brought fire hidden in a fennel stalk, to mankind. Esoterically, Prometheus symbolizes every human being, bringing the spiritual fire of life down to the earth plane of matter. "Fire in the plant stalk" is symbolically equivalent to "spirit in matter" and "the Word become flesh" (incarnation), as has been discussed in chapter 3.

Among the Aryans of ancient India, Agni was the brightest and most powerful of the gods, praised and revered in numerous hymns of the Rig Veda, the world's oldest mythic sacred literature.[2] He was the "flame born," visualized as a red giant with flames shooting from his mouth, and rays of light pouring out of his body. Sri Aurobindo, who synthesized the ancient Indian teachings with the modern worldview, stated: "Agni is the force or energy aspect of consciousness." Through sacrificial offerings of food in the Agni ceremonies, the Vedic priests cultivated a link to the gods. The practices referred to as *tapas,* usually translated as "austerity" and "penance," originally signified "heat," "fire," and "ardor." The austerities and penances generate inner heat, which is the technical process of Agni Yoga, as well as of many later yoga disciplines. According to the Rig Veda, "Out of the flaming *tapas,* order and truth were born." Thus, the practices *(tapas)* associated with the fire god Agni, brought about positive (orderly and truthful) transformations of consciousness.

The pervasiveness of sacred fire imagery among the early Indo-Europeans has been established by the researches of Georges Dumezil.[3] He found a threefold value system, each value associated with a particular caste or type, each type developing a particular kind of energy or fire and worshiping a particular deity. Today we can still recognize these distinctions and differences of orientation among different people. The priests and teachers cultivated "fire in the head"— wisdom, speech, prophecy, and memory—and worshiped the great Agni. They correspond in modern terms to scientists, intellectuals, and teachers—those who pursue truth. The warriors and rulers developed "fire in the arms," the power of royalty, majesty, and splendor, and worshiped Indra, the great father god, who used his lightning bolts to destroy limiting obstructions and demonic opposing forces. This caste corresponds in our world to politicians, the military, executives, "titans of industry"—those who pursue power. The merchant caste in ancient India was associated with the "fire in the belly and loins," the fire of digestion, sensual warmth, and the heat of passion. Their deity was Soma, the lunar god of sensory delight and nourishment, whose worship included a vision-inducing plant beverage. In our terms, these are the artists, the visionaries, the hedonists —those who pursue pleasure, wealth, and sensory experience.

In the later Indian literature, the mythology of the Puranas and the yogic texts of the Tantras, the great fire god is Shiva, the transformer, who, like Agni, is revered by priests and yogis; and as Rudra, the destroyer, Shiva takes on the warrior fury and demon-conquering qualities of the earlier Vedic Indra. Shiva dances in a ring of fire, trampling on a dwarf whose name means "Forgetting." Thus, he symbolizes the power of inner fire to overcome ignorance, to awaken, to destroy the limiting obstructions that "dwarf" our true potentials. As Agni was the patron deity of Vedic priests and seers, Shiva became the protector and prototype of yogis and ascetics, practicing the austere purification disciplines of raja yoga and tantra yoga. Shiva is a dualistic, paradoxical deity: both male and female, ascetic and erotic, destroyer and transformer.[4]

In Nordic mythology, we have the fire god Loki, who also has some decidedly ambivalent characteristics: he is the enfant terrible of the Nordic pantheon, forever mocking, tricking, and even betraying the other gods and men. In one famous incident, he enrages all the gods and goddesses at a banquet by pointing out their indiscretions and deceits; he also prophesies the eventual downfall of the gods, their Götterdämmerung. Loki thus is dangerous and tricky, but he also mirrors our defects and has far-seeing eyes. In these ways he reminds us of the American Indian Trickster-Coyote, who is the original fire bringer for many of the tribes and who also functions to expose our weaknesses and mirror our foibles, tricking us into self-knowledge.

In the Hebrew Old Testament, there are numerous allusions to the purifying power of fire and to the fiery nature of God. "The Lord our God is a consuming fire." God speaks to Moses from a burning bush and appears to the Egyptians in a pillar of fire. The prophet Elijah is taken up to heaven in chariots of fire; the prophet Ezekiel sees visions of a cloud glowing with inner fire and, within it, four gigantic living beings facing the four directions. Daniel sees a vision of a man whose "body gleamed like topaz, and his face shone like lightning, his eyes flamed like torches, and his arms and feet sparkled like discs of bronze."[5] Thus we get a picture, from the scriptures that form the basis of much of Western consciousness, of God and godlike beings made up of pure fire or energy, existing perhaps in another dimension, but visible in visionary states of consciousness. These fiery beings or manifestations of God can, and do, interact with and have an impact on human beings in this reality.

The chief impact of the fiery Spirit is purification, the burning away of tendencies and impulses to wrongdoing or falsehood. The author of *Psalms* says those who hate God flee before him like smoke in the wind; "like wax melting in fire, the wicked perish in the presence of God."[6] Taken in an interior sense, this can be seen to refer to evil tendencies in our own nature that are melted away when we invoke the presence of God or Spirit.

In the Gospels there are several references to Christ's nature as a being of fire. In the Gospel of Luke, Jesus says: "I have come to set fire to the earth, and how I wish it were already kindled. I have a baptism to undergo." Here Jesus seems to be referring to his own trial by fire. In other passages, he is the bringer of the purifying fire. Saint Matthew quotes John the Baptist as saying: "I baptize you with water, for repentance . . . but the one who comes after me . . . will baptize you with the Holy Spirit and with fire. . . . The wheat he will gather into his granary, but he will burn the chaff in a fire that will never go out." And in the Gospel of Thomas, Jesus says, "Whoever is near to me is near to the fire, and whoever is far from me is far from the Kingdom."[7]

This notion of Christ as a bringer of fire for the purification and transformation of the world is a far cry from the traditional image of the meek lamb of God or the sorrowful martyr. In these passages Christ is like the fire deities of the ancients: powerful, dynamic, a warrior Spirit who separates the "chaff" from the "wheat" among people. And, again taken in the interior sense, these passages say that through the fiery Christ Spirit within, the useless and trivial tendencies in our nature (the chaff) will be consumed, and only the truthful, valuable, and authentic (the wheat) will remain.

In many mythological traditions and in the Hermetic teachings, there is a giant serpent or dragon who guards the subterranean fires; this dragon is sometimes portrayed as the Creator Spirit of the world of nature. In alchemy, the fire dragon is one of the aspects of *Mercurius,* who is mythologically the god Hermes-Mercurius, the initiator and teacher; who is psychologically the energy of awareness or mind; and who, in terms of inner psychophysiological practices, is the elemental fire principle *(ignis elementaris)*. This alchemical fire was also referred to as "liquid fire," "living fire," or "invisible fire, working in secret." It was regarded as the force or principle of generation and regeneration in all organic life; as well as in inorganic matter, which to the alchemists was very much alive. One text refers to this energy as "the universal and scintillating fire of the light of nature, which carries the heavenly spirit within it."[8]

For the European alchemists, as for Chinese Taoists, yogis, and most shamanic native cultures, the world of spirit and the world of nature are unified, not separated, as they are in the Western rationalist mentality. Fire and light were unifying energies or elements, common to both worlds. As human beings we see and sense them around us, and we feel them within us as energizing, vitalizing forces.

In Chinese mythology there are two kinds of fire dragons, and neither is associated with destruction, danger, or evil, as is the dragon in Western mythology. The celestial dragons represent the cosmic generative power, referred to symbolically in the first hexagram of the *I Ching,* "The Creative." The Chinese believed that atmospheric electricity was a manifestation of this celestial dragon and that lightning was its procreative intercourse with the feminine Earth. The terrestrial dragons were regarded (as in the West) as guardians of the hidden wealth of the Earth. Their movements caused earthquakes, and their "veins" were the electromagnetic lines of force in the Earth and the streaks of precious metals and minerals. For the Taoists, as for the alchemists, meditation and spiritual practice consisted to a large extent of attuning and harmonizing with these fiery beings, who were the embodiments of natural forces and energies.[9]

An extraordinary unitary vision of the world as animated by divine spirit-fire, is found in the works of Jacob Boehme, the great seventeenth-century German mystic, an uneducated shoemaker whose transcendental visions had a profound influence on subsequent European philosophy and theology. Boehme held that all of life, all creation, all matter, all opposites come from and are based in a kind of primal ground, which he himself likened to the Hermetic ideas of chaos and *prima materia;* a conception similar in some respects to the Chinese Tao, the

Buddhist Void, and the Hindu Brahman. The unique aspect of Boehme's formulation is in the fact that he called this primal ground a *fire:*

> This Burning Fire is a manifestation of Life and Divine Love, through which
> Divine Love, as unifying principle, over-enflames and sharpens itself as the
> fiery aspect of the power of God. This ground is called Great Mystery or
> Chaos, from which originates evil and good, as light and darkness, life and
> death, joy and suffering, salvation and damnation, . . . for it is ground of souls
> and angels and all eternal creatures, the good and the evil, ground of heaven
> and hell and the visible world, including everything existing—since all come
> from that one source-ground.[10]

We have here a vision of ultimate reality, of God and the universe, that in
contrast to other formulations (including that of the physicists' "unified field")
is much more dynamic: a unified field of all-encompassing fire energy that provides the ground-matrix of the known and unknown universe. This primal fire
ground, in Boehme's vision, precedes the division into all the dualities of spirit
and nature, physical and metaphysical, good and evil, light and darkness—and
into it all these dualities and separations will, in the end, be resolved.

Purgatory and the Alchemical Fire of Purification

In the world's religious literature, whereas fire is associated with divine
spirit, with the origin and ground of all life, a very different kind of meaning of
fire is equally widespread. In almost every major religion, fire is an important,
though not necessarily the only, element of hell. In contrast to the soothing
warmth, sparkling light, and melting blissful feelings of divine love typically
found in descriptions of heaven, the inferno is typically a place of raging, smoking,
toxic flames, of burning lakes, of boiling oil, unbearable fiery torment, and un-
speakably disgusting demons. It is, however, also true that many descriptions of
hell, both in the Judeo-Christian and the Hindu-Buddhist traditions, include
extreme cold and eternal ice, as well as heat; and experiences of being crushed,
squeezed, torn, dismembered, prodded with sharp instruments, or forced to swal-
low burning and disgusting fluids.[11]

The significance of this universal imagery of heaven and hell for the experience of transformation is derived from the following psychological fact: both
heaven and hell are states of mind or states of consciousness—they are within us.
"Heaven" is a state of consciousness in which we experience blissful, ecstatic,
paradisaical emotions, sensations, and thoughts, whereas "hell" is a state in which
we experience their opposites—terror, rage, anguish, despair, torment, disgust,
horror, and so on. The depictions of these "places" in religious mythology and
art are clearly external representations of inner experiences.

I believe it was Aldous Huxley, in his book *Heaven and Hell,* who first
pointed out the similarity of classical descriptions, and depictions in paintings,

of these places to the experiences of people under psychedelics, in visionary states, or in the grip of psychotic terrors.[12] Psychotics typically describe having all the same feelings and sensations attributed to the residents of hell in the classical theological literature of East and West, including feelings of being on fire or of intolerable burning sensations all over the body. The parallels are so striking that one is led to surmise that "hell" is the prepsychological term for psychosis or madness. To be insane is to be in a state of consciousness marked by painful torturing sensations and feelings of hopeless despair and anguish—which are, after all, the defining characteristics of hell.

While there is a close experiential analogy between madness and hell, I am not saying that only psychosis is hellish. Since hell and heaven are states of consciousness, one can "enter" them from other states, dreams, for example, or drug-induced states. The nightmare is a dream of madness and of hell. Likewise, the ability of hallucinogenic drugs to trigger psychotic-like, hellish bad trips is so well-known that they were first referred to as psychotomimetic. A toxic delirium and illnesses marked by severe chronic pain are other conditions of psychological "hell."

In giving a psychological interpretation to the terms *heaven* and *hell,* I am by no means suggesting that these are nothing but inner states. Anyone who has had first-hand experience of war, imprisonment, torture, or other forms of individual or social violence, needs no reminder that hell can be, and often is, manifested externally in ways that can indeed drive one insane. It is perhaps the grimmest irony of our time that the specter of nuclear holocaust, which we all now confront in the twentieth century, is identical with the age-old myth and prophecy of a universal conflagration—truly a hell on Earth.

Traditionally, one of the distinguishing features of hell is its timelessness. Even when, as in the Buddhist traditions, hell is regarded as one of the six transitory worlds of *samsara,* the sufferer in hell feels trapped and doomed forever. It is a situation of "no exit" and no surcease from unbearable anguish. This no-exit feeling characteristically accompanies the psychological hell of schizophrenia. Gopi Krishna, when undergoing the hellish aspect of a kundalini awakening, also felt that the relentless, glaring, and searing heat would not end but would consume his body entirely. I myself have had an experience of "hell," under the influence of a short-acting psychedelic; subjectively experienced, this episode was unbearably unending, although it lasted only three minutes measured by the clock.

The difference between hell and the state referred to as purgatory would seem to lie in exactly this factor: hell lasts forever and there is no way out, whereas purgatory is a temporary stage one goes through in order to be purged and purified. Hell is usually envisioned as a pit or an abyss, whereas purgatory is seen as a path one must walk or, as in Dante, a mountain one ascends in purposive struggle and conscious suffering. From the perspective of the psychology of transformation, the hellish state of mind, the psychotic's feeling of being forever the victim of implacably hostile powerful forces, needs to yield to the recognition that one is involved in a temporary process, a stage of transition that has a definite purpose or "end," purification and transformation.

In LSD-triggered psychoses I have witnessed, when a resolution occurred, the crucial turning point seemed to be the recognition of being on a journey, in a process, or in a temporarily altered state. The purifying inner fires are then no longer experienced as torture, a shirt of flame one cannot remove, but instead are regarded as a necessary purgation, accepted—even welcomed—for the transformative power they bring. Grof observed that encounters with consuming fire are a frequent component of psychedelic experiences and are usually accepted as transformative. "The individual who has discovered all the ugly, disgusting, degrading, and horrifying aspects of his personality finds himself thrown into this fire or deliberately plunges into it and passes through it. The fire appears to destroy everything that is rotten or corrupt in the individual and prepares him for the renewing and rejuvenating experience of rebirth."[13]

This attitude of accepting the pain of purgation, of even welcoming it and seeking it, underlies much of the ascetic self-denial of mystics and monastics, expressed in deliberate renunciation of pleasure, in penitence, self-inflicted pain, and deprivation. It leads to the ecstatic paradoxical utterings of Saint John of the Cross: "O burn that burns to heal, O more than pleasant wound"; or to the alchemical philosopher's "sweet wound, soothing pain" *(vulnus dulce, suave malum).* Taken to an extreme, the attitude leads to the violent self-torture of the *flagellantes.* Nor are such practices limited to medieval Christianity: among the Plains Indian tribes of North America, sacrificial ordeals, such as the Sun Dance, in which the initiate is hung by hooks inserted into his flesh or has strips of flesh cut from his body, also fall into this category.[14]

For the average person undergoing a transformative experience, whether spontaneously or purposely, in the course of psychotherapy, the importance of what one could call the purgatorial attitude is this: pay attention to the pain, learn from it, remember your intention in this process, remember it has a beginning and an end. Consciously experienced purgatorial purification can teach us a posture of humility and receptiveness, as we learn to understand the messages of the body and the psyche and to regard its signals as a guide to growth. This is also the attitude of traditional Asian medicine and of modern "holistic" healing approaches: symptoms, pain, and illness are seen as signs that something is off balance in the totality of body, mind, and spirit; something needs to be purified.

In the writings of the mystics, the inner fires are described as purifying by burning off the coverings or accretions that cover the soul, which are comparable to the skins and veils discussed in chapter 2. A medieval Christian text, the *Treatise on Purgatory,* states, "the souls are covered by a rust, that is by sin, which is gradually consumed away by the fire of purgatory."[15] Jacob Boehme writes, "If the love of God but once kindle a fire within you, you shall then certainly feel how it consumes all that it touches; you shall feel it burning up yourself, and swiftly devouring all that you call I and me."[16] In modern psychological terms, in the purgatory experience, false identifications and self-concepts, egotistic habits and fixations are consumed.

In the Hermetic-alchemical tradition, the two analogies most often used for the purifying fire are the fire of cooking and digestion, and the fire of the smiths, which burns away the black dross in order to reveal the shining metal. An alchemical text entitled "The Sophic Hydrolith" states: "The old nature is destroyed, dissolved, decomposed, and, in a longer or shorter period of time, transmuted into something else. Such a man is so well digested and melted in the fire of affliction that he despairs of his own strength."[17]

The following report of an alchemically oriented psychotherapy session, which was amplified with the use of the experimental psychoactive substance MDMA, vividly illustrates the psychological and physical transformations that can occur, given the appropriate set, or intention, and preparation.

I became aware of major energy blockages in my spine just below my belly button. I had already had powerful energy releases after spinal massage, and I requested the therapist to massage my spine at the place I felt blocked. I was studying ancient alchemy at the time, and imagery from that tradition began to take on reality. The Neoplatonic concept of matter being the densest, darkest aspect of God's light became real. Not dark, but black, hard, dense, old, putrid, rotten material began to emerge from this place on my spine and flowed throughout my body. This contamination of my body was being released. It was like the base metal of the alchemists, gross, dense, hard, and black. . . . The therapist suggested I bring the purifying "philosopher's fire" to this place on my spine and so intensely heat the material as to transform it. I was ripe for this and experienced something like fire but not fire. It was like a fire of consciousness: bright, white, hot, intense, and eternally burning —like the center of the sun. The dark, dense matter blocking my spine became white hot, the impenetrable vault was being transformed by heat; its structure was being destroyed. All the details of my past had become condensed and packed into my body, and it was now all simultaneously being broken up in a blazing bonfire created by the heat of pure consciousness. Still now, but particularly for many days afterwards, my emotional reaction to ordinary events was and will always be different. The next day I was able to release pain that had been locked inside me for many years, by crying in a way that I don't remember ever doing. I also reexperienced the fire; it began to burn again spontaneously, continuing the process. I am still assimilating the material previously released, and I can still feel the fire glowing. Changes in myself and [in] people I am involved with have been accelerated. I don't compromise my feelings as much as I did previously, and I am in touch with them to an infinitely greater extent.[18]

While this man's experience was undoubtedly intensified both by his prior study of alchemy and by the chemical amplifier MDMA, purifying transformations of this kind are by no means limited to drug states. In a class on "Alchemy and Depth Psychology" I have taught, students who were reading and meditating on alchemical themes and symbols began to have dreams and inner visions that corresponded to many of the key processes of alchemical transformation.[19] One of these processes, *calcinatio,* the heating of a solid to burn off liquid, is analogous to the body's purifying fevers and sweats. Another, *solutio,* the dissolving of solid, crystallized forms, is analogous to the dissolving of rigid, fixed perspectives ("thought forms") and defensive structures.

One student in the class who was studying these fire-related processes had this dream:

> I was in a large vat of oil with a woman. On the far side a fire began to burn spontaneously. I began to run out of the vat, but the woman I was with fell and needed my assistance. We were surely in danger of burning alive. The flames were approaching closer. I stopped running, went back, and pulled the fallen woman up to the ladder and safety.

The dreamer definitely "knew" that this dream referred to and illustrated a purification process, akin to yogic *tapas* and alchemical *solutio.* The interaction with the woman indicated his need to confront and dissolve the separation from his anima, his feminine psyche.

The common theme, expressed in these accounts and confirmed in my experiences and practice of alchemical fire-yoga methods, is that there is a process experienced subjectively in the body as fiery and hot. This process brings about definite changes in the psychophysical totality, including the dissolving of emotional and mental fixations; the melting and release of hard, painful tensions in the body; the cleansing of the "doors of perception," so that inner and outer realities are seen more clearly; and the reduction of separative factors blocking inner unification. These changes are experienced as healing, both physically and psychologically, and as accelerating the individual's growth toward a more integrated, "whole" sense of self. The changes are universally experienced as good and valuable, though the process itself can be extremely painful.

What exactly this fiery process is has always been a mystery, and it certainly is not explainable within the paradigms of modern physical science or psychology. The alchemists used the metaphor of the transmutation of "lead," or "base metal," to "gold," which they said was accomplished by this "fire." Lead is symbolic of dark, heavy, dense, depressed states of consciousness; "gold" symbolizes the quality of consciousness that is shining, radiant, reflective, brilliant, valuable, and sunlike. The alchemical and purgatorial "fire" is obviously not the fire that burns in the sun or in the fireplace, but it is like those fires. And it can come under our conscious control or direction.

This fire is more like consciousness or awareness: we can learn to direct it;

we can focus it, concentrating it in those areas of the body and the psyche where its transformative action is needed. The philosopher J. Krishnamurti has, in recent writings, begun to talk of the "flame of attention" that can burn away attachments, prejudices, fears, hatred, violence, and programmed thinking that distort our perception of truth. This is a description of basically the same alchemical purifying fire.[20]

Kundalini and the Yoga of Fire

Kundalini is both an energy or fire, and a serpent. At the cosmic level the fiery serpent or dragon symbolizes atmospheric and terrestrial electromagnetic energy currents; at the individual level, the serpent fire represents generative and regenerative energy. According to the teachings of Tantric yoga, some of this energy is expended or expressed externally in sexual release. In order for it to be used for transformative purposes, however, it must be raised up internally, which is equivalent to a transmutation of the energy. Thus, the serpent fire of kundalini is said to rise up through the body. This is both a metaphor and an actual psychophysiological experience.

The healer-adepts of the ancient Near East and Greece adopted the symbol of the winged pair of serpents coiling around a vertical central staff as the emblem of the physician's art: this is the caduceus, the staff of Hermes, the master initiator. The staff represents the central axis of the body; the twin serpents represent the male and female aspects of the generative power. Brought up through the body, this power promotes healing and longevity; raised to the throat and head, where the serpents' wings are, it stimulates creativity and intuition. In Indian Tantra yoga, the solar and lunar energy currents (ida and pingala) coil around the central axis (sushumna), at the base of which lies the sleeping kundalini serpent. Thus, in the yoga practice, the kundalini energy is not only "raised," it is also balanced in its male and female polarity.

When the kundalini is awakened, through conscious yogic practice, the fiery energy passes up through the body's energy centers, energizing them and burning off the "coverings" that block or dwarf their expression, finally to unite with the spiritual consciousness in the "crown chakra" at the top of the head. This vertical rising of the kundalini serpent is a metaphor for the experience of sinuous, serpentine fire energy rising up through the body and bringing about profound changes in consciousness and personality. The transformations brought about are virtually identical with those described in the alchemical literature and its modern descendants: so much so that one can regard alchemy and Tantra yoga as the European and Indian expressions of basically the same process and method.

Gopi Krishna, a modern Indian scholar, has published a detailed account of his experiences with the awakening of the kundalini energy, including the painful and near-fatal effects of the energy when imbalanced or when the body has not been sufficiently purified prior to its activation. In recent years many individuals in the West—who have not had any prior exposure to or knowledge of the literature of Tantra yoga—have reported similar experiences of fiery heat rising and surging uncontrollably through the body. The American psychiatrist Lee Sannella has assembled a number of such cases and suggested that the "kundalini syndrome" may often be unrecognized for what it is and misdiagnosed as a psychotic episode—which it becomes only when not handled properly.[21]

Sannella's book is concerned with establishing the diagnostic criteria for distinguishing a kundalini process, which he regards as basically a healthy, powerful transformation, from the misguided and chaotic manifestations of energy psychosis. The underlying physical or physiological mechanism of the kundalini process is still totally unknown. The Czechoslovakian-born Itzhak Bentov, a biomedical engineer, has proposed a highly technical theory involving resonating circuits in the brain which is capable of accounting for some aspects of this phenomenon.[22] At this point, about all that can be said about the phenomenon, in terms of Western science, is that it involves some aspect of bioelectricity, or what Russian researchers refer to as "bioplasmic" or "psychotronic" energy. Nevertheless, experiential accounts of contemporary individuals, whether Western or Indian, show a remarkable degree of convergence with one another and with descriptions in the traditional Indian literature.

According to this literature, if the body is to tolerate the high-intensity energy of the activated kundalini, the *nadis,* which form a vast, intricate network of subtle nervelike energy channels, must be purified of obstructions and accretions. If this purification has not taken place, the energy becomes a violent, searing and corrosive flame that causes illness, fever, delirium, insanity, and eventually death, from the body's literally burning up.

Gopi Krishna describes his initial experiences thus:

> I found myself staring fearfully into a vast internal glow, disquieting and
> threatening at times, always in rapid motion, as if the particles of an ethereal
> luminous stuff crossed and recrossed each other, resembling the ceaseless
> movement of wildly leaping lustrous clouds of spray rising from a waterfall.
> . . . Sometimes it seemed as if a jet of molten copper, mounting up through
> the spine, dashed against my crown and fell in a scintillating shower of vast
> dimensions all around me.

Continuing over several months, the raging internal fires that he was unable to control in any way, brought him to the brink of death. He finally realized that the energy was one-sided: the solar, right-sided aspect alone was harsh and corrosive. When he consciously invoked the lunar, left-sided counterpart energy, as a soothing, cool luminescence, his experience changed dramatically into one of pleasurable internal stimulation, accompanied by heightened awareness and psychic perception; this shift brought about a rapid healing recovery. Gopi

Krishna's experience suggests that the balancing and harmonizing of the two polarities is as important to the transformation process as the activation and raising of the energy per se.[23]

Variations in the recommended patterns of energy flow are frequently found in the esoteric yogic literature as well as in the spontaneous experiences of modern individuals. In traditional Agni Yoga, in Aurobindo's synthesis of yoga principles, and in the teachings of Actualism, a modern Western school of yoga, the light-fire energy pours from above the head downward and is directed into the various parts of the body that need purification or healing.[24] In Chinese Taoist practices, both ancient and modern, the energy is circulated through and around the body, in what is variously referred to as "the circulation of the light" or "the microcosmic orbit."[25] In these systems the energy is channeled from the pelvic center up the back, over the head and down the front, in a continuing circuit. From the point of view embodied in these systems, the Indian kundalini method might be regarded as only half the process.

It is clear from these accounts of different yoga techniques that the subjective and psychological changes they stimulate are basically similar, even though the technical procedures may differ. These changes are also similar to the kinds of transformations we have seen within the metaphoric framework of alchemy. Here, for example, is an account by a student of Actualism Agni Yoga energy-work that has strong alchemical imagery:

> There were many experiences of sensing light energy in the centers, and radiating out, becoming flaming consuming fire, dissolving muscular tensions, emotional fixations, and crystallized image-forms. I could "see" two-dimensional images burn up like plastic sheets; sometimes I could hear soft crackling sounds and smell the odors of putrefication as toxic bodily fluids were being purified by "gentle cooking." During body work, I felt pulsing beams of fiery energy coming from the healer's hands, breaking off what felt like chunks of psychic debris, melting the icy grip of fear-based spasms or contractions. After this kind of experience I felt lighter in weight, almost floating, as well as cleansed inside and outside.[26]

We see, then, that such experiences of modern individuals are described in the same patterns of imagery, the same symbols and metaphors, that the ancient technologies of human transformation have used and elaborated. The imagery of alchemical purification through fire and of the serpentine healing fire seems to correspond to something inherent and natural in the human being.

In my view, this is true, even though in any given time, only a few people may have worked consciously with these processes in yogic practice. Many more may have experienced some aspect of the process without awareness that it is a transformation and that it can be deliberately developed and supported. The fact that the process and the method have their dangers (pain, illness, insanity) is true of any human endeavor, particularly those that aim at radical self-transformation.

The Mystical Fire of Union

What remains after the fires have done their work of purification? What is the nature and value of unitive experience brought about by and based on inner fire? Since God, in religious literature and sacred myths, is often identified as a fire being, or light being, who purifies and transforms us, the answer becomes startlingly simple and obvious: the fire of Divine Spirit is both the agent of transformation and its goal, or end.

The following passage from an alchemical tract called, appropriately enough, "The Glory of the World," can be interpreted as making this point. It refers to the adept's experience of God as fire, to the vitalizing and animating qualities of inner fire and the value in cultivating it, and to its purifying effect on the mind (symbolized by Mercury).

> Take fire, . . . wherein God himself burns by divine love. It is the most precious fire that God has created in the earth, and has a thousand virtues. . . . It has the purifying virtue of Purgatory, and everything is rendered better by it. . . . The fire should be able to fix and clarify Mercury, and to cleanse it from all grossness and impurity. The Sages call it the living fire, because God has endowed it with his own divine and vitalizing power. . . . This fire unites three things, namely body, spirit and soul.[27]

It is the mystics and alchemists who really personalize this theme of God as living fire: God is no longer an immense powerful being out or up there somewhere; rather, God is the fire of life within every being. The fire-spirit is our innermost essence. Saint John of the Cross expressed it:

> Oh flame of love so living
> How tenderly you force
> To my soul's inmost core your fiery probe.
> Oh lamp of fiery blaze
> To whose refulgent fuel
> The deepest caverns of my soul grow bright.

This inner flame is both a purifying, consuming fire and the fire of the soul's love for God. As the "Treatise on Purgatory," attributed to Saint Catherine, says, "As she, plunged in the divine furnace of purifying love, was united with the object of her love, so she understood it to be with the souls in purgatory."[28] The human psyche is purified, transformed, and loved by the fire of God, with which it becomes increasingly unified.

Like the purifying, purgatorial fires that generally come earlier in the process of transformation, this mystical fire of inner union is an actual, psychophysiological experience, not merely a metaphor: it is actual fire, felt in the body. This is emphasized again and again in experiential literature of all ages. The Englishman Richard Rolle, in his fourteenth-century tract *The Fire of Love,* gives this account:

> I cannot tell you how surprised I was the first time I felt my heart begin to warm. It was real warmth, too, not imaginary, and it felt as if it were actually on fire. I was astonished at the way the heat surged up and how this new sensation brought great and unexpected comfort. I had to keep feeling my breast to make sure there was no physical reason for it. . . . Before the infusion of this comfort I had never thought that we exiles could possibly have known such warmth. It set my soul aglow as if a real fire were burning there.[29]

This account is typical of the experience of many, many individuals to this day, who, either spontaneously or in the course of psychospiritual practice or psychotherapy, feel what is often called an opening, or awakening, of the heart.

The sequence in transformation by fire characteristically follows the stages presented in Dante: first the inferno, then purgatory, then heaven. In the first state we feel like victims of overwhelmingly powerful hostile, destructive forces, the fires of madness and hell; then we recognize that we are on the path of purification, that we have a purpose and our fiery suffering is intentional, and that the end is in sight; finally, the painful purgatorial fires change to the soothing, nourishing fires of divine love and union. We are, in T. S. Eliot's phrase, "redeemed from fire by fire."

Sri Aurobindo makes a similar point about these transitions:

> As the crust of the outer nature cracks, as the walls of inner separation break down, the inner light gets through, the inner fire burns in the heart, the substance of the nature and the stuff of consciousness refine to a greater subtlety and purity, and deeper psychic experiences become possible. . . . The soul begins to unveil itself and manifests itself as the central being which upholds mind and life and body.[30]

Several of our other metaphors are used here: in the first stage of hell and suffering, in which our defensive walls break down, we may "crack" (reducing separative tendencies). Next, the purifying fires in the heart transmute our emotions and perceptions; last, the loving fire of Spirit causes us to unveil, to unmask ourselves before the central Self.

The following image from the alchemical tradition encapsulates the difficult and paradoxical themes presented here. The alchemists' symbol for the central Self, the divine Spirit, is the King, the inner ruler. The image is twofold: in the foreground, the King is depicted lying on the ground as though dead; a wolf is gnawing at his side; in the background of the picture, the wolf is shown burning in a bonfire, from which the King emerges unscathed.

At first, our royal Self is as though lifeless; we are dis-spirited, our will and inspiration sabotaged by predatory, instinctual aggression and greed. Then these lower egotistic drives—animal tendencies—are burned away and purified. The divine inner Being is revealed and liberated. "At the end of the work, the King will go forth for thee, crowned with his diadem, shining, radiant as the Sun."[31]

5

From Darkness to Light

The one thing that frightens Satan is to see a light in your heart.

—SUFI PROVERB

Enlightenment—bringing light in—is implicitly and explicitly an aspect of the transformation processes we have discussed. In awakening, we open our eyes and perceive (with) more light. To become "lucid" (from *lux,* "light") while dreaming or in waking life is to bring a quality of transparent awareness to our experience. Similarly, when the cataracts that blind us, the veils or coverings, are removed, there is more light. Metaphorically speaking, when the clouds of ignorance are dispelled, the light of the sun, the light of spirit, shines in brightness. Imprisoned in a dungeon or a cave, we are trapped in darkness; when liberated, we are dazzled by daylight. And the alchemical purification by fire burns away the dross of conditioned, earth-bound consciousness to reveal the radiant "gold," illumined consciousness. This golden consciousness is like metallic gold in its brilliance, its reflectivity, its malleability, and flexibility.

For most people enlightenment is a process of imparting or acquiring information or knowledge about something. "That was an enlightening presentation you gave today." Historians of culture speak of the Enlightenment: the period in eighteenth-century Europe when a group of philosophers applied and promoted a rational, non-theological approach to problems of philosophy and society. This is not, however, the meaning of enlightenment for the mystics and visionaries of Eastern and Western spiritual traditions. For them, light is not an abstract symbol but an experience that is lived and felt in the mind, the heart, the body, and the inner recesses of the psyche. Enlightenment, then, is not merely a metaphor but, rather, an experience of one's own inner essence, the Self, as a being of light.

"Enlightenment," when defined as the rational acquisition of knowledge, deals with only a very limited aspect of human transformation. I follow the teachings of the ancients in proposing that the notion of enlightenment is meant to be taken much more literally: the process involves seeing more clearly, both internally and externally, so that there is more lucid awareness, a feeling of the light and warmth of love in the heart—ultimately a complete immersion in the ocean of light called God, Being, or Spirit. This aspect of self-transformation is actually a process of moving from darkness to more and more light.

The reader might object that these ideas of Spirit, or God, or Self as a being of light are mystical and arcane—that they are impossible-to-prove assumptions that modern people cannot apply to themselves. I myself once held such a skeptical view, when I was still under the influence of the rationalistic-mechanistic worldview with which I had been conditioned. Only through repeated personal experiences and the parallel accounts of friends, colleagues, students, and clients, was I eventually led to adopt a more open-minded attitude. I realized also that, contrary to my prior beliefs, mystics were not armchair philosophers, indulging in fantastic speculations. Rather, they were, without exception, speaking from their own experiences: they were describing interior perceptions. In many cases, these were not learned intellectuals but simple, humble men and women who led active and productive lives. The unanimity of the mystics' testimony and of the related images and symbols in the myths and sacred texts is far too pronounced to write off to chance.

It is an unmistakable fact that in the sacred literature and art of most religious and spiritual traditions, the symbolism of en-lightenment is central. The accounts of the mystics and seers of East and West are replete with experiences of and visions of light. The creation of the world, in the Judaeo-Christian tradition, begins with God's invocation, "Let there be light," and the emergence of light out of primal darkness. Modern science, in a rather parallel fashion, sees the universe beginning with an energy explosion of inconceivable force and radiance. The Creator works with light—is light. The Christ is seen as "the light of the world." The vision of the Lord in the Bhagavad-gita is of a cosmic being of overwhelming radiance, "brighter than a thousand suns." Solar deities of light and fire, such as the Indian Agni, the Iranian Mazda, the Egyptian Ra, and the Greek Apollo, play key roles in all the ancient sacred mythologies. Jung called light "the central mystery of philosophical alchemy."

In some traditions the duality of light and darkness is emphasized. In Taoism light is *yang* like the day and darkness *yin* like the night. "That which lets now the light, now the dark appear, is Tao." It is a natural process of cyclic change: the Earth turns its face toward and away from the Sun. Some of the dualistic religious teachings see an ongoing cosmic struggle between the "forces of light" and the "forces of darkness." This is true of the Zoroastrians; of the Essenes, from whom Jesus is said to have come; of the Egyptians, in their stories of Osiris/Horus and Set; and of the ancient Meso-American cultures, in their myths of the conflict between Quetzalcoatl, the Lord of the Dawn, and Tezcatlipoca, the Lord of the Smoking Mirror.

Medieval philosophers made a distinction between three kinds of light and three kinds of eyes. These philosophers held that we have eyes of flesh, which see with exterior light *(lumen exterius)* the physical world of sense objects and matter. Next, we have an eye of reason, which sees with interior light *(lumen interius)* the truths of reason, mind, and knowledge. Last, we have an eye of contemplation, which sees with higher or transcendent light *(lumen superius)* the ultimate reality of oneness, the ground of Being.[1]

The Enlightenment of the Body

"A man's wisdom makes his face to shine," says Ecclesiastes. It is a common observation that uplifting, affirmative emotions, such as joy and love, cause people's bodies and faces—their eyes especially—to "light up," to "radiate" or "shine." Conversely, moods of depression or despair cast darkening hues on a person's countenance, draining the visage of color and making the eyes appear to "lack luster." We could, of course, say that such expressions are merely metaphorical and do not have any real validity. On the other hand, there is the cogent testimony of those who report luminous energy phenomena, that is, light emissions from the body, of which present-day science is as yet unable to render an account. There are age-old traditions of subtle energy fields, or "auras," surrounding living organisms, and some of these phenomena have in recent years proved amenable to measurement and recording, through such means as the Kirlian photography effect, and other methods.[2]

Whatever the nature and origin of this "light" may be, it is apparent that it can, on occasion, suffuse the body with such intensity that it becomes visible to others, even those who are not normally clairvoyant. Or the light may become visible in certain altered states: in psychedelic states, as well as after prolonged periods of meditation, many people, myself included, have seen patterns of light and flame around the heads and faces of individuals. Thus, it appears that either the sensitized vision of the perceiver or the intensity of the phenomenon in the subject can make the inner light outwardly visible.

There is a universal tendency to depict saints and enlightened beings with haloes and auras of flame and light, and mystical literature is filled with accounts of yogis and prophets who were seen to be filled and overflowing with light. The nineteenth-century Indian saint Ramakrishna was frequently observed by his students to glow visibly. Some of these occurrences have been recorded in photographs, in which the body can be seen to have a distinct luminosity. In this century, a German traveler who visited Ramana Maharshi, another famous Indian yogi-saint, recorded his observations of the saint's transfiguration:

> While my eyes were immersed in the golden depths of the Maharshi's eyes
> . . . the dark complexion of his body transformed itself slowly into white. This
> white body became more and more luminous, as if lit up from within, and
> began to radiate. . . . With the same eyes which a moment ago were able to
> read some notes in my diary, I saw him sitting on a tiger-skin as a luminous
> form.[3]

An elderly lady of my acquaintance has told me of an experience where she saw the upper torso of her yoga teacher, who was sitting in front of her, literally become transparent and dissolve into shimmering fibers of light.

The prototype of this kind of occurrence in the Christian tradition is the event known as the Transfiguration, in which Jesus took the disciples Peter, James, and John up to a high mountain, where they saw him transfigured: "his face shone like the sun, and his clothes became white as light," and he was seen conversing with Moses and Elijah.[4] In trying to understand such perceptions, the explanation of Meister Eckhart makes simple and elegant sense: "The light in the soul's core overflows into the body, which becomes radiant with it."[5]

The individuals who are experiencing the light-in-the-body phenomenon usually agree that it is both like and unlike the physical light we see around us. Often, the light is felt more than seen, which makes the experience parallel to those of fire and warmth in the body, described in the last chapter. This light-fire energy is often perceived as being healing, as well as spiritually illuminating. Here, for example, is an account, by a contemporary student of light-fire yoga, of a breakthrough experience that came after many days of inner self-healing work:

> My body had again gone into a state of near collapse . . . and I felt sick and frustrated, working with healing energy in my abdominal area. Nothing but darkness, pain, and obstruction was being experienced, for what seemed like an endless period of time. . . . All at once something broke loose and I entered into what could only be described as a region of light. It was a vast curving plain, cool and full of delicious sensations and feelings, and it was filled with light, above, below and all around. My biggest shock came when I realized it was inside of me. "The Kingdom of Heaven is within you," it had been said, . . . and with a churning mixture of shock and exhilaration I knew what that meant, and I knew that it was true.

Shock, elation, gratitude, joy—these are the common accompaniments of this kind of unexpected illumination. An informant quoted in Cohen and Phipps' *The Common Experience* describes walking home one evening on a freezing night, when suddenly,

> it was a bit like a long electric shock, . . . but it wasn't mechanical, it was a person. . . . There was a feeling of heat and light rushing through my bloodstream, seeping over me and paralyzing me almost, as if some person were blowing something in me to white heat, and I was sobbing with tears of love and gratitude. There were no visions or voices, but the person communicated. . . . ideas or certainties, with a sort of close intimacy, much more closely than into my ear or imagination.

The light is felt *in* the body; it brings healing and feelings of love and tremendous well-being, and it is perceived as personal, alive, aware, and as having a deeper knowledge of self than the normal personality or ego.

Arthur Young has pointed out the simple but profound truth that we do not see light; instead, we see by light or with light.[6] We usually think of light as coming into the eyes, the eyes of flesh, with which we see the world. However, in states of illumination, light seems to pour through the body and flow outward —at times to the intensity where it is visible to others. The eyes radiate, the face shines, and the heart "sees." There is said to be an eye in the heart: presumably this is the heart center, where we see with inner light. Experiences of the heart-center opening are almost always accompanied by sensations of warmth and light, as well as of openness and lightness.

Corresponding to this kind of experience are many expressions in the world's sacred literature which speak of the Self, or Spirit, as a light in the heart. In one of the Upanishads we read that *Atman* is "the person here who is the knower among the senses, the light within the heart [*antaryotih*]." The notion of the light in the heart is expounded also by the Vedantist philosopher Shankara: "*Atma* rises in the heart like the sun of knowledge, destroying darkness, all-pervading, all-sustaining."[7]

Islamic mysticism also refers to the light in the heart. The fourteenth-century Sufi Mahmudi Kashani writes of the light of truth that is ordinarily veiled by our humanness: as long as it shines through this veil, we call it faith. "If this same light attains directly to the heart and the veil of humanness does not intervene, then it is the light of certainty. . . . The black cloud of human attributes rises up constantly . . . and covers the face of the sun of truth. When it is uncovered, . . . then the heart directly experiences the effulgence of that light."[8]

Shamanism, which some scholars regard as the original religion on this planet, describes the initiatory experiences of shamans in training, or in healing trances, as involving light. The explorer Rasmussen quotes an Eskimo shaman as saying, "Every real shaman has to feel *qaumaneq,* a light within the body, inside his head or brain, something that gleams like fire, that enables him to see in the dark, and with closed eyes see into things which are hidden, and also into the future."

Healing, self-knowledge, clairvoyance, and precognition have all been associated with this kind of inner light, especially when focused, as it were, through the heart center or the midbrain "third eye" center. Light in the body is natural: it is perceived also in animals and plants, if we are to believe shamanic seers and the kind of work reported in *The Secret Life of Plants,* by Peter Tompkins and Christopher Bird.

European alchemists, particularly Paracelsus, spoke of the "light of Nature" *(lumen naturae).* Paracelsus claimed that psychic perception and clairvoyant dreams in man, and the instinctive prescience ("the auguries") of animals were brought about by this light of Nature. "Nothing can be in man unless it has been given to him by the light of Nature." Elsewhere, Paracelsus distinguishes the light of Nature from another light, "outside the *lumen naturae,* by which [man] can search out supernatural things." He says these lights appear in our experience as *scintillae,* "fiery sparks." They come from the world soul and are "seeds of a world to come," sprinkled throughout the great cosmos. In man, the little cosmos, the sparks come from what Paracelsus calls the *astrum,* the "star in man."[9]

In all the great religious traditions, as we know, light has been the primary symbol, or manifestation, of God, Divine Being, Spirit, the Immortal, the Eternal. In some traditions, notably the Hindu and Buddhist Tantras, as well as Chinese Taoism and European alchemy, divine light "descends" to nature and into the body. Yaqui Indian shamanism, as described in the books by Carlos Castaneda, involves painstaking and disciplined practices aimed at heightening the apprentice's ability to see the human form as a being made up of luminous fibers. Alchemy, as mentioned, involved the purification and illumination of the dense matter of the body (symbolized by the alchemical furnace), carried out until the *scintillae,* the sparks of light, begin to appear and produce visions and insights.

In the yoga systems of Tantra, the practitioner visualizes geometric configurations of light (triangles, stars, diamonds, circles, spheres) in the various centers and in the energy channels *(nadis)* that link these centers. Agni Yoga methods involve the channeling and focusing of light-fire energy of different frequencies in the centers as well as directly in the physiological organ systems of the body, for healing and purification. In Tibetan Buddhism, the Vajrayana (the "Diamond-Lightning Way") teachings particularly emphasize light-energy yoga practices. It is said that as a result of these practices, "one's body becomes like a rainbow of divine light and emptiness." Likewise, Taoism advocated the "circulation of light" (or fire, or energy) through the body in certain distinctive patterns.

The experience of light-throughout-the-body is something that can and does happen to people spontaneously, as an integral part of a transformation process, regardless of religious or cultural belief systems. When this experience does occur, it is always felt to be something immensely positive, healing, and inspiring. It is, in fact, such a common experience that it has been incorporated into the language of all the great religious traditions and has become the central preoccupation of certain groups—shamans, alchemists, yogis—who might be regarded, in Eliade's words, as "technicians of the sacred."

The Illumination of the Mind

In very broad terms we might say that en-lightenment of the body is associated with healing and physical transformation, whereas illumination of the mind is associated with wisdom and greater self-knowledge. It is important to emphasize again that those who have experienced this kind of enlightenment insist that the experience is literally and actually en-lightening, that the expression is not just metaphorical. As strange as this may sound to one who has not experienced it, the contents of the mind itself, its thoughts and images, can become filled and suffused with light, just as body structures and tissues can. Thus, the notion of the "eye of reason," or the "mind's eye," which perceives with *lumen interius,* inner light, makes good sense, experientially.

The distinction made between exterior light (of the body, the flesh) and interior light (of the mind, the consciousness) parallels the distinction between the light of Nature and the light of Spirit developed by Paracelsus and other philosopher-mystics. In the eighteenth century, these ideas were given cogent expression in the writings of that great clairvoyant scientist of consciousness, Emmanuel Swedenborg, who wrote:

> It has often been granted me to perceive and also to see that there is a true light that enlightens the mind, wholly distinct from the light that is called natural light. I have been raised up interiorly into that light by degrees; and as I was raised up my understanding became so enlightened as to enable me to perceive what I did not perceive before, and finally such things as I could not even comprehend by thought from natural light.[10]

The Indian Vedanta philosophers also equate the "light in the heart" (enlightened body) with the "sun of knowledge" (illumined mind), as was shown in the passage quoted from Shankara. This inner knowledge-light is said to be "all-pervading, all-sustaining, radiating throughout the world"—very much like the networks of thought energy, the collective tapestry of consciousness that links all humans and all forms of life. These are paradoxical utterings, because the reality is difficult to convey. The enlightening of the body and the illumination of the mind are different experiences, but the light involved in both is the same. Modern teachers speak of a spectrum of consciousness, a spectrum at each band of which light energy is expressed with a different frequency rate.

Buddhist texts, although they deny the independent existence of any self or ego, are remarkably similar in their descriptions of interior light. The Tibetan Book of the Dead describes the radiant light that appears to a person at the moment of dying: "this mind of yours is inseparable luminosity and emptiness in the form of a great mass of light, it has no birth or death."[11] Another text states that when in meditation, Buddha had "a ray named the ornament of the light of knowledge rising from the cranial suture, shining above the head."[12] Again, the integration or equivalence of mental and physical experiences is demonstrated here.

In the Tibetan Book of the Dead, careful distinctions are drawn between the visions of "lights" that one sees in the after-death state, which signify the different realms of conditioned existence; and the "clear light" of Buddha-nature, or Spirit, that is "radiance from the seed of emptiness, the radiance in the realm of knowing and the light of self-generating wisdom."[13] The person experiencing the in-between *(bardo)* state is advised to stay with the clear light, to recognize it as the light of his own beingness, and to allow it to illuminate the *skandhas,* the thought forms and perceptions that make up our ordinary consciousness. All this suggests an infusion of light into the mind, which is altogether analogous to the infusion of light into the body.

In the New Testament there are many well-known sayings that refer to Jesus as the "light of the world"; yet there are an equal number that make it abundantly clear that, according to Christ's teaching, every man and woman has, and is, a being of light within.

> Ye are all children of light, and children of the day . . . therefore let us not sleep, but let us watch and be sober.

> The light of the body is the eye; if therefore thine eye be single thy whole body shall be full of light.

The Gnostic Gospel of Thomas reinforces this interpretation of the Christ teaching. When the disciples ask Jesus to show them where he is, he answers: "Within a man of light there is light, and he lights the whole world. When he does not shine, he is in darkness."[14]

The significance of these passages is that they point unmistakably to the light and divinity within the human being. They are consistent with many others in the Gospels and in Gnostic literature, where Jesus deflects the disciples' attempts to idealize him as the only enlightened one or as the only son of God. "Is it not written in your law, 'I said, you are gods'?" (John 10:34). Each human being is, in essence, a divine Spirit, of pure light. This light can come "down" or "through," into mind and body, into outward expression and manifestation.

Christian mystics and theologians make it abundantly clear that light is not an abstract symbol but an actual energy that is known in the mind, felt in the heart, sensed in the body, and that comes from, and is, Spirit. Saint Augustine writes: "I entered into the secret closet of my soul, led by Thee . . . and beheld with the mysterious eye of my soul the Light that never changes. . . . It was not the common light that all flesh can see, but different. . . . It was higher because it made me, and I was lower because made by it. He who knoweth the truth, knoweth the Light: and who knoweth it, knoweth eternity."[15]

We noted earlier the Gnostic and Hermetic image-symbol of "light sparks," *scintillae:* they are called "germs," or "seeds," of the soul. Seeing with the eye of flesh and the light of nature, our first experiences of light are likely to be in the form of sparks, points of light in swarms, like fireflies in the night sky. Seeing with the eye of mind and the interior light, we understand these sparks to represent visions, flashes of insight, awakenings, moments of truth, and lucid awareness. Jung suggested we could think of ego-consciousness as "surrounded by a multitude of little luminosities." For him, as for Paracelsus, the unconscious, the "darksome psyche," was like "a star-strewn night sky"—a great, dark unknown, studded with brilliant gemlike points and stars of light. These are messages from the luminous realm of archetypes.[16]

In Gerhard Dorn, an eighteenth-century alchemical philosopher, we read of the illumined seeker: "Little by little he will come to see with his mental eye a number of sparks shining day by day . . . and a growing into a great light that thereafter all things needful to him will be made known. . . . For the life, the light of men, shines in us, albeit dimly. It is in us, and not of us, but of Him to whom it belongs, who makes us his dwelling place. . . . He has implanted that light in us that we may see. . . . Thus the truth is to be sought, not in our selves, but in the image of God within us."[17]

The sparks, or light seeds, or starlike flashes, can be regarded as the visual representation, or visual perception, of moments of discovery, insight, or creative inspiration that all of us have. Studies in the psychology of creativity and on the process of invention and discovery have amply documented that creative ideas and discoveries are not so much made up or imagined; rather, they are typically experienced as something that "came through," "just happened," or was first seen in a dream. In other words—consistent with the idea of the *scintillae,* or sparks —creative ideas seem to come from the unconscious, the nonpersonal realms, the subtle dimensions of consciousness.[18]

Some mystics have reported experiences of enlightenment coming after prolonged periods of intense inner struggle, analogous in many ways to the hellish and purgatorial experiences described in the last chapter. A classic example of such an experience is offered by the great seventeenth-century mystic Jacob Boehme, the shoemaker whose first illumination occurred when he was struck by the brilliant reflection of sunlight off a burnished copper plate. He described struggling for a long time with his "corrupted nature," trying to overcome his "evil will." "Now while I was wrestling and battling, being aided by God, a wonderful light arose within my soul. It was a light entirely foreign to my unruly nature, but in it I recognized the true nature of God and man, and the relation existing between them."[19] This kind of transition is characteristic of "breakthrough" experiences, where after a prolonged inner opposition of "good" and "evil" aspects of the psyche, there can occur a sudden opening to the light—a light that embraces both the polar opposites.

Often, the struggle of opposites is a struggle between fear and love. We want to love—to love others, ourselves, God—but we are afraid. The fear is experienced inwardly as a wall, an immovable block of resistance, or as a threatening force. When the power of love finally prevails and the light dawns in the heart, then the walls of fear are dissolved, the threat disappears, the heart opens. This is why it was said that Satan, who represents the principle of opposition and whose chief weapon is fear, is threatened when he sees the light in the heart. And this is why the Indian sages of the Rig Veda sang, "May I reach that light on reaching which one attains freedom from fear."[20]

When conflicting and depressing emotions prevail within the psyche, our experience is consistently one of darkness and gloom. The color and vibrancy may fade out of visually perceived objects; things may look foggy, gray, muddy, and obscure. This is the interior, or subjective, counterpart to the darkened visage, the lackluster eyes, that may be seen in people who are experiencing such heavy, oppressive moods. There have been many expressions and symbols to describe such a state. The alchemists called it *nigredo,* the "blackness," as well as *massa confusa,* a "confused mass"; or the "chaos of the elements." The "elements" symbolically represent psychological functions—thoughts, feelings, perceptions, and the like. In this pre-enlightenment phase, then, our inner psychic energies and tendencies are in chaotic conflict and confusion, and we may not even recognize the chaos as such until it begins to change, to become illumined.

This kind of experience also relates to "the dark night of the soul," which Saint John of the Cross described: this is regarded by students of mysticism as an experience that typically occurs *after* the initial awakening and purifications but *before* the final illumination and union. It is, as Saint John expressed it, especially poignant to the soul that has already experienced some degree of illumination and already knows the intense ecstasy that is possible and promised. "What we call the dark night is the absence of pleasure in all things. For as night is the absence of light . . . so it can be said that the mortification of the appetites is night for the soul."[21]

In interpreting this passage, we should remember that the word *soul* has undergone a number of changes in meaning over the centuries. The passage makes clear that the frustration or mortification of "appetites," wishes, desires, cravings, and so on, is being described—and these are now not usually conceived of as components of the "soul." We are dealing with a personal, mind-created prison, hell, or chaos. For this reason, it has been suggested that the famous "dark night of the soul" could better be called the "dark night of the ego," for it is the *ego* that is frustrated, pained, and confused.[22] According to this view, which I share, the soul is never in darkness; rather, it lives always in light, since it *is* light. This parallels the Gnostic conception of the soul, as a self-luminous sphere.

A graphic description of an enlightenment experience is found in R. M. Bucke's *Cosmic Consciousness,* first published in 1901:

> I was in a state of quiet, almost passive enjoyment, not actually thinking, but letting ideas, images, and emotions flow of themselves through my mind. All at once, without any warning of any kind, I found myself wrapped in a flame-colored cloud. For an instant I thought of fire, an immense conflagration somewhere close by in that great city; the next I knew the fire was within myself. Directly afterward there came upon me a sense of exultation, of immense joyousness accompanied or immediately followed by an intellectual illumination impossible to describe. Among other things, I did not merely come to believe, but I saw that the universe is not composed of dead matter,

but is, on the contrary, a living Presence; I became conscious in myself of eternal life.[23]

This account makes clear, once again, the consistent claim of the mystics: what they describe is not imagining or theory or philosophy or belief. It is, rather, the testimony of their direct experience: it is marked not by a character nebulous and obscure but by luminous clarity and irrefutable certainty.

The Self as Light

The basic feature of the experience of enlightenment appears to be a sensing, feeling and knowing that one's body, heart and mind are being infused, usually from "above," with inner light of a spiritual nature. Light coming in from above is a literal, direct perception in many instances of body enlightenment, and in some light-yoga practices, as noted, the light-energy is chanelled into the body from above. When speaking of mental or spiritual illumination, "light coming in from above" is a metaphorical expression. The spatial metaphor is based on the understanding that the light is of spiritual origin, that it comes from a part of our being, our totality, that is "higher" than body or mind. Thus *Atman,* Spirit, which is Self, which is Light, comes into and suffuses throughout the body, the emotions, and the mind—the entire psyche. Thus it is transformation by illumination.

Sri Aurobindo describes the process as follows, using the word *enthusiasm,* which means, literally, "to be infused with god force" *(en-theos):*

Into the consciousness, with a fiery ardor of realization . . . a downpour of inwardly visible light envelops the action . . . the vision of light accompanying inner illumination is not merely a subjective visual image, or a symbolic phenomenon: light is primarily a spiritual manifestation of the Divine Reality illuminative and creative. There is also in this descent the arrival of a greater dynamic, a golden drive, a luminous "enthusiasmos" of inner force and power which replaces the comparatively slow and deliberate process of the mind by a swift, sometimes vehement, almost a violent impetus of rapid transformation.[24]

Here Aurobindo makes the point that once the light of divine spirit is received and perceived, the process of transformation takes almost a quantum leap forward in intensity and rapidity. This leap might occur spontaneously and unexpectedly, or it might occur after years of deliberate and purposeful practice, but with the dawning of the inner light of Spirit/Self, a new and higher phase is initiated. The individual is now "fired with enthusiasm" because connected to the divine source or ground of all life.

We saw how the mystics often perceive ultimate reality as a kind of fiery ground that precedes all divisions into dualities and opposites. Light and fire are always experienced as two aspects of the same basic energy. We know that on the level of physical reality, the sun and other stars are all massive spheres of both light and flame. Considered psychologically, when the fiery aspect of the primal life energy is emphasized, we have the fires of purification; when the luminous aspect is emphasized, we have illumination.

That the innermost spiritual essence in man is of light is emphasized again and again in the sacred literature of ancient India. "Like the sun when the clouds are removed—*Atman* is revealed shining when our ignorance is dispelled," wrote the Vedantist philosopher Shankara. And further, these texts affirm, this Self that is a "light in the heart," is one with the macrocosmic spiritual principle (*Brahman*). "The light that shines beyond this heaven, beyond all, in the highest worlds beyond which there are none higher, is truly the same light that shines within the person," according to the Chandogya Upanishad.[25] This identification of the individual Self with the cosmic Self, which the Indian sages discovered and described, came later to be referred to as cosmic consciousness. In this state one sees and realizes that God stands in the same relationship to the universe as Self stands to the body and personality.

The idea that the Light/Self/Atman is identified with, or unified with, the cosmic divine principle is consonant with the statements of the mystics. They declare that the light they sense is eternal and infinite, a light beyond the duality of light *versus* darkness—just as Boehme's fire ground is beyond all dualities. "It is an infused brightness, a light which knows no night, but rather it is always light, nothing ever disturbs it," says Saint Teresa.[26]

Gnostics and Neoplatonists often referred to the soul as a sphere that is *augoeides*—a word meaning "radiant," "brilliant," "shining," "possessing splendor," "raylike," or "lucid." G. R. S. Mead quotes the Gnostic philosopher Damascius: "In Heaven indeed our *augoeides* is filled with radiance, a glory that streams throughout its depths lends it divine strength. But in lower states, losing its radiance, it is dirtied, as it were, and becomes darker and darker and more material."[27] These expressions refer to something like what esoteric philosophies and transpersonal psychologies call a higher, or subtle body. Because it consists of light, it is referred to in some traditions as a "radiant body," a "rainbow body," a "body of light," or a "diamond body."

Probably the hardest part of such teachings for a modern Westerner to accept is the claim that every human being has an inner light or a light body. Many people feel that such concepts, metaphors, or descriptions don't apply to them, because, of course, they have not had any direct experience that corresponds to such ideas. The accounts offered here have demonstrated, I hope, that such experiences are not at all rare and correspond very closely to the descriptions given in the literature of mysticism and religious experience, both Eastern and Western.

Some of these teachings see the soul as the more individualized form of the Spirit—"higher" than mind and body but not as cosmic or universal as Spirit.

The lower levels of mind and matter are then perceived as obstructions or dirt on the soul, the denser material acting as a kind of sheath, skin, covering, or even cage or dungeon for the soul. The enlightenment experience then involves light from the highest or innermost center of pure beingness, that flows down into and through soul, mind, emotions, and body. As Eckhart says, "God pours himself into the soul, and the light at the core of the soul grows so strong that it spills out, even passing the outward man."[28]

The autobiography of Yogananda, one of the first of the Indian yogi-teachers to bring the Indian spiritual teachings to the West, describes such an experience. It was triggered in the yogi by a touch on the chest from his guru, Sri Yukteswar. He describes how his awareness left his body and his vision transformed to a spherical sight that saw everything in the environment as light and pure vibration, melting into a "luminescent sea." The ocean of light was interrupted at certain points by materializations of form. The experience continued, with an increasing expansion of awareness that included continents, the earth, planets, stars, and constellations: the outer cosmos becomes visible to inner sight. Yogananda saw "the entire cosmos, gently luminous, like a city seen afar at night, glimmering within the infinitude of my being."[29]

Here again, we find that in the experience of cosmic consciousness, the individual Spirit realizes its identity with the macrocosmic Creator Spirit. When, during this kind of illumination, awareness shifts from the individual to the cosmic perspective, then the objects of the outer world (including planets, stars, and galaxies) are seen to be *within* the field of consciousness of the individual. At this point, then, the sense of identity also, the sense of who "I" am, has shifted: I am no longer just an individual; at this level I am also unified with divine reality, the reality or being that sustains the universe. Or in the words of A. R. Orage, "God is the I of the universe."

6

From Fragmentation to Wholeness

When the ten thousand things are viewed in their oneness, we return to the origin and remain where we have always been.

—ZEN MASTER SENGSTAN

One of the major themes in the literature on the transformation of consciousness is the notion that the disjointed, separated, fragmented parts of the psyche can be and need to be synthesized into a harmonious, integrated whole. An initial condition of confusion, disorder, and chaos gradually gives way to a state where we are functioning from a clear center within ourselves. In this state, the different parts or aspects of our psychological and physical totality are functionally coordinated and unified. William James spoke of "The Divided Self and the Process of Its Unification," and Jung wrote of the process of *individuation,* becoming in-divisible or whole. The experience of feeling scattered, fragmented, and confused is surely familiar to all of us at times, and this is the psychological and experiential basis for the metaphor of integration.

Because people often feel themselves, their psyche, and their whole lives to be scattered or splintered, a significant aspect of the experience of healing and growth is the synthesizing, the gathering together of these fragments. As an example, here is the account, by a twenty-five-year old college student, of his experience during a deep altered-state psychotherapy session:

> I put together all the bits and pieces of my past knowledge of my father, my mother, and brother, . . . and in an instant of realization I saw my fragmented emotional interior become a whole gestalt. I "saw" my childhood history with an adult mind and unified the fragmented pieces of my emotions. . . . I have waited many years for such deep understanding.[1]

The English words *whole, wholesome,* and *wholeness* (as well as the more recent variants *holism* and *holistic*) are derived from the Old English *hal,* which means "sound," "complete," "healthy"; the Old English root is also ancestral to the German *heil,* "safe," to our *hale,* and to *hail,* as a greeting. Thus, wholeness, in the sense of integration, overlaps considerably with the concept of health. We might say that health *is* whole, complete functioning. Furthermore, the English *holy* and German *heilig* also derive from the same root, *hal.* Thus, health, wholeness, and holiness are all associated with the fundamental underlying concept of integration and togetherness, which is contrasted with its polar opposite of dispersion, scattering, and fragmentation.

There are pertinent links between this metaphor and some of the other themes we have already discussed. Fragmentation and dividedness are often seen as identical with captivity and defense: the knots and nets that trap our awareness are the same defensive mechanisms that also separate and divide our personality. The process of inner purification burns or strips away the blocks and barriers that produce the state of dividedness. This metaphor is also related to the notion of opposites and their reconciliation. From the many to the one, from duality to unity—the direction of growth and evolution is toward integration, toward oneness. Transformation toward more fragmentation, greater internal dividedness, is seen as regressive or pathological; with one important exception.

In shamanic and yogic traditions, there exist practices of intentional fragmentation in which practitioners purposefully allow themselves to be divided and dismembered—psychically. This kind of conscious, guided dismantling of ego structures is regarded as part of the work of learning to function in different realities. We are dealing, then, not with psychotic disintegration but with shamanic initiation and intentional yogic practice.

A further crucial point here is that separation or dissociation in the psyche is regarded as an inevitable and necessary consequence of incarnation, just as imprisonment is. Man's nature is originally one, single, whole, and unified with God. Through entry into the world of forms, however—through embodiment—we become involved with multiplicity. We live enmeshed in the thousand petty details of ordinary existence. Meister Eckhart wrote: "This treasure of the Kingdom of God has been hidden by time and multiplicity . . . and by creaturely nature. But in the measure that the soul can separate itself from this multiplicity, to that extent it reveals within itself the Kingdom of God."[2] In the core of our being we are singular and unified; at the surface of our interactions with the world, we are multiple and dispersed. In transformation we seek to recover that original unity.

Fragmentation in Everyday Consciousness

Numerous expressions in our language attest to the belief that our personality, our psyche, our mind is something that is brittle, that it can be broken, or fragmented in some way: we may be "shattered" by an experience; we may think we are "falling apart," "coming apart at the seams," or "falling to pieces," to the point where we have a "nervous breakdown." We may "break" under cross-examination, "break up" with laughter, or "break off" a relationship, which may also make us feel "brokenhearted." I may be "shaken" by some bad news, feel "torn" between conflicting demands, be "crushed" by a rejection, "crumble" under stress, until my mind "snaps"; I can get "smashed" on liquor and the next morning have a "splitting" headache. Colloquially speaking, we tell ourselves we need to "get our act together." Relationships, too, are fragile structures, as is seen by how often couples "split up."

Alternatively, instead of breaking down, we may "crack up." The word *crack* is based on Middle English *crasen,* "to break," which is the ancestor of our words *craze* and *crazy.* Insanity and psychosis, therefore, are related in common language and thought to the notion of psychic fragmentation. Equally indicative of the fragmentation metaphor is the etymology of *mad,* which is based on the Indo-European root *mait,* "to hew," which we find related to the words *main, mayhem,* and *mangle.* This is particularly interesting in view of the connection, discussed below, between psychic fragmentation and the symbolism of bodily dismemberment.

We tend to deplore states of mind in which our thinking is scattered; we feel confused when we have a multiplicity of choices or have mixed motives for something; on the other hand, we tend to admire those who are "single-minded" in their pursuit of some ideal or in their practice of a devotion. We search, with varying degrees of awareness, for a unifying vision or purpose in our life. William James spoke of several "selves" that constitute a personality:

> Now in all of us, however constituted, . . . does the normal evolution of
> character chiefly consist in the straightening out and unifying of the inner self.
> The higher and the lower feelings, the useful and the erring impulses, begin
> by being a comparative chaos within us—they must end by forming a stable
> system of functions in right subordination.[3]

Many psychological theories contain ideas similar to this. Starting with the common observation that human personality and behavior are constituted of many parts and functions, psychologists have developed lists of "traits" or "needs" to account for the multiplicity and diversity of human activities. In the psychoanalytic theory of personality and its later derivatives, a person's adult personality structure represents an accumulation of numerous identifications with various role models, who were imitated at various stages of development— starting with our parents. In adult life we find then ourselves with a multiplicity of roles. It is not necessary to go into the details of these theories of human nature to appreciate the common theme of multiplicity.

Roberto Assagioli, who developed his theory of psychosynthesis based partly on the esoteric teachings of Alice Bailey, spoke of the existence in the psyche of a number of differing, and at times conflicting, subpersonalities. In his view, we are at first unconsciously identified with these subpersonalities; in time, as we become aware of them, we see them as roles we consciously play out. Some have suggested the apt metaphor of the self as a kind of orchestra, with many different parts playing together. The task of transformation, then, is to attune and harmonize the different musicians and instruments of the personality.[4]

In Jung's psychology, there are certain chief actors in the drama of the psyche, such as the shadow, the anima or animus, the persona, and the ego. The many varieties of consciousness and identity are accounted for in his model by the multifarious images and symbols in the collective unconscious. Each one of us has access to an enormous number of archetypes, myths, and symbols, which live in our psyche. These archetypes and symbols serve as signposts, or centers, around which are crystallized our wishes, hopes, fears, ideals, and impulses. They are as numerous and varied as the facets of our personality.

It is a common observation that we identify with different parts or organs of the body as well. For example, if I say, "I hurt" rather than, "my foot hurts," I am identified with my foot at that moment. Each part of the body has "ego," a sense of identity. Sometimes an individual is so identified with a bodily subpersonality that this becomes a recognizable and characteristic feature. We may then speak of someone "coming from the heart" or being "in his head," or being "nervous" or "nosey" or "all ears"—and other, similar expressions that reveal identity localized in an organ or area of the body.

Older typologies of human temperament were often based on the assumption that people were identified in parts or subsystems of the body. In the humoral theory, for example, we had "sanguine" (blood-related) or "phlegmatic" (lymph-related) dispositions. There were typologies in the nineteenth century that distinguished digestive, cerebral, muscular, and reproductive characters.[5] Colloquially, people use genital and anal organ names as terms of abuse. We can, by self-observation, come to an awareness of where in the body our identity is centered, and this kind of awareness is very helpful in charting our course through the process of transformation. In psychotherapy, for example, it is valuable to ask someone who reports feeling fear, where in the body the fear is located.

I am inclined toward the view that sees each structural unit of the body, each organ, each cell, as having a sense of identity. Each organ and cell has its "ego," that is the subjective center of its aliveness. Because there is such an enormous number of these egos, it is easy to see how a sense of being scattered, disjointed, or fragmented can arise. This idea, which I adopted from the Actualism teachings of Russell Schofield, is also found in the writings of Georg Groddeck, the German physician from whom Freud derived his theory of the "It" (or "id"). "I go so far as to believe that every single cell has this consciousness of individuality, that every tissue, every organic system, every kidney cell and every nail cell has its "I" consciousness."[6]

Probably the most forceful statement of the fragmented nature of man's personality is found in the Russian mystic Gurdjieff's teaching:

Man has no permanent and unchangeable I. Every thought, every mood, every desire, every sensation, says "I." . . . There are hundreds and thousands of small I's, very often entirely unknown to one another, never coming into contact, or, on the contrary, hostile to one another, mutually exclusive and incompatible. Each moment, each minute, man is thinking or saying "I." And each time the "I" is different. Just now it was a thought, now it is a desire, now a sensation, now another thought, and so on, endlessly. Man is a plurality. Man's name is legion. . . . There is nothing in man able to control this change of I's, chiefly because he does not notice, or know of it; he lives always in the last I. . . . This explains why people so often make decisions, and so seldom carry them out.[7]

Gurdjieff goes on to argue that the arising and functioning of these different egos is controlled by such temporary factors as weather and other external accidental circumstances, as well as by the longer-lasting influences of education, imitation, religion, caste, tradition, and so forth. In this view of the variegated multiplicity of human personality, our everyday consciousness is seen as scattered and fragmented.

The physicist David Bohm, in discussing the prevalence of fragmentation on the level of the individual, of the group, and of society, points to the "rather interesting sort of irony [that] fragmentation seems to be the one thing in our way of life which is universal, which works through the whole without boundary or limit." Bohm goes on to make the important point that in talking about changing from fragmentation to wholeness, we are not talking about wholeness as some sort of ideal to be attained. Rather, wholeness is the original fact, which we want to reestablish. "Wholeness is what is real, and fragmentation is the response of this whole to man's action, guided by illusory perception, shaped by fragmentary thought."[8]

We need to become aware of our fragmented consciousness, to pay attention to our fragmented way of thinking and understanding reality. We need to learn to "view the ten thousand things in their oneness."

Dissociation and Splintering in Madness and Illness

The notion that normal, everyday consciousness is characterized by scattering and fragmentation is difficult for many people to accept, and it is not a comforting realization when we observe it in ourselves. In the area of mental illness or psychological disturbances, however, we can readily see that dissociation and dividedness are a key feature. In these states, in addition to extreme separation or disconnection between different parts of the psyche (to a much higher degree than in "normal" individuals), there may also be conflict—active opposition, between the different subpersonalities. Psychological researchers have referred to "the shattered language" of schizophrenia in describing the loose associations, the incoherence, the attentional gaps and intrusions, the nonlogical, non-reality-oriented speech of these patients. Schizophrenia is literally the "split mind"; indeed, the "psychotic break" is regarded by some as simply a more intense and radical version of the normal, neurotic "nervous breakdown."

What "breaks" in a psychotic break is the usual relationship between a person's thought and the external physical and social reality. Some psychologists argue that the contact is broken, that there is diminished contact with "reality." Modern theories of psychopathology distinguish schizophrenia from the "dissociative disorders" such as hysteria and multiple personality disorder. A different kind of psychological "splitting" occurs in these disorders. According to a standard psychiatric dictionary,

> In hysteria (and other dissociative disorders), the splitting . . . consists of division into complicated and relatively complete subpersonalities. In the schizophrenias, on the other hand, individual psychic functions are split off from the personality as a whole and attain an autonomy of their own which is unrelated to and often contradictory to the major personality trends.[9]

The actual dissociative mechanism is probably quite similar however, nor is it unknown in normal consciousness. Indeed, as we have seen, this kind of fragmentation is an inherent feature of all human consciousness.

In multiple personality disorders, the individual appears to have two or more relatively complete personalities manifesting at different times; these personalities are separate from one another, often of different ages, sex, characters, and names. The psychologist Ernest Hilgard, in his book *Divided Consciousness,* has argued that dissociative states, including multiple personalities, may be much more common than psychoanalytically oriented psychiatry believes. One could say we are all "multiple personalities" to a certain extent, since we all have several roles and identities.

This brings us to the highly important role of disorganization and fragmentation in physical, as well as psychological and psychosomatic, illness. If we were simply to describe the physiological changes occurring in someone who is ill, we would readily agree that there is a breakdown of the normal relationships between different subsystems; the functions of the liver and the kidney, say, might have become disconnected or desynchronized. The newly rediscovered "holistic" approach in medicine argues that it is a serious mistake to consider the health or illness of any organ or system of the body separately from the whole organism, *or* from the mental, emotional, and spiritual aspects of the human beings, *or* from the social and environmental factors impinging on the individual.[10]

Whatever the causes of illness may be, it seems clear that when we are sick we feel disorganized, "out of sorts," and drained of energy. We may even get a sense of a kind of internal battle going on, in the case where antibodies are fighting bacteria, for example. The transition from being physically disordered or sick to being well, whole, and healthy is analogous to, and a metaphor for, the transition from ordinary consciousness to integrated, unified consciousness: in both cases, we are going from fragmentation to greater wholeness.

Furthermore, becoming sick or the fact of being ill can be a major catalyst to an individual's psychospiritual transformation. We have all known people for whom a physical illness was the major turning point setting them off onto the journey of self-transformation. Even the illness itself, its precise nature and symptoms, can become a kind of message or guide through the healing transformation the individual needs to undergo. The bodily location of a disease can have profound personal meaning to the individual. For instance, most people would consider the possibility that a man or woman who develops cancer on the genitals has some conflicts and concerns around sexuality that are being expressed; which is *not* to say that the disease is psychogenic in origin.

I am not saying that diseases are psychologically caused, only that there are psychological, social, and spiritual aspects to physical illness. This is not the place to enter into the debate about internal versus external causes of disease. The relevant point here is that with a certain kind of attitude and a redirection of attention, and intention, the experience of being ill can catalyze a transformation. This brings us to the theme of the next section, which deals with initiatory sickness and fragmentation symbolism in shamanism and yoga.

Dismemberment and Fragmentation in Shamanism and Yoga

The experience of psychological and psychosomatic fragmentation is symbolized in a very direct, concrete manner in the ancient images and rites of shamanism. Following the lead of historians of religion such as Mircea Eliade and anthropologists such as Michael Harner, we can regard shamanism as a set of practices in which altered states of consciousness are induced by various means, including chanting, drumming, dancing, and use of hallucinogenic plants. Such an altered state is experienced by the shamanic initiate as an inner journey in which he enters another world for the purpose of connecting with a source of power, of obtaining a vision, or of bringing about a healing. The metaphor of the shamanic journey as a transformative altered-state experience will be discussed in more detail in chapter 7. Here we are concerned with the shamanic initiation experience of being symbolically cut up or dismembered, and with the related concepts of initiatory sickness and the "wounded healer."

Eliade has amply documented the occurrence of dismemberment initiations in shamanic cultures of North and South America, Africa, Australia, Central Asia, and Indonesia. In these cultures, it is an accepted and expected part of shamanic apprenticeship to suffer an illness or a wound, or to experience being dismembered, and then reconstituted. The illness of the shamanic seeker can be very real, and by going through it and overcoming it, the would-be healer is in a way following the ancient adage "Physician heal thyself": The shaman's healing power is being tested and demonstrated for the members of the tribe. In some cases, the illness may be more psychological. The parallels between some shamanic vision accounts and psychotic experiences have often been remarked upon. The differences, however, are equally important: the shamanic experience is intentionally incurred, as part of a training sanctioned and approved by the tribe, while the psychotic experience is involuntary and unwanted, and has no social support.[11]

Thus, physical dismemberment and physical sickness are metaphors for psychological fragmentation and breakdown. Shamanic initiations often involve the shaman apprentice becoming mysteriously ill, or even apparently dying. Shamans may have visions in which they see and feel themselves being dismembered, or cut open, or flayed, or reduced to a skeleton. In some of the Australian aboriginal tribes, the would-be medicine man is symbolically "cut open" with stones; the abdominal organs are "removed" and replaced by crystals, which give him curing and clairvoyant power after he is put back together. In Siberia and among the Eskimos, the initiate is divested of flesh and contemplates his skeleton before being reassembled. In other cultures there may be a "stripping" of the skin, followed by its being washed or replaced by a new one. It is important that such apparently gruesome inner experiences are sought out by the shaman in training, for they are followed by a feeling and vision of the body being renewed and by the acquisition of magical or healing powers.

To the practitioner who is a member of that shamanic culture such visions are in the nature of a religious experience. The initiate feels he is being delivered from the limitations of the ordinary world and empowered to perform visionary, healing, and protective work for himself and the members of his tribe. Michael Harner has for several years conducted training workshops in shamanic practice for modern Westerners and has found that altered-state journeys and dismemberment visions can readily occur in a contemporary context and are usually experienced as being both healing and renewing. I have attended several of these workshops and verified this observation. According to the shamanic teachings, when the person's body is reconstituted, it is given new organs that are healthier, stronger, and free from disease. Interestingly, the technique of working with cancer by interior visualizations, developed by Dr. Carl Simonton, has many similarities with these shamanic altered-state practices, as well as alchemical operations.

Perhaps the most dramatically powerful of such rituals that has been documented is the *chod*, or "cutting-off" rite, of the Tibetan Lamaist tradition, which represents a fusion of the original Bön shamanism with Vajrayana Buddhist ideas from India. In this rite, the initiate retires alone to a deserted cemetery or charnel ground, invokes demons and "wrathful deities," and invites them to cut up and devour his body. Here are the instructions for one such rite:

Then imagine this body, which is the result of thine own karmic propensities, to be a fat, luscious-looking corpse, huge enough to embrace the universe. Then visualize the Radiant Intellect, which is within thee, as being the Wrathful Goddess and as standing apart from the body, having one face and two hands and holding a knife and a skull. Think that she severs the head from the corpse, cuts the corpse to pieces and flings them into the skull as offerings to the deities. Then think that by the power of mantras, the offerings are wholly transmuted into *amrita* [divine essence or nectar], sparkling and radiant.[12]

This text makes clear that the dismembered body is transmuted to a higher, "lighted" form, just as the substitution of crystals for internal organs among the Australian medicine men symbolizes their becoming filled with light and power. In these examples, such ritual visualizations of personal destruction are regarded as an inherent and inevitable feature of the transformative initiation. Dismemberment is always followed by renewal, fragmentation by integration, death by rebirth.

In the Tibetan and several other shamanic traditions, the destruction of the body is often visualized as being accomplished by demons or monsters; the healing and reconstituting may be done by the practitioner's teacher or guru or by a spirit ally or power animal. From another point of view, the destructive demons or "wrathful deities" are in essence also allies: they assist in the labor of transformation and liberation. They are personifications of the fiercely energetic forces of "breakthrough"—even though to the ego experiencing their violent power, they appear to be causing breakup and breakdown. The shaman-yogi must learn to tame these demons, which reside, of course, within the psyche, and he or she must learn to redirect their energies toward enlightenment and transformation.

In the Indian yoga tradition, one of the *siddhis,* or "powers," of an advanced yogi is that of separating the body into different pieces and reassembling them again at will. In the biography of the nineteenth-century saint Sai Baba of Shirdi, there is an eyewitness account by a man who entered the yogi's quarters and found his limbs and head scattered around the room. Departing in fear and amazement, he returned several hours later to find Sai Baba sitting on his usual seat. Apparently this yogi's power was such that he not only experienced the dismemberment himself, he made it externally visible to others. This particular *siddhi* is recognized in books on yoga as *nava-kantha siddhi.* [13]

Closer to our own Western roots, dismemberment symbolism also occurs in the religion of the ancient Hebrews, as, for instance, in Ezekiel's vision of "the valley of dry bones."[14] Here the prophet sees the skeletons of many dead men, whom the Lord reanimates: "I will put breath into you and you shall live. I will fasten sinews on you, bring flesh upon you, overlay you with skin, and put breath in you and you shall live; and you shall know that I am Lord." And, according to Ezekiel, there was "a rustling sound," and the bones fitted themselves together, and the Lord called the winds from the four quarters to breathe into the skeletons; "and they came to life and rose to their feet, a mighty host . . . these are the people of Israel." The connection between the reduction to bones, or dismemberment, and the theme of resurrection, found in most of the Near Eastern mystery religions of ancient times, is here suggested.

Fragmentation in the Myths of Osiris and Dionysos

The relevance of these ancient shamanic rituals and practices to the modern individual lies in their emphasis on transformation and awareness. Such is the power of these vivid and dramatic inner visions that they can give a new center and a new direction to the psyche of the practitioner. A similar role is played by myths of dying and dismembered gods and by the mystery cults based on these myths.[15] The myth of a god or hero functions as a prototype, or exemplar, for the individual, telling us to follow the example of the god who can let himself be dismembered and then reconstituted.

We have already discussed the myth of Osiris, who was trapped inside a coffer, a tree, and a house, as a metaphor for the human experience of embodiment. In another part of the myth, the symbolism of dismemberment and reintegration is elaborated. The story goes that Osiris was captured again by his adversary Set; this time he was cut up into fourteen fragments that were scattered all over the world. His consort Isis again saved him, by finding and reassembling the pieces—except that his generative member could not be found. So Isis fashioned a new one and became impregnated by it. Osiris goes on to become the Lord of the Underworld; their son Horus continues the struggle against Set in the natural world.

Such a myth has many levels of meaning: for example, the fact that there are fourteen fragments has been related by some to the lunar month, which has twice fourteen days; Osiris is, among other things, a lunar and vegetation deity, and his fragmentation was symbolically related to the apparent cutting up of the moon. On the psychological level, his dismemberment is a metaphor for the dispersal and fragmentation of personal identity in the world of ordinary existence. We have psychic pieces of ourselves all over the place. Isis, in putting Osiris back together, represents the feminine spiritual counterpart, the female soul, or *anima,* capable of synthesizing and integrating our scattered selves. The myth applies equally to men and women: the dynamic, expressive aspect (Osiris) gets scattered and lost in the toils and splinters of material existence; the nurturing, receptive aspect (Isis) heals and "makes whole." The cure for dismemberment is re-membering: remembering who we actually are. This is the process of self-remembering and re-collection that plays such an important role in Gnostic and Sufi teachings.[16]

In the Greek myth of Dionysos, the connection between the experience of bodily fragmentation and the psychic dissociation of insanity is clearly revealed. Like Osiris, Dionysos is a lunar god of vegetation and fertility; like Bacchus, he represents intoxication and ecstasy. In the words of Walter Otto, Dionysos is "the wild spirit of antithesis and paradox, of immediate presence and complete remoteness, of bliss and horror, of infinite vitality and the cruelest destruction."[17] He is the god, the spirit, the archetype, of divine intoxication, ecstasy, *enthusiasmos*— as well as of madness, *mania,* dismemberment, dissolution, and death. He was referred to as the "divided and undivided spirit." As Erich Neuman says, "madness is a dismemberment of the individual, just as dismemberment of the body . . . symbolizes dissolution of the personality."[18] Dionysos, like Osiris, has several births and several deaths. The variant of his story most relevant to the present theme is that of Dionysos-Zagreus, whose name means Great Hunter. At the instigation of Hera, who was jealous because he was the offspring of Zeus and a human woman, he was captured by titans as a youth. Before being caught, he changed himself rapidly from one animal form into another, ending with a bull. In this form he was caught, cut to pieces, cooked in a cauldron, and devoured by the titans. His father, Zeus, managed to save his heart and remake him from this one organ. In another variant, the pieces were reassembled by his grandmother Rhea. Since he is a god, however, the story of Dionysos' fragmentation, like that of Osiris, must be seen as an expression of the archetype of conscious, intentional dismemberment. It is part of the myth of Dionysos that he drives mad those who do not acknowledge his divinity. This can be interpreted as a statement about the psychological importance of acknowledging one's own instinctual, violent, and ecstatic impulses. If we do not acknowledge or recognize them, they can drive us mad. If, however, we recognize and acknowledge them, those violent and paradoxical impulses within us can be transformed and integrated. In modern literature the character of Zorba the Greek is a prime example of the Dionysian temperament: we may recall his statement that you have to be a little bit crazy to really cut loose and be free.

We can see the titans not as destructive forces but, rather, as master initiators who lead the youthful Dionysos through the kinds of experience his followers later incorporate in the rituals of the mystery cults. Dionysos, like every human being, is part god, part human. In childhood he is dismembered, just as we all become fragmented and dissociated as a result of the conditioning processes of ordinary existence. And through the intervention of the divine principle, in the form of either the divine father (Zeus) or the divine mother (Rhea), the human life is saved and healed. Like Osiris, Dionysos becomes Ruler of the Underworld, equated with Hades. He is the one who crosses and recrosses the boundaries between worlds, who shatters our carefully constructed conventional realities, driving us into madness or liberating transformation—depending on our level of preparedness and the quality of our intention.

A role similar to that of Osiris and Dionysos is played by Kali in the mythology of India. This goddess shares the same mixture of life-giving and death-dealing qualities, the same imagery of dismembered and decapitated bodies, the same paradox of gruesome destruction and astonishing capacity for self-transformation and regeneration. Individuals in the midst of a transformation process that includes fragmentation or dismemberment experiences would do well to study the mythic imagery of Osiris, Dionysos, and Kali, for in these myths we can see how such a madness-inducing experience can be transformed and how it can eventually lead to integration.

Alchemical Separatio in Meditation and Psychotherapy

In the Hermetic tradition, the process of *separatio* most nearly corresponds to dismemberment symbolism. Through *separatio,* the elements of our nature, which are initially in a state of undifferentiated chaos, are carefully distinguished, separated, discriminated. It is a kind of sorting out of the separate parts of our totality, seen as a necessary prerequisite to subsequent integration. Or, to put it another way, the destructuring of the old personality, both physical and psychic, must precede the restructuring of transformation.[19]

As used in alchemy, the "elements" have both physical and psychological meanings. Physically, they represent component states of the body: earth the solid, water the fluid, air the gaseous, and fire the bioelectrical. Identifying and then integrating these aspects through meditation, imagery, and discriminative awareness is the first phase of the alchemical integrative process. Psychologically, the four elements correspond to Jung's functions, or the dimensions of consciousness: earth the physical body and sensation, water the emotional or feeling level, air the thinking or mental level, and fire the intuitive or perceptual level. Thus, the alchemical process of transmuting the elements consists of first distinguishing and analyzing these functions, and then balancing and integrating them; in Jung's theory this is an aspect of individuation.[20]

Separatio is akin to the process of *solutio,* as a way of releasing the spirit that has been trapped or bound. Jung wrote: "The *anima mundi,* imprisoned in matter, . . . was set free by 'cooking,' by the sword dividing the 'egg,' or by the *separatio,* or by dissolution into the four 'roots' or elements. The *separatio* was often represented as dismemberment of a human body." He also points out the connection between *separatio* and the modern concept of psychic dissociation, "which, as we know, lies at the root of the psychogenic psychoses and neuroses."[21]

An example of a dismemberment-*separatio* image occurred to a psychotherapy client who, after an emotional encounter with a psychotic, dreamed of seeing himself with his torso opened and his intestines pouring out. Subsequently he imagined his depression as a pit of darkness, out of which light was beginning to emerge. Other experiences in the same vein, which have been observed in psychedelic states, in psychotherapy, as well as in dreams of persons undergoing radical transformations, include: seeing parts of one's body, especially the arms and hands, becoming elongated and flying off into space; seeing another's or one's own body as a skeleton; feeling one's skin being turned inside out and washed; or feeling as if penetrated and transfixed by hundreds of needles or sword or arrow points simultaneously (as in the legend of Saint Sebastian).

In the model of personality transformation developed by Stanislav Grof, the dismemberment and *separatio* imagery stems from the third phase of the birth process, in which the fetus is being actively and vigorously, though often with enormous pain and struggle, propelled through the birth canal.[22] Experiences derived from the memory of this stage are characterized by feelings of "titanic struggle," "cosmic suffering," "volcanic ecstasy," explosions, orgies, bloody war-fare, battles, dangerous adventures, dying and being reborn, and religious sacrifice as in the Aztec, early Christian, and Dionysiac traditions. Clearly these are all characteristic dismemberment and fragmentation images; in psychotherapeutic transformations, they occur just prior to the experience of rebirth into a new and better kind of life.

An example of healing, liberating *separatio* imagery is found in this account, by a twenty-six-year-old college student, of part of a psychedelic therapy session:

> I felt shattered, broken up. . . . It was as if a sledgehammer had been slammed down on the crystallized, granitelike structures of my deepest and earliest emotional pain and trauma—something that was previously rocklike and unchangeable, like cement that had solidified in my being.

In other words, healing takes place as some psychic complex is disintegrated through a cutting and breaking down process, applied to the area of hardened defenses and resistance.

Almost all these images can be found in alchemical texts and illustrations —another factor that supports the notion that the alchemists were in fact practi-tioners of consciousness transformation. For example, in a seventeenth-century tract entitled *Splendor Solis (Splendor of the Sun)*, we are told of a vision of an alchemical practitioner, Rosinos, in which he sees a man lying on the ground, his limbs and head cut off. Next to the dead man stands the killer holding a blood-stained sword. In the killer's other hand is a paper on which is written, "I have killed thee, that thou mayst receive superabundant life. . . . And the body I will bury, that it may putrefy, and grow and bear innumerable fruit."[23] Another alchemical text advises us to "destroy the bodies until they are changed." This is conscious, deliberate destruction of psychic structures, leading to intentional reconstruction.

Jung pointed out the parallels between this symbolism and that of Job's sufferings and Christ's passion—and, he might have added, with the early Chris-tian martyrs. The martyrs' devout, even ecstatic, acceptance of torture and death might in part have been stimulated by a perception of the similarity of Christ's martyrdom with the slain and dismembered divinities of the mystery religions of Osiris and Dionysos.

Approaches to Wholeness

There are three major keys to what could be called the strategy of transformative reintegration. These keys are also central in the other varieties of transformative experience discussed in this book. The first point is that one must recognize the fact of scattering and dissociation in one's ordinary consciousness and everyday life. The second point is the need to focus intention toward the transformative integration: this aware intention makes the difference between a psychotic experience of psychic disintegration and a shamanic, yogic, or alchemical process of change that involves purposeful use of images of disintegration and fragmentation. The third point is that an inward orientation is necessary: we get scattered into multiplicity because our attention is directed toward outer things and events in an imbalanced manner. In turning within, we find the single source of wholeness.

All the various technical procedures of yoga, alchemy, and shamanism are utilized in the process of reintegration and healing. This includes methods of visualization, of vocalization *(mantra),* and of breath control. It is often said that the power of breath, as the animating wind, or *spiritus,* of Divine Presence, is the medium through which the healing actually takes place. For example, an apprentice shaman may feel that his or her "power animal" reconstitutes the body by breathing into it. A yogi may use various breath control techniques *(pranayama)* to bring about a new balance of inner energies and perceptions. Breathing into deadened or disconnected parts of our body image is perhaps the surest way to awaken and reanimate them.

The feminine principle, in women and men, symbolized as mother, nurse, sister, or consort—plays a principal role in the healing process. It is usually the masculine, outgoing principle (in men or women) that gets dissipated, scattered, or dissociated from the source or Self. In many of the ancient myths and texts, the healing woman or goddess exemplifies qualities of nurturance, synthesis, order, containment. However, it is not necessarily always the feminine principle that heals. Indeed, in many mythologies, the devouring, destroying force is the Great Mother—Kali, Cybele, Hecate, Lilith, for example. In the best-known version of the Dionysos myth, Father Zeus is the agent who reconstitutes the son who has been killed. And Osiris was often worshipped as the one who has made himself whole: "I have knit myself together. . . . I have renewed my youth. . . . I am Osiris, Lord of Eternity."[24]

Transcendence and the imagery of ascension is also a major aspect of the unification. We "rise into" oneness. Meister Eckhart wrote: "The whole scattered world of lower things is gathered up to oneness when the soul climbs up to that life in which there are no opposites."[25] As mentioned earlier, in the ancient wisdom teachings, the highest, source level of consciousness is an undivided unity. As differences and multiplicity arise inevitably in the course of the descent of Spirit into material forms, evolutionary transformation then involves a return to the original state of undivided wholeness, a theme to which we shall return in chapter 8.

As we recognize that the fragmentation to which we are subject is due to a disconnection from the source of our life, the Immortal Self, it follows that our path to wholeness must involve a "re-membering" of that Self. Christian contemplatives gave the name *recollection* to the process by which "the scattered interests of the self" are gathered together. And in the Islamic Sufi tradition, the term *dhikr,* also usually translated as "recollection," similarly encourages "remembering God," by the repetition of key prayers or mantras.

Finally, singleness itself is regarded as a quality of consciousness that can be cultivated. Ancient Greek authors used the term *monachos,* "single," to describe the Gnostic (this word entered into English in *monk* and *monastic*). Origen, one of the early Christian Fathers, said, "Where there are sins, there is multitude ... but where virtue is, there is singleness, there is union." The Gnostic Gospel of Thomas speaks of a person who "finds himself single, then he will be full of light; but when he finds himself divided, he will be full of darkness."[26]

This singleness, perhaps single-mindedness—the undividedness of the individuated person who has a unifying vision that integrates all of life's experiences —was beautifully expressed by the American mystic and transcendentalist Walt Whitman:

> There is, apart from mere intellect, in the make-up of every superior human identity, a wondrous something that realizes without argument ... an intuition of the absolute balance, in time and space, of the whole of this multifariousness, this revel of fools, and incredible make-believe and general unsettledness, we call the world; a soul-sight of that divine clue and unseen thread which holds the whole congeries of things, all history and time, and all events, however trivial, however momentous, like a leashed dog in the hands of the hunter.[27]

Whitman calls this single-mindedness a "root-center for the mind," and "soul-sight." It is indeed, as we have seen, a vision that seems to come from soul or spirit, and one that fosters a feeling of being rooted in the very ground and core of our beingness.

7

Journey to the Place of Vision and Power

I am afoot with my vision. . . . I tramp a perpetual journey.

—WALT WHITMAN

The sense of our movement through the ever-changing flux of life's events as a journey or path is certainly an almost universal human experience. Our life is a journey, with a beginning, middle, and end. It is a going out, extending into the world, and a returning, or settling down. The process of self-transformation is a journey within that journey, a branching out from the main trunk, a new growing. Numerous metaphors in the literature of mysticism and in myths the world over speak of transformation as a journey to another land, along a river, up a mountain, through a wilderness, into the depths of the earth, or searching for the castle of marvels. The experience of change and the experience of wandering, of traveling, are very similar. In German, "to change" is *wandeln;* "to wander" is *wandern.* As we wander we change. The pilgrim who arrives at the sacred place is not the same man who left home. The seeker who returns to her family or tribe, bringing gifts of power, healing, or vision, is a transformed individual.

This metaphor is employed in all the spiritual traditions. The ancient Chinese sages spoke of Tao as the "way" or "track." It is "the way that cannot be told," the way of heaven and earth, that man is to follow. This Tao-way we cannot perceive; we can only see its tracks and traces in Nature—in patterns of flowing water, in swirls of wood, lines of stone, curling smoke, the veins of leaves and clouds. The Indian teachings of transformation speak of three "paths" *(margas)* that seekers pursue: the path of knowledge, the path of love, and the path of action. In the oldest *Upanishad* we read, "Long and narrow is the ancient path —I have touched it, I have found it—the path by which the wise, knowers of the Eternal, attaining to salvation, depart hence."[1]

The symbolism of journey, path, and way is pervasive in the Western religions as well. The journey of the Israelites out of Egypt to the Promised Land exemplifies the pattern of the journey as an escape from imprisonment or slavery;

which is a natural extension of the metaphor of liberation we have already discussed. The biblical prophets show people the *way* of God, the way of truth, and of righteousness, and warn them to desist from false ways, the ways of the wicked. Jesus Christ proclaims, "I am the way" and "The Kingdom of Heaven is as a man traveling into a far country."[2]

In Islam, the prophet Mohammed describes his own mystical journeys and leads the way to Mecca, the Holy City. The Islamic Sufi is also said to be on a path *(tariqat),* the end of which is dissolution of the ego in divine union *(fana).* In Islamic mysticism a distinction is made between "those who are drawn up-ward" *(majdub),* raised up passively to higher stages of consciousness; and "those who stride" *(salik),* who must make their way with suffering and labor.[3] This parallels the distinction between a transformation that occurs through grace and one that occurs through intention.

The same imagery appears in the mythology of native cultures, whether in the form of the "Red Road" of the Sioux Indians, the "Blessing Way" of the Pueblo, the "Holy Path," the "Way of the Heart"; all these are terms used by native cultures to describe a way of life that follows the guidance of the Great Spirit. In the words of Black Elk, "For you see the birds leave the earth with their wings, and we humans may also leave this world, not with wings, but in the spirit."[4]

There is the mythic hero's journey, told of with masterful eloquence by Joseph Campbell in his *Hero with a Thousand Faces.* The pattern of the myth is always similar: departure, arrival, and return. The departure involves what Campbell describes as a "call to adventure": the hero leaves "home," the safe world of conventional reality. The journey includes many tests, obstacles, challenges, and battles. The goal is a place where the hero is given knowledge, magical power, healing, or a priceless gift. The hero then returns with this gift or power to the everyday world of family, tribe, or village. This returning with a gift or power means, metaphorically speaking, that after the mythic journey we are changed, we have a new identity—we are now empowered as teachers, healers, or seers. Similarly, the pattern of the mythic journey is also found in the practices of the shaman. As Mircea Eliade has pointed out, "Through his own ecstatic experience, [he] knows the roads of the extraterrestrial regions. . . . Sanctified by his initiation and furnished with guardian spirits, the shaman is the only human being able to challenge the danger and venture into a mystical geography."[5]

Since experiences with psychoactive plants or drugs are among the most powerful altered states of consciousness, it is not surprising that the young people experimenting with psychedelic drugs in America in the 1960s spontaneously began using the metaphor of the "trip" to describe the states of consciousness induced by these drugs—as shamans and medicine men had done for thousands of years. In our time, psychedelic trips have played a major part in the transform-ative process of thousands of individuals.

Then there is the archetype of the "lost soul," the psychotic seen as one who has lost his way on the journey through inner space. Like the mythic hero, the mystic, and the shaman, the schizophrenic has departed from the everyday world of conventional reality; he has "gone" or has had a "break." But unlike shamanic or yogic seekers after knowledge and power, the poor madman has gone on an involuntary journey, one for which he had no preparation, and for which he finds no familial or cultural support. As R. D. Laing has written:

> In our present world, which is both so terrified and so unconscious of the other world, it is not surprising that when "reality," the fabric of this world, bursts, and a person enters the other world, he is completely lost and terrified and meets only incomprehension in others. . . . Most people in inner space and time are, to begin with, in unfamiliar territory and are frightened and confused. They are lost. . . . They try to retain their bearings. . . . The person who has entered this inner realm (if only he is allowed to experience this) will find himself going, or being conducted—one cannot distinguish active from passive here—on a journey. The journey is experienced as going further "in," as going back through one's personal life, in and back through and beyond into the experience of all mankind, of the primal man, of Adam and perhaps even further into the beings of animals, vegetables and minerals. In this journey there are occasions to lose one's way, for confusion, partial failure, even final shipwreck; many terrors, spirits, demons to be encountered, that may or may not be overcome.[6]

Each of the many kinds of journeys, with its mythic variations, provides a recognizable symbolic description of a type of transformation experience. The completed journey always ends with a return, a homecoming, to the ordinary, world of conventional reality that was left behind. This world has been transformed, if our journey has been successful, into a new world, seen with fresh eyes. The end of the journey is the beginning of a new, empowered way of life.

This theme of returning home connects to an important variant of the journey metaphor: the idea that in ordinary life, we already are on a journey, that we come from a faraway place, that we are in exile. In this pattern, the mystical journey of enlightenment is actually a return to our original home, to a place we have forgotten. This metaphor will be discussed in the next chapter, "Returning to the Source."

The Myth of the Wanderer

The image of man as a traveler or wanderer is an ancient one, perhaps rooted in ancestral memories of the hundreds of thousands of years our species spent wandering in nomadic bands of hunter-gatherers. People differ greatly in the quality of their experience of life's journey, and for each one of us, there may be differences in the type of journey at different stages of life. Some of us—

probably all of us at some time—wander restlessly and aimlessly through life. At other times we may be seized by a sudden sense of destiny: we start off and aim for a destination, a definite goal. Perhaps our purpose is to escape some intolerable situation. Or the goal may be worldly: to attain power, wealth, fame, or love. Or it may be supernatural and mystical: a quest for meaning, a longing for God, a thirst for wisdom, a need to heal. The Islamic Sufi sage Ibn al'Arabi wrote, "Know that since God created human beings and brought them out of nothingness into existence, they have not stopped being travellers."[7]

The mythic wandering hero represents the human ego exploring and discovering the world of reality as he or she grows up to adulthood, traversing the rites of passage and the transitions and challenges of each phase. This journey of growth and development follows parallel lines for people in all cultures. The spiritual quest, the transformational journey, begins when the hero leaves home, leaving behind the familiar, conventional world in order to journey into the "far country," to the magical castle, the sacred city; to ascend the holy mountain; or to cross the great seas and deserts. A striking literary exposition of this theme is Lewis Carroll's *Alice in Wonderland;* the heroine's subterranean wanderings, initiated by her drop down a rabbit hole, lead her into a realm where the usual dimensions of time, space, and logic do not apply.

There are several different types of wanderers on the path of transformation, having different purposes for their journeys. Some feel they have been instructed to wander. Like the biblical Abraham, whom God commanded to migrate from the city of Ur, they may hear an inner voice that directs them. Others may feel impelled to escape, to seek a "way out." These are the stories and myths in which one escapes from a prison or a labyrinth, or flees the threatening attacks of mortal enemies. In modern terms this corresponds to the story of a person who seeks to escape a career "rut," a relationship trap, or a situation threatening bodily harm or legal difficulties.

Then there are those unfortunate souls, like Odysseus, who are doomed to wander because they have incurred the wrath of a deity. Wandering as a kind of divine punishment is the theme of the folktale of Ahasuerus, the Wandering Jew. This story, current in the European Middle Ages, told of a man who refused to help Christ when he stumbled while carrying his cross on the road to Calvary. For this, Ahasuerus was condemned to wander homelessly for centuries. These legends correspond to the situation of a person wandering restlessly, driven by guilt or remorse about some misdeed, and unable to settle anywhere because of an uneasy conscience.

Very often the death of a loved one or one's own illness and approaching death serves as the catalyst that propels a person on a kind of existential quest to discover the meaning of mortality or understand the nature of loss and grief. Gilgamesh, the hero of Babylonian myth, departs on his journey when Enkidu, his closest friend and companion, dies. "Bitterly Gilgamesh wept for his friend

Enkidu; he wandered over the wilderness as a hunter, he roamed over the plains."[8] Three famous goddess myths express the same archetypal pattern: those of the Babylonian Ishtar, the Egyptian Isis, and the Greek Demeter, who all wander disconsolately over the Earth, looking for their lost son, lover, or daughter. As they wander, the earth is barren; cold winds ravage animals and humans, and the forces of death and darkness hold sway. Until the earth-mother goddess actually confronts Death in the Underworld, life is held in the balance.

These myths point to loss of love and grief over separation as a main theme of the journey: this loss and grief can be such a shock to the emotional nature, that severe illness and depression, symbolized in the myths by the barren lands and cold winds, can ensue.

We can understand from all this that the "path" or "journey" of both mysticism and mythology is an explicit metaphor for the process of self-transformation. The different phases of this process are named in accordance with the metaphor: the pilgrim, the strider, the once-returner, the never-returner, the one who has stopped wandering.[9] The writings of the mystics are quite explicit about the interior nature of this "journey": they tell us that the terrain to be explored and traversed is our own psyche. They give detailed landmarks for those who know they are on the inner journey and who need further guidance and information. They tell us that the "castle" is "interior," that there is a "valley" of "detachment," a "swamp of despair." The mystics offer interpretations that reveal the psychological meanings of their symbols and metaphors.

On the other hand, the myths and folktales that describe the hero's journey are not explicitly psychological: in myth the journey is described as an outer journey, carried out in real time and space. Therefore, the inner, psychological meaning of the mythic journey, as a process of consciousness transformation, is not directly stated. Instead, it is communicated to the deeper, imagistic layers of our subconscious minds. The imagery of the path, the journey, the traveler's adventures, evokes in the psyches of the listeners or readers the recognition and remembrance of their own journeys of personal transformation, of their own life process. Because we identify with the hero or heroine, these stories awaken us to the process of transformation occurring in us. We can readily identify with the misadventures of Odysseus, seeking to return to his wife and family, with Demeter, searching disconsolately for her lost daughter.

Just as the poetic imagery of the journey evokes ancient and personal resonances in us, an actual outer journey to a faraway land can have a similar effect—the outer stimuli perceived by the voyager by symbolic resonance can evoke corresponding inner experiences. For example, a thirty-five-year-old woman teacher found herself at a turning point in her life when she took a sabbatical leave from her job, dissolved a nine-year marriage, and began to plan a trip to Nepal. Months later she wrote, "I began to refer to my trip as a 'journey.' . . . Subsequently I realized that my outward trip was a mirror of my inward journey. My experiences . . . in Nepal and Europe reflected a personal transformation of equal magnitude—a spiritual awakening."[10] Later, while reading Joseph Campbell, she saw that she was getting the "call to adventure" and received "supernatural aid" in the form of visions: she started seeing mountains in her meditations, as well as a magic wand. In dreams and waking thoughts, she began anticipating both "treasures and dangers."

Some cultures have institutionalized such journeys of personal transformation. The vision quest of the American Indians is such a journey of self-discovery, in which the youth spends three days and nights alone in the wilderness, fasting and praying for a vision. On such a wilderness journey, into terrain far removed from human society, not only is there a stimulation of the inner journey by analogy and mirroring, there are also profound alterations of consciousness induced by sensory deprivation and social isolation. The year-long "walkabout" practiced by some of the Australian aboriginal tribes, like the "year walk" among the Basques, extends the vision quest into a much longer journey, for the dual purposes of learning to survive in nature and finding the personal vision.[11]

In other cultures the journey may be ritualized as a group project. The Huichol Indians of Mexico go annually on the three-hundred-mile peyote hunt, in which they travel as a whole village to find the hallucinogenic plant that provides them with visions. While on that journey, through purification and meditation, they consciously engage in harmonizing their relationships with one another as a community. Pilgrimages by groups of people to holy places— whether Chaucer's rowdy band of travelers on the road to Canterbury, devout Christian monks on the way to Jerusalem, or Muslim caravans on the road to Mecca—all share the same purpose: travelers seeking God, seeking to find the Self. In some traditions it is left deliberately ambiguous whether the goal of the pigrimage is an actual outer place or is instead "only symbolic." The Tibetan Buddhist Lamaist teachings concerning the mythical kingdom of Shambhala, which may be hidden somewhere beyond the most desolate Asian mountain ranges or may exist only as a "state" of consciousness, is an example of such an intentionally ambiguous metaphor.[12]

In medieval legends of the quest for the Holy Grail, it seems clear that both outer and inner journeys are being described. Knights definitely wandered through strange forests and wastelands, came to hidden castles, and fought actual battles. But the frequency with which the natural landscape in the tales changes to a magical one indicates that altered states of consciousness, visionary, and meditative experiences, were also being described. King Arthur's fellowship of the Round Table may have been a military and political alliance, but in legend it was also a spiritual fraternity of mystical seekers. The Castle of Marvels that Gawain and Percival both visit, with its moving furniture and visible spirits, is clearly an inner place, a place in consciousness, something like Saint Teresa's "interior castle." On the other hand, Montsalvat, the supposed home of the sacred chalice, which was never found, is also an actual mountain in the Pyrenees.

The journey of transformation enters a crucial new phase when we realize that the journey is, in fact, interior; that the places we seek "out there," the dangers we fear "out there," are only within us. Recognize, says the Tibetan Book of the Dead, to the traveler in the *bardo* (intermediate realms), that both the peaceful and the wrathful deities are within your own mind. The demon that you meet and battle with is the shadow of your ego. The damsel in distress that you rescue is your own anima, the knight in shining armor for whom you long, your own animus.

The stories of the wanderings of the hero contain many metaphors for the interior processes of transformation. The experience of the individual on an actual journey in the real world of space and time may also become highly significant catalysts of deep inner change. Or the inner journeys can take place without any outward travel: the hermit who meditates in his cave may be roaming the world in his mind. On the other hand, we also know that outer journeys can take place without any psychic echoes or spiritual overtones, as is the case for most vacation and tourist travel.

Departure and Threshold Crossing

The departure, the "call to adventure," can come in many different ways. It signifies, according to Joseph Campbell, that "destiny has summoned the hero and transferred his spiritual center of gravity . . . to a zone unknown."[13] It signals the separation from home and family, from the "familiar" world of relatives and friends, the world of our culture or tribe, of convention and stable expectations. The call may be a subtle inner prompting, a vague sense of needing to leave, to withdraw from external commitments, to "make changes." Or the call may be a dramatic and unavoidable challenge, a command, or even a compulsion—"I've got to get out of this rut" or "I have to get on with the rest of my life." The first clue that a metaphorical journey of transformation is beginning may be a dream of embarking on a voyage. Or the first clue may be a kind of awakening, a realization that the first step has already been taken.

This first step may occur as the result of a pain, illness, loss, or separation. Something occurs that makes us sense a lack or dissatisfaction, whether with self, with relationships, or with lifework. This pain or discomfort stimulates us to search for healing or comfort—to *move* somewhere. The woman quoted earlier wrote: "Prior to my departure I experienced great anxiety, reflected in moods of fear, confusion, fascination, compulsion, expectation, yearning. I was afraid to be separated from the known and familiar; I was also afraid of becoming someone new."[14]

The twelfth-century German Benedictine mystic and seeress Hildegard von Bingen gave a most poignant description of the mystic journey as one of escape from imprisonment, from the torture dungeon of worldly existence, with its sufferings, outrage, and pain. Describing her vision, she wrote:

I saw that the soul dwelling in the human body was overwhelmed by many storms, that bent it down to the ground. But the soul gathered its strength, straightened itself with courage and resisted vigorously. Sighing deeply, the soul spoke: "Pilgrim that I am, where am I? In the shadow of death. On what path do I wander? On the path of error and illusion. What solace do I have? The solace of those who are in exile."[15]

The soul, in this vision, after enduring many hardships and insults, devotes itself "with great care to seeking narrow paths, on which to escape from evil associates and wretched imprisonment." These "narrow paths" symbolize the careful choosing, the wise discrimination required of the traveler who would escape from the imprisonment of worldly existence.

The departure on the journey may be associated with anxiety and apprehension about the many unknowns that lie ahead. But it may also be filled with excitement and a sense of adventure, since it is an opportunity to find what we have been lacking. R. M. Rilke, in a poem entitled "A Walk," captures the sense of mysterious anticipation that we may experience as we leave on a journey of transformation:

My eyes already touch the sunny hill,
going far ahead of the road I have begun.
So we are grasped by what we cannot grasp;
it has its inner light, even from a distance—

and changes us, even if we do not reach it,
into something else, which, hardly sensing it, we already are;
a gesture waves us on, answering our own wave . . .
but what we feel is the wind in our faces.[16]

Closely associated with the theme of the departure on a journey of transformation is the symbolism of the doorway, threshold, gate, entrance, or passage. There is the "eye of the needle," through which the rich man cannot pass: and the "crack between the worlds," through which the sorcerer stealthily moves. Every time we enter an altered state of consciousness, even when falling asleep or waking up, we cross a certain border or threshold; this is even more true in those prolonged changes of consciousness that are experienced as a journey. At these gateways or thresholds, there is often a special heightened sensitivity or receptivity. For example, the twilight stage before sleep is a fertile source of creative imagining. When we heed the call to adventure, our senses come into fine tuning—we don't, after all, want to miss any signposts or clues that might help us on our journey.

Sometimes the threshold may be a dangerous narrow passage, as between Scylla and Charybdis, where Odysseus found himself between a seven-headed serpent and a devouring maelstrom—caught between the "devil and the deep blue sea." Or it may be, as in many myths, a bank of fog or a cloudy, indistinct region where we feel confused and disoriented. This is the region that William Bridges, in his work *Transitions,* calls the "neutral zone": one phase of our life has ended, but the shape of things to come is not as yet clear. In some traditions there are elaborate interior geographies that refer to these in-between states. The Tibetan Buddhist teachings refer to *bardo,* the "intermediate states" between death and rebirth, where we have to negotiate many tricky and hazardous points of choice. And medieval theologians spoke of *limbo,* the in-between realm where the ghosts of the recently deceased hover. We feel we are in *limbo* when we are "neither here nor there," when we are not sure whether we are "coming or going."

The ideas of *bardo* and *limbo* imply that dying is a kind of departure. Indeed, death as a journey—the ultimate journey—is a nearly universal metaphor. In this context the threshold experience is often symbolized as the crossing of a river, like the Styx, which the dead were obliged to cross, according to the Greeks. As dying is definitely the crossing of a threshold, so is being born the violent, tumultuous beginning of the long journey of our lives. Each phase of the journey has its passages and gateways. Each consciously guided new beginning is a threshold of initiation.

Each of these phases of transition requires us both to see and to seize the opportunity for transformation. Often we are afraid to venture forth; we may wait for others to precede us, or we delay and make excuses. And yet, as Walt Whitman wrote in *Leaves of Grass,* "Not I, not any one else can travel that road for you. You must travel it for yourself. It is not far, it is within reach. Perhaps you have been on it since you were born, and did not know. Perhaps it is everywhere on water and on land."[17]

Most Eastern teachings, however, warn of making too much of an attitude of striving, of the spiritual ambition so characteristic of the Western psyche. A poem by the Indian *bhakti* mystic Kabir tells us: "What is this river you want to cross? There are no travelers on the river road, and no road. There is no river, and no boat. There is no ground, no sky, no bank, no ford."[18] This seems to be a caution not to get caught up in the external trappings of transformation, not to make it an ego-achievement. Remember that everything is within you; all the old familiar structures of reality are being left behind.

Or, in the words of Zen Master Mumon,

> The great path has no gates,
> Thousands of roads enter into it.
> When one passes through this gateless gate,
> He walks freely between heaven and earth.[19]

The paradoxical phrase "gateless gate" captures perfectly the strange mixture of the familiar and the new that we find at these threshold crossings. There is nothing "to do," and yet, when we have done it, we are altogether transformed. We can walk freely between heaven and earth, between the spiritual and the worldly realms.

Descent into the Depths

The "lower world journeys" that are so important in the shamanic traditions are clearly a kind of altered state of consciousness. Most commonly they
are induced by hallucinogenic plants, rhythmic drumming, or prolonged dancing.
They are referred to as lower world journeys because the shaman's experience in
the altered state is that of walking, crawling, or falling down, not physically (the
physical body is lying on the ground), but in consciousness. The sensation of
downward movement may be accompanied by images of a cave, a tunnel, a stream
bed, a well, or another opening into the ground—which then gives way, after a
while, to an interior landscape of some kind.[20]

Lower world, or underworld, journeys also have a significant place in
mythology: many a hero or heroine, god or goddess, has to descend to the inferior
regions for the purpose of healing and salvation or to obtain some vital piece of
knowledge. Psychologically, one is inclined to say that these lower world journeys
represent experiences in the subconscious layers of the psyche, "below" normal
waking consciousness; these are the layers that are plumbed through dreams and
"depth" analysis. These levels of consciousness are often (though not invariably)
experienced as more constricting, arduous, painful, and frightening than either
"middle world" or "upper world" journeys or states of consciousness. Typically
in mythology, both hell and the land of the dead are found in the lower region,
beneath the surface of the earth. Religious heroes, including Jesus and Muhammad, generally have to traverse hell at some point in their initiatory career. The
prototypical Christian mystical journey, as portrayed in Dante, begins with a
descent through the nine layers of the *Inferno*.

The lower world journey may be a descent into the depths of the ocean. In
psychological terms, the ocean symbolizes the vast collective emotional unconscious, since the element of water is associated with affect and feeling. In dream
journeys we may find ourselves descending into the watery deep, following the
way of many a mythic hero. Gilgamesh has to descend to the bottom of the sea
to find the herb of immortality. Theseus goes into the sea depths to obtain from
the ocean goddess Thetis the gift of a crown of gold, which he uses to illuminate
his travels through the labyrinth. Jonah is drowned and swallowed by the whale:
"The waters compassed me about, even to the soul—the depth closed me round
about . . . yet thou has brought my life up from corruption. O Lord my God."[21]
These stories suggest that while experiences of descent into the fluid depths of the
emotional psyche are often arduous and frightening, they are potentially healing,
cleansing, and liberating as well, providing us with essential insights and tools of
transformation.

In some instances, lower world altered states may actually be excursions
into the interior geography of the body. This is especially evident in the markedly
physiological imagery found in many myths and shamanic accounts. For exam-

ple, the Siberian Yakut shaman must travel through the throat and body of a serpent monster, whose gullet and bowels are lined with sharp spikes. As Joan Halifax has documented in her book *Shaman: The Wounded Healer,* on lower world journeys "the shaman and the soul must brave icy winds, burning forests, stormy rivers, and bloody streams."[22] These and related images, such as the river of blood, the inner sea or swamp, the heaps of bones, the wind-swept caves (lungs), the sloping, gulletlike tunnel, are suggestive of symbolic visualizations of internal physiological structures and functions. This idea is consistent with what we know of the material and organic preoccupations of shamans and alchemists. It is furthermore highly appropriate, from a common-sense point of view, that healers, or heroes on a healing quest, would need to tune their awareness to the biological processes occurring within their own bodies.

Besides healing, the other main objective of a lower world journey, as described in countless myths, is to find the land of the dead and contact dead relatives or ancestors. Orpheus journeys down to Hades to find and recover his lost love Euridice, pacifying the beasts and monsters of this world with his soulful music. Odysseus visits Hades in order to speak to his dead mother and to consult the seer Tiresias for prophecy concerning his fate. The Sumerian Inanna and the Babylonian Ishtar descend to the land of death to find and bring back their lost son or lover. The girl-child Kore is forcibly abducted into the nether world by Hades, the Lord of Death: the involuntary lower world experience of this story, marked by violence and terror, might be a metaphor for the altered state of consciousness induced by a near-fatal injury or illness.

The myth of Demeter, the goddess-mother of Kore, or Persephone, who wanders disconsolately over the earth searching for her lost daughter, thus causing the world's vegetation to wither and decay, has been interpreted as a metaphoric account of vegetative seasonal cycles. Barren winter alternates with fruitful spring and summer, these seasons corresponding to Persephone's alternating sojourns, first in the cold underground of Hades, then in the warmth of the Earth Mother's blooming valleys and fields. Demeter and Persephone-Kore are two aspects—mother and virgin—of the ancient Great Goddess of Grain and Nourishment.

Yet the myth has another interior dimension: it concerns transformation-individuation as well, particularly of the way of women. Seen from this perspective, Demeter and Persephone are two aspects of the feminine psyche— the mother and the girl-child (the Jungian *puella*). Demeter's disconsolate wanderings in search of her lost daughter, while Earth's vegetation withers and decays, is a metaphor for a woman's shock at the physical and psychic loss of fruitfulness, the longing for lost youth, as fear and grief overtake the soul. Support for this interpretation exists in a poignant detail of the myth: as the wandering Demeter calls her daughter's name in the mountainous wilderness, only her own name is echoed back—as if to say, "It is your own Self, your own identity that you seek."

In the myths of the Sumerian Inanna and the Babylonian Ishtar, the descent into the land of death has the same connection to seasonal vegetation cycles and rituals, but it is also motivated by the longing search of the woman for her lover or son, who has died. This represents a different, equally important phase of the transformational journey: the search for androgynous union of the male and female principles into a complete whole. In the ancient Near East, the priestesses of these mother-goddess cults imitated their divinity in the rites of lamentation, crying and calling the name "Tammuz, Tammuz" in the cold darkness of the midwinter season. In such rites of lamentation, they not only evoked the grief and loneliness of women who had actually lost sons or lovers, but also gave expression to the eternal longing for the soul companion, the animus or anima who will complete us. These myths embody an aspect of the quest for the alchemical conjunction of the king and queen, the sacred marriage with one's own internal counterpart, which has "died," that is, has become separated or disassociated.

The story shows the initiatory character of the descent of the goddess by the requirement that Inanna remove seven garments and ornaments from her body before confronting, in nakedness, the Terrible Dark Goddess Ereshkigal. The stripping of the ornaments at the seven gates on the way into the lower world represents the process of stripping the psychic energy centers (the yogic chakras) from obstructions and superimposed coverings and distortions, to reveal the naked truth about oneself.[23]

This lower world journey of the goddess is a metaphor for the often painful and laborious self-examination and self-confrontation that accompanies the quest for inner unification. Ishtar does not succeed in regaining her lost lover-son until she has hung as dead for three days and until the great god Ea, "Lord of the Sacred Eye," intervenes. This means, psychologically speaking, that the woman must die to her old self and open herself to the guidance of higher wisdom (the god Ea) in order to be restored. Again, for modern women and men, such an opening up might be catalyzed by an experience of near-fatal illness or deathlike depression, in which one learns to give up all attachments to past identities in order to reconnect with one's other half in the union that restores love and regenerates life.

"Flying" and the Upper Realms

What shamanism calls upper world journeys or magical flight are altered states of consciousness with the general theme or experience of ascent, rising, climbing upward, or gliding effortlessly through space. Dreams of flying also fall into this category of states of consciousness, as do experiences we describe as "highs." Milder versions might be states in which we feel "uplifted" or "elevated" in moods of ecstatic reverie. I propose that we regard such states as an expansion (or "heightening") of awareness into the subtler, also known as "higher frequency," levels of consciousness. Sometimes one has the experience of ascending through several layers, steps, or rungs of a ladder—which would correspond to the several levels, or planes, of consciousness that are known and described in both Eastern and Western esoteric spiritual traditions. Rising upward in space is a metaphoric image for the process of raising the vibratory frequency of consciousness—which is analogous to the raising of a musical tone to a higher frequency or pitch.

Dreams of flying are everyone's upper world journey. We have already noted that waking up, as well as other kinds of heightening of awareness, are almost always experienced and described in metaphors of upward motion. In flying dreams we usually feel exhilarated, "high," exceptionally lucid, and observant—we seem to have the vision of eagles, or of hawks. This kind of dream can be regarded as a simple, involuntary version of states pursued intentionally by shamans, yogis, and mystics. These are states especially valuable for "seeing," for clairvoyant perception, and for prophetic and prognostic visions. They are akin also to the states of consciousness studied by parapsychologists under the categories of "out-of-the-body" experiences (OOBE) and "remote viewing" experiments.[24]

Many mystics and poets have described spiritual visions metaphorically as being like the flight of birds. Recall, for example, the words of Black Elk, "For you see the birds leave the earth with their wings, and we human beings may also leave this world, not with wings, but in the spirit." His words echo those of the mystic theologian Gregory of Nyssa, who wrote, "The human soul has but one vehicle by which to journey heavenward, that is to make itself unto the flying dove."[25] Gregory goes on to say that the same "dove" is what Scripture calls the Holy Spirit. A poem by R. M. Rilke evokes the feeling of a life in which there are cycles of visionary spiritual states:

> I live my life in growing orbits
> which move out over the things of the world.
>
> I am circling around God, around the ancient tower,
> and I have been circling for a thousand years.
> And I still don't know if I'm a falcon,
> Or a storm, or a great song.[26]

The shaman, mystic seer, or dream flyer typically finds him- or herself flying through the air *like a bird;* riding *on a bird,* such as an eagle or a giant goose; or, transformed magically, flying through the air *as a bird.* To the ancients, the intentional pursuit of this path was known as sky magic, in contrast with the earth magic involved in lower world journeys. Mircea Eliade recounts the ritual of the Altaic Siberian shaman, who speaks while in a trance of his experience flying on the back of the great goose that is his vehicle: "Under the white sky, over the white cloud, under the blue sky, over the blue cloud, rise up to the sky, bird!"[27]

North American Indian stories tell of vision seekers, including Castaneda's Don Juan, who become a crow or a raven and fly thus, unrecognized, in conscious journeys of "seeing" or "remote viewing." Tibet's great yogi Milarepa writes in his autobiography of learning to transform himself into any shape desired and flying through the air: "By night, in my dreams, I could traverse the universe unimpededly . . . and I saw everything clearly as I went."[28]

Other modes of ascent are also found: one may find oneself riding a winged horse (this metaphor is often used to describe the powerful LSD-driven "trips") or flying a plane or a spaceship. I have heard of dreams and visionary states in which the person feels as if rising up through a chimney or curling upward on the smoke of a fire. The latter sensation is reminiscent of the idea, taught by Native American elders, that when one smokes the sacred pipe, one's prayers rise up with the smoke to the Great Spirit.

Other variants of the ascensional journey are: climbing a tree (with seven or nine branches), a pillar, a ladder (e.g., Jacob's ladder), or a vertical rope (as in the famous Indian "rope trick"). In the *Upanishads,* the spider's upward movement on a self-generated thread is a metaphor for the heightening of awareness practiced in *mantra* meditation: "As a spider mounting up by means of his thread . . . thus assuredly does the meditator, mounting upward by means of OM, obtain liberation."[29]

The upper world traveler may ride great clouds, where ancient people envisioned the gods and goddesses living and moving. The psalmist wrote, "O Lord, my God . . . who maketh the clouds his chariot, who walketh upon the wings of the wind."[30] The North American Indian theme of the "Windwalker" and our modern epic film hero Luke Skywalker are other versions of this mythic image. The sixteenth-century Chinese Taoist Master T'u Lung wrote:

> One who travels does so in order to open his ears and eyes and relax his spirit.
> He explores the eight states and travels over the eight countries, in the hope
> that he may gather the divine essence and may eat of the plant of eternal life,
> and find the marrow of the rocks. Riding upon wind and sailing upon aether,
> he goes cooly wherever the wind may carry him."[31]

For someone involved in a transformative journey, experiences of "flying" or upper world journeys are particularly valuable. They tend to be experiences in which we are granted a preview or vision of our life or of some aspect of the world. They are usually accompanied by insights, intuitions, and new images; and they often instigate a mood of playful and euphoric creativity.

On the other hand, the immoderate or egotistical pursuit of high states and visionary phenomena can be distracting *hubris,* so the ancient teachings tell us. Some traditions, including Zen and Protestantism, are likely to dismiss visions as "illusions," or the "devil's work." The possibility of a flying journey that leads to a fatal mistake is shown in the myth of Icarus, who "flew too high" and burned his wings at the sun's fire.[32] We enact the tragedy of Icarus when we get "carried away" by our own narcissistic moods of self-aggrandizement, by pride and vanity, or by "flights of fancy," or ego-inflation, as the Jungians call it.

Collective expressions of misguided sky magic also exist. The existence and prevalence of UFO cults whose members believe in a superior race of advanced beings who will descend from the skies to save us, can be seen as a collective example of this kind of grandiosity. The technology of nuclear missiles is perhaps another manifestation of the Icarus complex on a mass scale: phallic weapons rape the sky, impelled by reckless ambition and suicidal arrogance.

Journeys into Nonordinary Reality

We turn now to the third of the three great "cosmic zones," as Eliade calls them: the regions of consciousness in which transformational travelers may find themselves. Shamanism, alchemy, and yoga, which have mapped out these various inner domains, situate one between the upper and lower worlds: it is the intermediate world, or Middle Earth, in which things and presences have a human scale. Ordinary men and women live in this world, and on our journeys in this world, in dreams and visions, we see and meet one another, converse and relate as humans do. As with upper and lower world journeys, middle world journeys can, and often have, magical qualities that make them of particular interest to those on a transformational quest. In these journeys, which take place in dreams, meditations, or reveries, we may travel to faraway, exotic, and unfamiliar places, or we may travel in our local environment, among family, neighbors, and friends.

It is my belief that the transformative potential of such experiences is a function of our intention: if we explore these states with respect and openhearted attentiveness, we begin to discover all sorts of valuable pieces of knowledge. If we wander in aimless curiosity or unconsciously flit about, without awareness or attention, we experience "spacey" trips. "Things are not always what they seem" is a useful motto or *mantra* for these realms or states. An aura of unreality may surround ordinary objects: there are enchanted forests, interior labyrinths, castles of marvels, hallucinatory deserts. When we have an intention for self-transformation, these sequences of nonordinary images we perceive are symbolic representations of the lessons we are to learn. They show us the interior landscapes of the mind.

As mentioned before, there can be a correlation or synchronicity between inner journeys, which are altered states of consciousness, and outer journeys. The external journey may serve as a catalyst to definite inner changes; these, in turn, are symbolized in dreams and visions by journeys. For example, in certain moods or hypersensitive states, an ordinary landscape may suddenly assume an aspect of mystery or numinosity or have unexpected personal significance. Ramakrishna once said, speaking of such states, "meaning seems to leap out of matter, like a tiger out of a dark cave." The hidden glow in the landscape paintings of the old Dutch masters reflects such visions, as does the swirling exuberance of Van Gogh's fields, trees, and skies. When we see a landscape in this light, whether internally or externally, we are moved to walk with wonder and respect, "in a sacred manner," as the American Indian elders teach.

Holy mountain. The theme of the holy mountain is both a middle world journey experience as well as a variant of ascension imagery. Some of the sacred mountains have been actual geographical mountains that are believed to have supernatural power: Mount Fuji, Chomolingma (Everest), Mount Ararat, Mount Olympus, Mount Sinai—all play a central symbolic role in religious myth. In other cases, such as the Hindu Mount Meru, we are dealing with a symbol of the world axis, the central pivot or pillar of the world. This image is analogous to the symbolism of the World Tree, discussed in chapter 10. On the microcosmic, or individual, level, the corresponding central axis, which has the *chakras* (energy centers) on it, is referred to as the "staff of Meru" *(merudanda).* Climbing or approaching the holy mountain is a pilgrimage to the center of the world— psychologically speaking, to the center of our existence.

The French philosopher René Daumal, a disciple of G. I. Gurdjieff, traced the mountain climbing metaphor with literary elegance in his *Mount Analogue,* subtitled *A Novel of Symbolically Authentic Non-Euclidean Adventures in Mountain Climbing.* This so-called novel is actually a thought-provoking guidebook for those who would find and climb the interior mountain.

> You cannot stay on the summit forever; you have to come down again. . . . So why bother in the first place? Just this: what is above knows what is below, but what is below does not know what is above. In climbing, always take note of difficulties along the way; for as you go up, you can observe them. Coming down, you will no longer see them, but you will know they are there if you have observed them well. One climbs, one sees. One descends, one sees no longer but one has seen. There is an art of conducting oneself in the lower regions by the memory of what one saw higher up. When one can no longer see, one can at least still know.[33]

Here Daumal is reminding us that the ascent to higher levels of consciousness brings visions. The knowledge of these visions can have a salutary and inspiring effect on our frame of mind and behavior when we return to ordinary reality.

Seven valleys. Traversing the seven valleys is another ancient allegory for the mystical path, described in luminous imagery by the Persian Sufi Poet Attar in his The *Conference of the Birds.* He speaks of a gathering of birds, who make many and various excuses for why they cannot go on this long journey to what is called "the hidden palace of the King." This is a metaphor for a common occurrence: the path of mystical transformation is pointed out by a guide or teacher, but because people don't feel comfortable with following the guide's vision, all kinds of resistance to making the journey arise. In Attar's tale, a small number of birds finally do venture forth together through seven distinct "valleys": first is the Valley of the Search, a long, desolate, purgatorylike stage; second is the Valley of Love, a kind of earthly paradise of beauty and joy; third is the Valley of Knowledge; fourth, the Valley of Detachment; fifth the Valley of Unity; sixth the Valley of Amazement; and seventh, the Valley of Annihilation, where all vestiges of ego are dissolved.

This metaphor of traveling through seven valleys, with all its beautiful, poetic elaborations, is a classic description of the mystical journey, consisting of definite stages, that has ego-transcendence and union as its final goal. In a profound allegory, Attar tells how the birds who arrive at the hidden palace of the King, now reduced to only a handful of those who departed, see themselves and one another as God: "in the reflection of each other's faces these thirty birds of the outer world contemplated the face of the Simurgh [God] of the inner world." The goal of the journey, as always, is our own Self (the King), our center, the core of Being.[34]

Wilderness. Perhaps the most poignant expression of the metaphor of the journey is the theme of wandering in the wilderness. Old Testament literature is filled with the imagery of man lost in wild, unknown, inhospitable regions. Job laments, "He taketh away the heart of the chief of the people of the earth, and causes them to wander in a wilderness where there is no way."[35] So often we feel that we have lost our way, we are disheartened and roam aimlessly. Like the children of Israel under Moses, who wandered in the desert for forty years strenuously seeking the Promised Land, we are searching for a way out. Individually and as a family or group, we seek to escape from the prison of worldly existence (symbolized by "Egypt" in the Bible). During this aimless wandering in the wilderness, we endure many hardships and sufferings; but we are also saved and rewarded with God's gift of "manna from heaven"—the unexpected blessing that nourishes both body and soul. The voice of God, speaking through Hosea, another of the great Hebrew prophets, proclaims: "That is why I am going to lure and lead her [Israel] out into the wilderness and speak to her heart. I am going to give her back her vineyards, and make the valley of Achor [misfortune] a gateway of hope."[36]

The mythic hero Gilgamesh, on his journey to discover the meaning of life and death, had to cross vast steppes and pass through a mountain fastness guarded by monstrous scorpion men. The knights of the Arthurian legend, on their quest for the Holy Grail that would give salvation, wandered dejectedly through the "gray lands," finding in the desolate wilderness of dim light and sparse vegetation no clues and no hope for their search. The mystic visionary Hildegard von Bingen wrote of the soul's quest to escape from the dungeon of sinful life, finding "narrow paths" through the stoney wilderness, hiding in small cracks in the rock, climbing through thorns and thistles, and avoiding poisonous snakes and scorpions.[37]

All these are images of our psychological condition, our state of consciousness when we are in the midst of a transformative process but have lost our way. We are trying to leave behind our past, highly unsatisfactory way of life, with its sufferings and insults, "the slings and arrows of outrageous fortune," but we have not yet found the promised land; we have not fully healed the ancient wounds, and we have lost hope and heart. T. S. Eliot captured the haunting feeling of this experience in his poem *The Wasteland:*

> What are the roots that clutch, what branches grow
> Out of this stony rubbish? Son of Man,
> You cannot say, or guess, for you know only
> A heap of broken images, where the sun beats,
> And the dead tree gives no shelter, the cricket no relief,
> And the dry stones no sound of water.

Perhaps one reason why this theme is so stirring to the modern psyche is that the wasteland symbolizes the modern Western condition of alienation, discouragement, and existential despair. We all at times feel ourselves to be wandering dejectedly through a life journey devoid of meaning and beauty. Since water is the great symbol of emotional and spiritual nourishment, the absence of water, as in a desert wasteland, is suggestive of emotional deprivation and lack of spiritual inspiration or enthusiasm.

This kind of experience of despair and hopelessness, symbolized by being lost in a barren wilderness, is represented somewhat differently in the Eastern traditions. In Buddhism, for example, we have the analogy of life as a senseless round, a repetitive wheel of existence *(samsara)*. This endlessly turning wheel, fueled by greed, anger, and desire, symbolizes the ordinary human condition, lost in utter unconsciousness *(avidya)*. From this we are to escape by practicing the ways of meditation, by turning inward to the source of light within.

Mysterious castle. The theme of finding and exploring a mysterious castle is also widespread: in folktales ("the castle of no return"), in myth ("Castle Merveil"), and in mysticism ("The Interior Castle"). The latter work, by Teresa of Avila, is considered a classic of Western mysticism. In it, the human soul is likened to a crystalline castle surrounded by seven concentric "mansions." The innermost circle is that of the King of Glory, the indwelling Spirit who is the Sun, the Light that is at the center of our Being.

Each mansion has many rooms, many doors, passages, gardens, mazes, fountains: these are the many aspects and facets of our nature, which, according to Teresa, the soul must be permitted to explore. The outermost mansions, which symbolize the surface personality, the masks and roles that we act out, are uncared for and dark—in other words, we neglect the development of our persona, so that there is quite a discrepancy between it and the beauty and light of the indwelling Spirit. The governors of these outer mansions, whom Teresa describes as blind, unruly, and inefficient, are our own petty impulses of egotism, pride, and vanity.

Maze or labyrinth. The maze, or labyrinth, which many a hero (Theseus, for example) has to walk through, is an apt symbol for the tortuous windings of our psychological defense mechanisms: the negations, displacements, concealments, projections, regressions, compensations, that have to be unraveled and reversed if we are to come to the center of our being (the center of the maze) or if we are to escape from the crippling limitation that the defensive maze creates in our personality.

Climbing the holy mountain, traversing the seven valleys, wandering in the wilderness, finding and exploring the interior castle, tracing the psychological maze or labyrinth—each of these metaphors points to a change in point of view, a reorientation of awareness, a new sense of direction, as the crucial shift that takes place in the process of transformation. Through this change of consciousness we learn to escape from the cycles of meaninglessness and the wastelands of hopelessness. When this shift occurs, we recognize that we are not the victims of uncontrollable external circumstances: the journey is within us; therefore, we choose the destination and are in charge of our own destiny.

A famous Zen saying points to this realization: "I am on the bridge, and O marvel! It is not the river which flows, it is the bridge which moves over the torrent." Up to this point I have experienced life events flowing past me or under me, like a river; I have been passive and detached. Now, with this realization on the bridge—which is a crucial phase of transition—no longer do life's events flow past me. Instead, I move through life, passing through experiences. Active, involved, and empowered, I am crossing over thresholds and limits.

Returning home. The final phase of the mythic or mystical journey is returning home. Even if the hero/ego is successful in the difficult quest for knowledge or healing, this homeward journey can be equally fraught with difficulties. On his return path, Gilgamesh had the herb of immortality, which he had found at the bottom of the ocean, stolen from him by a serpent as he lay sleeping near a spring. The woman quoted earlier who took a trip to Nepal wrote:

> I feared my return as much as I had feared my departure; both were entries into the unknown and unexpected. What had been familiar was now unfamiliar; nothing had changed but me. . . . I returned with "nothing" to show for my experience. By understanding my journey I gained confidence to make the necessary—and difficult—separations from the old life structures which were no longer meaningful. . . . I returned from the journey to begin another.

In the famous Ten Ox-Herding Pictures by Kaku-an, a twelfth-century series of Zen illustrations and text, the sixth picture is called "Riding the Ox Home." This comes after (1) the initial search, (2) the finding of tracks, (3) the glimpse of the animal, (4) the capture of the animal, and (5) the taming of the animal. Now the man rides the animal home. The wild animal is a symbolic representation of our own ego, our emotions, desires, and impulses. When we have come to terms with them, "tamed" them so that they come under our direction, rather than vice versa, then we are ready to return home. "Riding on the animal" symbolizes living in an integrated way with our animal strength and vitality. In the seventh picture, the man is sitting outside his home, and the ox is gone. There is now no more separation between the human being and the instincts; at this stage we are at peace with ourselves and with others.

At the end of our journey of transformation, we return to where we started. We bring back to family or tribe the gift that we found or were given on our journey. This gift may be the power to heal; it may be the ability to see, to prophesy; or it may simply be a new feeling of contentment and balance. With this new attitude, this new sense of our own power, we are indeed transformed.

8

Returning to the Source

I once was lost, but now am found, was blind and now I see.

—Traditional hymn

In the previous chapter we discussed the journey as a metaphor for the experience of transformation. You leave your home in the ordinary, familiar world, travel to a faraway place where you are changed, and then you return to the world of your family and friends, to live in a new way. The metaphor we are now considering conveys the quality of transformation as a homeward journey rather than an outbound journey. It sees human life is a kind of exile, an alien environment in which you feel like a stranger and from which you return to your true home, to the place where you came from, your source and origin. In accounts of profound transformative experiences, whether mystic, psychedelic, cosmic, or ecstatic, it is not uncommon to read or hear such expressions as: "a feeling of having been here before," "this is like coming home," "I've been away from here so long," "this is my true home." People often feel their usual state of consciousness to be one of alienation, especially in comparison with this new, changed state of "being found."

An example of this kind of experience is described in the following account by one of the contributors to the *Common Experience* anthology:

> When I was sixteen I had an experience I can only describe as mystical.
> . . . The feeling was that I suddenly, that very moment, became aware of the answer to the mystery of life, and the knowledge of it made me want to shout with joy. As if I had been dead before that moment, and suddenly I was alive.
> . . . Always this same feeling leaving me weeping with great joy and feelings of deep reverence, and feelings of worship and love, I think best described as a sort of homesickness, a nostalgia for some-other-where, almost as if I had known an existence of such great beauty and indescribable happiness, and am yearning and homesick for it again.[1]

This contemporary account is indistinguishable from similar experiences described in many mystical writings. The Chinese Taoist and Japanese Zen masters frequently use the imagery of returning to the origin, to our true home, to the primordial beginning, in describing the experience of enlightenment.

Another example is provided by the following dialogue, which occurred in the deep phase of a psychotherapy session amplified by the empathogenic substance MDMA.

Client: "This feels like before."

Therapist: "You mean in previous psychedelic experiences?"

Client: "No, earlier than that."

Therapist: "Like in childhood?"

Client: "No, before that."

Therapist: "You mean like in the womb?"

Client: "No, before . . .—this is where it all starts."[2]

This woman later described having felt somehow connected back to her source, the center from which her ordinary personality and behavior are created and expressed. As a matter of fact, this type of experience is somewhat characteristic of this particular substance, which has acquired the code name "Adam." The name seems apt for the sense of primordial beingness, ancestral wisdom, and groundedness often reported with this substance. The experience is reminiscent, too, of the Zen koan: "what was your original face before you were born?"

When this kind of experience occurs during a prolonged journeylike transformative phase, the traveler may feel as if on a homeward journey, returning to his or her roots. Life itself is seen as the great journey, initiated at birth; and the spiritual path is one of turning inward, yearning to go back to whence we came. In the Gnostic Gospel of Thomas, Jesus says, "Blessed are the single ones [*monachos*] . . . for you shall find the Kingdom; because you came from it, and you shall go there again."

The associated image is that of ordinary life as a kind of exile, where we are separated from our true spiritual home. The great Flemish mystic Jan van Ruysbroek wrote: "Knowledge of ourselves teaches us from whence we came, where we are and where we are going. We come from God and we are in exile." The transformation to a new way of being is compared to the process of one who leaves exile or leaves imprisonment and slavery (a closely related metaphor) and returns to the place of origin. The New Testament parable of the prodigal son who returns to his royal parents also fits this pattern.

We are all prodigal sons and daughters, insofar as we forget our origin and lose our sense of purpose and our vision in life. When we finally awaken and begin the process of self-transformation, much of the journey seems like a retracing of our steps, an undoing of knots tied before, or an escape from a prison we had inadvertently created, to rediscover a long-lost treasure. T. S. Eliot's famous lines echo this theme:

> We shall not cease from exploration
> And the end of all our exploring
> Will be to arrive where we started
> And know the place for the first time.
> Through the unknown, remembered gate
> When the last of earth left to discover
> Is that which was the beginning.[3]

This experience is consonant with the idea of "recollection," the regathering of scattered pieces that have been lost; with *anamnesis,* the "overcoming of forgetfulness"; and with self-remembering, the remembering of our primordial self.

In a remarkable essay on "The Awakening of a New Consciousness in Zen," the Buddhist philosopher D. T. Suzuki unites several of these metaphors:

> The awakening is really the rediscovery or the excavation of a long-lost treasure. . . . [The awakening] is no other than consciousness becoming acquainted with itself. . . . Consciousness itself turns inwardly into itself. This is the homecoming. This is the seeing of one's own "primal face" which one has seen even before birth. This is God pronouncing his name to Moses. This is the birth of Christ in each of our souls. This is Christ rising from death. The Unconscious, which has been lying quietly . . . now raises its head and announces its presence through consciousness.[4]

The return journey of transformation is here compared to an awakening and to a death-rebirth; it is described also as a raising of consciousness. In both Western and Asian traditions, the theme of return is an essential component of spiritual teachings.

This image is so pervasive and so consistent across many traditions that we may safely conclude that we are dealing with an archetype. We find the image associated with a model for the development of consciousness, with two phases: an outward movement, a descending arc (often called involutionary), and an inward movement, an ascending arc (called evolutionary). In the latter we return to a paradisiacal state that we had left. The evolutionary path of the mystics involves a going back to Spirit, to the ground of Being, to Brahman, to the Tao, to Ain Soph, to the Godhead.

Often in such experiences of "return," the person may feel that he or she has contacted some special inner companions, who seem to be one's "true family," a kind of spiritual family. Sometimes these may be perceived as deceased relatives or ancestors. This sensed inner family, these beings with whom we have a special spiritual rapport and communion, may be quite different from those we call family in the "real," everyday world. These inner world companions may not even have a physical incarnation, and we know them only in these special states of mystic vision, dreams, or meditations; we might call them "guide," or "ally," or "muse," or "voice."

Shamanic cultures and those traditions that cultivate a closeness to nature, such as Taoism, believe that you can contact deceased parents and grandparents, so that they can help you, in a way similar to the way a "power animal" can. The feeling of the presence of inner family and friends probably also underlies the widespread custom (found in many indigenous cultures) of addressing spirit beings as "father," "mother," or "grandparents." In such practices, sometimes referred to as "ancestor worship," members of the tribe communicate with spirit beings they regard as their true or original parents and grandparents. The mythic hero Gilgamesh, when he goes forth to find the answer to the questions of life and death, searches for Utnapishtim, the ancient one called "Faraway" who survived the great flood, and addresses him as "father." Likewise, Black Elk addresses the "Powers of the World" that he sees in his vision as the "six grandfathers." American Indians pray to Mother Earth, Grandfather Fire, Father Sky, Grandmother Ocean, and so forth. We come home not only to a place but to our great and original family.

Man as Stranger, Life as Exile

In a typical transformation process, after one has the awakening vision, the everyday world of reality, family, and culture may be experienced as strange and *unfamiliar* ("not of the family"). Seekers or travelers, having obtained some insight, or even a small glimpse into higher realms of consciousness, having seen the daytime sun outside the Platonic cave—may feel lost because they can no longer relate to the old, illusory shadows within the prison-cave. They become wandering strangers, filled with longing for a faraway home, the memories of which lie in the heart. Generalized, this feeling becomes one of life on earth as exile, banishment, or expulsion from a paradise state, of being lost and abandoned.

Becoming aware of the exiled or alienated condition we are in is, as always, the necessary first step to returning on the homeward journey. Thus, paradoxically, the closer we come to the source from where we originated, the more acutely we sense our estrangement. This paradox is beautifully expressed in the following saying by the great thirteenth-century Chinese Zen Master Ekai, also called Mumon:

> When you understand, you belong to the family;
> When you do not understand, you are a stranger.
> Those who do not understand belong to the family,
> And when they understand they are strangers."[5]

The first two lines refer to the ordinary man who awakens, who questions, and experiences inner realities that make him feel like a stranger in the conventional world. As he begins to understand, to have insight into his destiny, he finds his "inner family," the family of others like him who are alienated seekers. He aligns himself with this family, who are for him what Goethe called *Wahlver-wandschaften,* "chosen relations" (or "elective affinities").

The second pair of lines refer to the seeker's affiliation with this true family. They are the family made up of those who realize they do not understand. They understand only that they are strangers in this world, and because they understand this, they do, in fact, in the eyes of the unawakened, become strangers. This is why in so many cultures there are traditions of the "holy fool," the "wise idiot," the eccentric, quirky person who turns out to be the wisest and most enlightened one of all.

Undeniably, many sensitive individuals come to feel at a certain point in their lives that a mistake has somehow been made: they are in the wrong place, or they are in exile, or lost in the wilderness, or adrift on an ocean of *samsaric* illusions. This theme occurs in many contemporary works of mythological fiction, testifying to modern man's condition of profound existential alienation. We need only think of books such as Albert Camus' *The Stranger,* Colin Wilson's *The Outsider,* or Robert Heinlein's science fiction classic *Stranger in a Strange Land.* Films also express this theme: *The Man Who Fell to Earth* gave a vivid, affecting portrait of an alien, whose story has all the features of the classic exile myths. The popularity of these stories attests to the deep, essential nature of the myth they embody.

The psychoanalyst Otto Rank, who was one of Freud's closest disciples, wrote a classic analysis of the exile motif in *The Myth of the Birth of the Hero.* In this book he pointed out the striking parallels between the fantasies of many neurotic patients, who imagine that their parents are not their real parents, and the pattern found in many myths of a hero (e.g., Moses), who is born of royal parents but raised in exile by foster parents under conditions of early poverty and anonymity. This suggests that the neurotics, who are among society's most sensitive individuals, are experiencing a highly personalized and distressing version of this stranger/exile motif. The challenge of psychotherapeutic transformation is to change the sense of loss, abandonment, and exile into the yearning for the homeward journey.

An even more extreme form of alienation is found in madness. As we have seen, transformation in a regressive mode leads to psychosis. The sense of alienation is so characteristic of insanity that in the nineteenth century, physicians who specialized in this field were known as "alienists." The schizophrenic has "lost touch" with "reality": to him the world of consensually validated symbols in which we normally move with grace and familiarity seems totally strange and largely malevolent. In psychedelic research, the ecstatic LSD trip is typically described by imagery of homecoming and returning to the source. The psychotic psychedelic trip, on the other hand, typically involves visions of being lost among dehumanized, lifeless, alien automata, and unfamiliar phantoms.

Because the feeling of alienation is so widespread in our time in Western culture, when a powerful, affecting story about it is told in fiction or film, it often touches deep chords and may even on occasion have healing effects. The mother of a twenty-year-old autistic "child" wrote to the producers of the enormously popular film *E.T.* to say that her son, who normally talked with nobody and never cried or laughed, "in the darkness [of the theater] came out of himself. He screamed, he clapped, he laughed, and then he cried—real tears . . . and talked, nonstop." She said that her son had always liked movies about spacecraft and aliens, and that seeing *E.T.* had changed his life. "It has made him relate to something beyond himself. It's as though Tommy has also been an alien life form and trying to find his way home, just like *E.T.*"[6]

The feeling of alienation and estrangement in human life is by no means limited to neurotics and psychotics, nor is it found only in modern consciousness. In fact it is one of the oldest themes in mythology and literature. Walter Kaufmann, in a brilliant essay on "The Inevitability of Alienation," traces the history of this concept in the writings of philosophers such as Plato, Descartes, Leibnitz, Pascal, Hume, Kant, Hegel, Nietzsche, Russell, Sartre, and others. He states, "philosophy is born of estrangement. It need not be alienation from other human beings, it could be estrangement from oneself or the universe."[7] Kaufmann adds the following observation, interesting in its connection to the theme of the exiled or lost child:

> Descartes lost his mother when he was one year old; Spinoza was six when his mother died, and Leibnitz was six when his father died. Pascal's mother died when he was three; Hume's father, when he was three. Rousseau's mother died soon after his birth, and when he was ten his father left him. Both Kant and Hegel lost their mothers at thirteen. Nietzsche was four when he lost his father. Russell's mother died when he was two; his father two years later. And Sartre lost his father at two.

Thus there is, with remarkable consistency, a personal history of parental loss in early childhood, which could be the psychological basis for the philosophical emphasis on alienation in the works of these influential thinkers.

Similarly, Kaufmann argues that the alienation idea is central in most of the key myths and stories of our culture. Oedipus, for example, "is a stranger to himself; . . . when he discovers who he is, he is filled with such loathing that he destroys his own eyes." Shakespeare's Prince Hamlet is dominated by a pervasive sense of alienation, as is Goethe's Faust. Modern writers, such as Joyce, Beckett, Sartre, Hesse, Rilke, and many others, as well as modern painters, musicians, and other artists, often strike us as haunted by a sense of being disturbingly different, lost, confused, and estranged.

When we delve into religious literature, we find that this theme is widespread here as well. The old Hebrew prophets, Kaufmann points out, seers like Moses, Elijah, Amos, Hosea, and Jeremiah, "not only remind their people that they were strangers in the land of Egypt; they themselves are strangers among their own people."[8] The prophets were sensitives, visionaries; in the words of Mumon, "When they understand they are strangers."

Religious teachers have consistently emphasized this theme, pointing to humanity's alienation from God. Saint Paul wrote, "They are darkened in their understanding, alienated from the life of God because of the ignorance that is in them, due to their hardness of heart."[9] This is the alienation of everyday life, based on forgetfulness and unconsciousness of our true nature.

Then there is the alienation of the mystics, which is of an anguished intensity close to that of the psychotic, especially in the phase of transformation referred to as "the "dark night of the soul [psyche]." The English mystic Richard Rolle wrote, "Be it known to all manner of people in this wretched dwelling-place of exile abiding. . . ."[10] In one of her visions, Hildegard von Bingen spoke of the soul as an exile far from home; in its home, the soul was companion to angels, and knew and sensed God's Presence. Then, however, when the eyes of awareness became fixed on external things, the soul laments: "I am imprisoned, deprived of my sight and the joy of knowing. My garment is torn. I am driven out of my inheritance. I have been abducted into alien territory, where there is no beauty and no honor. I have been delivered into degradation and slavery." The main difference between the mystic and the psychotic, in terms of this metaphor, is that the former has a sense of where he needs to turn—inward, to God—whereas the psychotic is totally lost.

It is among the Gnostics that we find the strongest expressions of the theme of alienation and estrangement. There is even a key text, among the Nag Hammadi scrolls, entitled *Allogenes,* which refers to the speaker, or author, of this tract and means "Stranger." According to the editors, this appellation, which literally means "of another race," was a common one in this period for semidivine revealers of higher wisdom.[11] To the Gnostics, the whole process by which this world was created was fundamentally flawed: humanity was a mistake perpetrated by demiurge creators who falsely imitated the image of God and misplaced us into this gloomy world, which they called a "circle of dark fire." To quote Jacques Lacarrière, "we are exploited on a cosmic scale, we are the proletariat of the demiurge-executioner, slaves exiled into a world that is viscerally subjected to violence; we are the dregs and sediment of a lost heaven, strangers on our own planet."[12]

Gnostics taught that all men suffer this fate, and *gnosis* is the aware recognition of this state of affairs; "and when they understand they are strangers." The sense of alienation, so widespread in Western culture and so particularly acute in twentieth-century consciousness, can be seen as the inevitable and perhaps necessary starting point for personal transformation. Estrangement leads to questioning, searching, and wondering. The quest or search may lead, if we are graced, to an awakening; the journey homeward may lead to the source of our beingness.

The Outgoing Path and the Return Path

The spiritual and mystical traditions of both East and West have consistently distinguished between two aspects of development or two phases of the process of transformation. Using the metaphor of a path or journey, these are expressed most simply as the outgoing journey and the return journey. Ordinary life is an outward journey—into matter, physical bodies, and worldly existence; we often get lost, imprisoned, or exiled while on this journey. The return journey is the quest for our origins, the quest to remember our purpose and to find again the light within, from which we have become separated. In a text by the first-century Neoplatonist philosopher Philo Judaeus, we read of this twofold journey:

> All whom Moses calls wise are represented as sojourners. . . . Their way is to visit earthly nature as men who travel abroad to see and learn. So when they have stayed a while in their bodies, and beheld through them all that sense and mortality has to show, they make their way back to the place from which they set out at first. To them the heavenly region, where their citizenship lies, is their native land; the earthly region in which they become sojourners is a foreign country.[13]

The metaphor of the return journey for the process of transformation implies, therefore, that an outward journey, into the alien world of conventional reality, has preceded this inward turning.

Jung drew a similar distinction between two kinds of development, relating them to two major phases of the life cycle. In the first phase, which normally lasts from childhood to middle adulthood, we are becoming individuals, in the sense of learning the ways of the world and involving ourselves in the demands of family, work, and society. In the second phase, which begins, according to Jung, with the midlife crisis, when we may find ourselves, like Dante, "lost in the middle of a dark forest," we begin the process of individuation, which involves turning inward. Now we have to integrate the shadow, balance the anima and animus, and reconnect with the Self, which has been all along and remains at the center of our being. Of course, there are always exceptions to the general pattern, and there are certainly many individuals who begin the return journey of inner transformation in earlier adulthood, even in youth or childhood.

In the ancient philosophies of India, these two paths of human development are seen against the backdrop of two parallel cosmic processes, interweaving cycles of Nature, inherent in every form of life. They are sequential, occurring one after the other, and simultaneously coexisting. One is called *pravritti,* literally "out-turning"—the unfolding externalizing process of emanation and creation. Also called the "out-breath of Brahman," *pravritti* is the outflowing of impulse and desire into matter and form. The other, complementary process is called *nivritti,* literally "back-turning"—the enfolding, internalizing process of transcendence and transformation. Also called the "in-breath of Brahman," *nivritti* is an inward orientation, a releasing of attachments to matter and form, a returning from the manifest world back to unmanifest, invisible essence.[14]

The reader may, with some justice, protest that these philosophical distinctions are abstract and seemingly of little relevance to us today. The pervasive metaphor of the two types of path, found in many myths and allegories both contemporary and historical, is often associated in our experience, with an underlying cosmic duality, such as posited by ancient Indian philosophy. It is, in fact, a consistent and recognizable feature of most people's experience of transformation that they become aware of the wide cosmic or universal dimensions of human life. It is not uncommon for individuals who have had no prior interest in metaphysical questions to begin examining these issues of ultimate reality, regardless of whether they prefer a theistic framework or a cosmic, non-theistic one.

Theories concerning a twofold process of consciousness transformation are also found in other ancient spiritual traditions, in occult systems such as theosophy, and in the writings of mystics and those of a very few modern scientists. Such theories usually suggest that the second phase, the return path, in some way leads back to the beginning of the first phase, although in a new way. People in this phase of the process may feel that they have returned to a place they knew before, but that they now know it with a new and different quality of awareness. Much has been learned, they may feel, on the outward journey, and these insights and lessons learned about the external world now form the background for a new transition.

In the writings of Sengtsan, also known as the Third Zen Patriarch, we read, "To return to the source is to find the meaning, but to pursue appearances is to miss the source."[15]

In the texts of the mystics, visionaries, and transformationalists, the home or origin or source we return to is often described as "behind," "within," "underneath," or "above" the usual world of phenomenal appearances. "Behind" suggests that our origin home is veiled from our knowing by perceptual screens and filters. "Within" points to the external orientation as having brought us into the state of exile. "Underneath" suggests that the source of our existence is a kind of ground, the ground of Being, of which the existentialists speak. "Above" suggests that we have come into the world of limits and forms from higher realms, from God, the Infinite, the Absolute.

Some teachings speak of the first, outgoing phase as evolutionary and the second, return phase as involutionary.[16] To *evolve* is literally to "roll out" or "unroll"; so in this phase, Spirit, or consciousness, is turning outward, unfolding, developing, into matter and form. To *involve* is literally to "roll up" or "envelop." Therefore, in this second phase there is an inward turning, enfolding, enveloping, of external matter and form back into formless infinity.

A modern scientific theory that fits this general paradigm is David Bohm's theory of the implicate and explicate orders. According to Bohm, the explicate order is the world of our time-space oriented sense observations; and an implicate order, exists that is more "subtle" and cannot be reached through reasoning or thought, only through direct insight. The implicate order is concerned with the whole; it is a *holomovement*—the unmanifest ground of the manifest world. "What is manifest is, as it were, abstracted and floating in the holomovement. The holomovement's basic movement is folding and unfolding."[17]

Other teachings seem to say the opposite: in theosophical and other esoteric formulations, the movement from Spirit into matter is described as involutionary, a "descent" into form, into embodiment, a building and inhabiting of form, the clothing or wrapping of the Spirit into bodies, the Logos into flesh. In this model, the evolutionary movement is an unfolding of the spiritual essence within material and biological forms; it is a series of successive self-transcendences that lead us, over countless aeons, to the divine home from which we came.

Among modern scientists, Arthur Young's theory of the "reflexive universe" gives a rational, considered, and elegant version of this theme. He posits a downward, involutionary arc from photons, to particles, to atoms, to molecules; followed by an upward, evolutionary arc, through plants, animals, and humans. "To throw off compulsive embodiment, to disconnect from specific function, to become universal, a total being, is the role of man."[18]

The apparent contradiction between these two interpretations of the evolution-involution process, can, I suggest, be resolved if one regards them as each describing different aspects of a process that actually has two pairs of movements, involutionary and evolutionary, occurring simultaneously. There is the evolution of spirit into matter: the *pravritti,* out-turning, unfolding, explicating. There is also the involution of spirit into matter: form building, creating, embodying. There is an evolution of matter toward spirit: enlightening, spiritualizing, transcending. And there is an involution of matter toward spirit: the *nivritti,* turning back inward, internalizing, implicating. Sri Aurobindo has expressed this paradox as follows: "In a sense the whole of creation may be said to be a movement between two involutions—Spirit in which all is involved and out of which all evolves downward to the other pole of matter, Matter in which also all is involved and out of which all evolves upward to the other pole of Spirit."[19]

The homeward, or return, path is an evolutionary transformation, because through an unfolding of latent capacities the individual becomes personally aware of his or her unity with the original source-Self. The return path is an involutionary transformation also, in the sense that it is a retracing, a refolding of personality back into the vast, all-embracing, all-containing context or ground of pure Being. The homeward journey always returns us to Spirit: this is an *un*folding, *de*veloping process—and an *en*folding, *en*veloping process, depending on our point of view.

The Gnostic text *Allogenes* makes it clear that it is describing the vision of one who has turned within: "I was very disturbed and I turned to myself. Having seen the light that surrounded me and the good that was within me, I became divine." The seeker Allogenes was instructed: "O Allogenes, behold your blessedness, . . . in silence, wherein you know yourself as you are, and seeking yourself, ascend to the Vitality that you will see moving."[20] This passage is typical of the kind of experience modern seekers often report: a growing sense of awe at the sacredness and numinosity of the inner realms of Spirit that they are entering, coupled with a recognition that this *is* the true Self.

To recognize is to *re-cognize,* to "know again," to discover again that which was in the beginning. On the return path we get the "shock of (self-)recognition." The homeward journey is one of self-revelation, in which we gain insight into our true nature and awareness of the alienation of our previous condition. We may see, if we are so graced, "the primordial face we had before we were born."

The Homeward Journey

The *Zen Ox-Herding Allegory* may be regarded as a metaphor for the process of unifying human and animal consciousness. The ox symbolizes the wild animality of the body-ego. As has already been discussed, the steps of the process were: (1) searching for the ox, (2) seeing its tracks, (3) perceiving the ox, (4) capturing the ox, (5) taming the ox, and (6) riding the ox home. The sixth step represents the stage where the wild animal within has been transformed into a trusted ally. In the next phase, the seventh picture, the man sits contemplating in the moonlight outside his hut, and the animal is gone. The ox, the commentators tell us, is "symbolic only," or it has been "transcended." If the ox represents the animal body-ego, then here is shown the first step on the inward/homeward journey: after the passionate nature has been tamed, it is transcended.[21]

The *eighth* picture shows only a perfect circle. "Both ox and man transcended," the text says. "Everything merges into no-thing, like a snowflake in a raging fire." Here the seeker-mediator passes into the realm of formlessness, where there is no perception of "things," only pure consciousness without an object. We note that there is transcendence here, although there is not yet complete transformation of the individual, which will come only with the last step.

The *ninth* picture shows a stream (there is no man) and is entitled "Returning to the Source." Here one perceives the manifest origin of external things. The commentary says, "better to have been born blind and deaf"—meaning that if the "sensory gates" had been closed off from the beginning, we would not become so separated from the source. We also read, "Dwelling in one's true abode, unconcerned with that without. . . ." In other words, at this stage we are no longer estranged; we have found the true home at the still center of being.

The *tenth,* and final, picture shows a man walking; it is subtitled either "In the World" or "Entering the City with Bliss-Bestowing Hands." This portrays the situation of one whose personality is completely transformed and who gives freely of his energy now for the healing and enlightenment of others. This represents the ideal of the Buddhist-Taoist sage, who, no longer attached to the results of his actions, is freed from the limitations imposed by ego concerns. It is also akin to the ideal of the adept of *gnosis,* who was said to be "in the world, but not of the world."

The *myth of Odysseus* is the story of the hero on the homeward journey toward wholeness. Odysseus is the archetype of the lover-warrior, seeking to return to the unitive state of consciousness, just as Gilgamesh is the prime exemplar of the wanderer on the quest for knowledge. The psychologist William Bridges has written perceptively on the meaning of the Odyssey for the midlife transitions of the modern individual. Odysseus is separated from his wife, Penelope, who symbolizes the anima, the inner counterpart with whom he wants to unite. Thus, this is a journey toward androgyny, the inner union of male and female, as well as the return journey to the origins. Because of the wrath of the sea-god, Poseidon, Odysseus experiences numerous difficulties on the way back. The myth portrays most insightfully the psychological tests and challenges that confront anyone, man or woman, on the way toward wholeness.

The journey of Odysseus begins "far from home"; he is in a "foreign land," waging war. He incurs the wrath of Poseidon for injuring one of the god's offspring. This represents the situation of a person (man or woman), who has become so wrapped up in various external activities and battles, that he/she loses contact with his/her inner being, or soul; the way of return seems blocked off. The obstacles encountered are the direct karmic consequences of their injurious and destructive actions. It is their fate to have to deal not only with dangerous monsters and strong opponents but with the temptations and distractions of erotic pleasure as well; these are portrayed in the myth in the form of a siren, a nymph, a goddess, and a princess. Odysseus represents the person who has turned away from his true inner nature in reacting to the attractive sense stimuli of the external world.

But the longing of Odysseus for union with his feminine half keeps awakening him and reminding him of his homeward journey. In the meantime, his palace at home is overrun by Penelope's suitors, who try to persuade her to forget Odysseus and marry one of them. These suitors symbolize the intrusive, predatory thoughts, images, and impulses that usurp our consciousness when we feel as if something alien had invaded our minds. Alchemical texts referred to this mental condition as having "enemies in the house" and stressed the need for the conjunction of opposites, the union of male and female, as the means to evict the "enemies."[23]

The final test Odysseus must pass in order to regain his kingship (his Selfhood) may be a symbolic allusion to a yogic awareness process. It will be remembered that the climactic contest challenge was to shoot an arrow through twelve ax heads that had been lined up. The foreign suitors could not do this— only Odysseus could. This can be seen as a metaphoric description of the process of aligning the energy centers and piercing them with enlightened awareness, a process that allows the ego to reconnect with Spirit or Self and to eliminate the degrading and destructive influences (symbolized by the suitors) that have kept separate the royal pair, the inner male and female.

The *Gnostic parable* variously known as the Prodigal Son, the Hymn of the Robe of Glory, or the Hymn of the Pearl speaks eloquently of the return journey, which in theistic terms is a journey back to God.[24] The account given in the Bible is a greatly truncated version of a much longer and more interesting narrative. The verse story tells of a royal couple who send their son out into the world. The "royal couple" are the divine inner parents, the Mother-Father Self from whom we "descend"—to go forth into the world. The "son" is the human ego, the personality, that grows up forgetting its origins.

We are told the son "wasted his substance with riotous living." In the longer versions, he is actually on a mission to obtain a pearl from a venomous dragon, and he forgets that mission also. The pearl symbolizes the shining nugget of wisdom and insight that is contained in the instinctual, animal consciousness. The dragon represents this instinctual nature, especially the reptilian sexual and aggressive drives; but also the "wisdom of the serpent." The son was given a robe of many colors (hence the title of one of the versions) to protect and inspire him; but he forgets this as well. Instead, he dissipates himself among the "Egyptians," who symbolize the stimuli of the sensory-material world. He eats of their food —namely, follows the dictates of greed and lust—until he is groveling in the field with the swine, in total oblivion to his purpose.

Then comes the turning point: asleep, drunk, and stupefied (the metaphor for our ordinary condition of consciousness), he receives a letter from his father, sent at the urging of "Princes from the East"; the letter urges him to "rise up and awake out of sleep . . . and remember that thou art a son of kings; thou hast come under the yoke of bondage." He is reminded of the pearl, of the robe, and of his agreement to return to the kingdom that he left. Rousing himself, overcome with guilt and shame, the son-hero takes the pearl from the dragon while it sleeps, then directs his way homeward.

Miraculous things happen on this return path—a sure indication that we are dealing with a sacred story of transformation, a mystic journey: the letter that had awakened the son-hero turns into a light that guides his way; the multicolored robe he'd lost sways before him in a vision, also encouraging him along his journey. "At once, as soon as I saw it, the Glory looked like my own self. I saw it all in all of me, and saw me all in all of it—that we were twain in distinction, and yet again one in one likeness." This is probably a Gnostic reference to the inner "light body," or "garment of light," an illumined, transpersonal form of the

Self. "And I stretched forth and received it and adorned myself with the beauty of the colors thereof and in my royal robe excelling in beauty I arrayed myself wholly."

The homebound voyager moves on, learning and making discoveries at each step of the way. He is ecstatic, as are all those who have knowingly embarked on the journey of returning to source. He is finally received into the palace of his parents, "the brightness of the Father which had sent me." He has fulfilled his promise: he has obtained and brought back the pearl of great price, which is the pearl of the wisdom of nature (the dragon). The Father then fulfills his promise: to receive the prodigal son who has wasted himself but has now returned; to receive him with gladness and rejoicing into the palace, "which was from the beginning." In the Gospel version, the father says, "For this my son was dead, and is alive again; he was lost and is found." The divine inner parents rejoice when the personality finally returns, recognizing its true Self.

In the *Navaho prayer* "I Was Lost and He Found Me,"[25] Hasji-Alte (God) moves up out of the Emergence Pit conversing with the grandchild. This symbolizes the Great Spirit within, walking and talking with the small, personal self. The Great Spirit reminds the small self of the return journey to be undertaken, provides him with the "rainbow cloak" (here also!) of protection, and leads him into the land where all is beautiful. This is clearly a reference to a state of consciousness where one's perceptions have been cleansed and purified to such a point that everything wears the vestments of beauty.

> "I came searching for you—
> You and I will begin our return, my grandchild;
> We two are leaving now, my grandchild,"
> Hasji-Alte says to me. . . .
>
> Encircling me sunwise with a rainbow,
> He turns me, sunwise, toward himself,
> And shows his compassion for me. . . .
>
> "This is your home, my grandchild,"
> He says to me as he sits down beside me.
> "I have returned with you to your home,"
> He says to me as he sits down beside me.
> "Your home is yours again.
> Your fire is your fire again.
> Your food is yours again.
> Your people are your people again.
> Your parents are your parents again.
> Your sacred mountains are yours again.
> Your creatures are yours again.
> The beauty of nature is yours again to enjoy, my grandchild,"
> He says to me as he sits down beside me.

"From the dwellings of the Holy Ones
Kind feelings will come to you as you go about in life,"
He says to me as he sits down beside me.
"Guided by these things, you shall find protection,
In all places as you live on, my grandchild,"
He says to me as he sits down beside me.

All is beautiful behind me
All is beautiful before me
All is beautiful below me
All is beautiful above me
All is beautiful all around me.

For I have been found and everything is beautiful.

In this serene and simple song of the heart, we find expressed in an incomparable fashion all the themes of the homeward journey: emergence-awakening out of the darkness of the external world; the guidance and protection of the Ancient One, the Grandparent, the Spirit; the perception of a new-old familiarity in all things and people around one; the multicolored garment of light; the feeling of being lost in the world transmuted to being at home in the world; the overflowing of feelings of love and compassion toward others; the exaltation and delight at finding oneself again in the shining presence of the inner family and in the realm of beauty from which we originated.

9

On Dying and Being Reborn

*As long as you do not practice it, this dying and becoming,
you are only a dreary guest on the dark earth.*

—J. W. GOETHE

To die and to be reborn is the metaphor for the most radical and total transformation that consciousness and identity can undergo. In one sense, as William Bridges has pointed out, any kind of "ending," whether that of a career, a relationship, or a project with which we have identified, is a kind of dying; and as a culture, we do not handle such deathlike endings very well.[1] When our self-image or self-concept, the sense of identity with which (and *as* which) we have lived, comes to an end, then we feel as though the ego or self is dying. The pattern of this metaphor is: everything that I call "me" is finished and dying; then, after a period of anxiety, turmoil, and uncertainty, there is the "rebirth" of a new identity, a new sense of who "I" am. The transformation involves all aspects of the psyche, because it involves the central organizing principle of selfhood. The new self that is born is naturally of a childlike nature, filled with the wonder, joy, and spontaneity of childhood.

Whereas in some Christian fundamentalist circles it is customary for people who have made a commitment to Christ to refer to themselves as "twice born," the original meaning of that concept goes much deeper than simply a profession of renewed faith, however sincere. It refers, in fact, to the second half of the transformation process we are talking about. Ironically, many fundamentalist "born-again" Christians do not appreciate that the rebirth experience, to be genuine, must of necessity be preceded by a metaphoric experience of "death." The first phase, the dying, is inevitably more anxiety provoking and problematical for most people.

In the mystery religions of ancient times and in many traditional cultures, "death-rebirth" was and is the name of an initiatory experience. Associated with it are ritual practices, such as entombment, profound isolation, or painful ordeals, through which the initiate would pass. Afterwards, it was customary for the initiate to adopt a new name, perhaps a new garment, and sometimes a new role in society, all of which expressed the newly reborn being. Although we no longer perform the ancient rituals of death and rebirth, many people, in changing their name, life-style, or work, are publicly signaling that a transformation has occurred.

In the mystical literature of Eastern and Western cultures, we find descriptions of many death-rebirth experiences. They are not just described—they are seen as something to cultivate, encourage, and practice. A saying of Zen master Bunan goes, "While living, be a dead man, thoroughly dead; whatever you do then, as you will, is always good."[2] Death-rebirth experiences, though painful, are highly valued because they lead to increased understanding, health and long life, peace, and inner freedom from fear. In modern literary and autobiographical accounts of transformative experiences, whether occurring spontaneously or induced by psychedelic substances, individuals may actually feel and sense themselves to be dying, then being reborn, renewed, or rejuvenated.

There is naturally a great deal of fear accompanying such experiences, because the person undergoing them does not realize that the "dying" is psychological, or metaphorical. They fear that they are literally, physically, going to die. The process is felt to be "out of control"—and indeed, from the ego's point of view, it is. Images of surrender, of self-sacrifice, or of letting go come naturally to mind.

As an example, here is the experience of a twenty-year-old college student, on his first LSD trip (for which he was not prepared). The setting was the back-seat of his friend's car, driving down the freeway.

> I had an extraordinarily powerful sense of expansion and ascent and at one point realized that I was faced with a choice of holding onto my limited identity as J. P., or going far beyond it into a space from which I might never return. In that moment my life unfolded with untold clarity. I was neither my name, nor the sum of my experiences accumulated during the past twenty years. I was not my parents' son, I had not grown up in San Jose and I was not a student at U.C. Santa Cruz. Each identification fell by the side. An irresistible force was impelling me beyond this illusion. I was to die to everything I thought was me—all I had to do was to say yes and there would be no turning back. I saw, too, in that moment, that to try to hold on against such a force could create madness. So I assented and ascended. I lost track of space and time and at some point found myself watching what seemed to be the center of creation—a massive luminous sphere that was radiating out concentric circles of light. It seemed that creation was being recreated in every moment, and I was part of that creation. . . . I felt profoundly happy and at peace in a way I never had before. I was established in truth, light, and the unshakeable knowledge of my own identity. . . . I have never stood so consciously upon the threshold of death and stepped across it. I felt as though I was leaving behind my familiar personality like an old suit. The sense of exhilaration was quite powerful.[3]

This kind of experience, which is not uncommon in the LSD literature, has all the hallmarks of radical self-transformation, what William James would have called a conversion experience. There were long-term, positive personality changes. One set of self-images ends, and true identity, or Self, is recognized. The feeling of crossing a threshold and the sense of participating in the processes of the creation of the world are both universally reported in the literature on mysticism and spiritual transformation. The idea that resisting the intense process could lead to madness, is one we shall return to later.

The Value of Death and Intentional "Dying"

For the majority of people, the idea of death—death in general and their own in particular—is surrounded by fear and denial. In the teachings of the great spiritual and religious traditions, however, we consistently find a positive and affirmative attitude toward dying. The following epitaph was found at Eleusis, the center of the greatest mystery religion in ancient Greece, "Truly the blessed gods have proclaimed a most beautiful secret: death comes not as a curse but as a blessing to men."[4] Spiritual teachers have always insisted that the commonly held negative view and fear of death are based on ignorance and must be changed for spiritual transformation to occur.

Mystics and teachers even go beyond the acceptance of death as an inevitable fact of existence to assertions of the necessity and desirability of dying with awareness, of the value of awareness of dying, and of growing through death. In a famous saying where he anticipates his own death and resurrection ("The hour has come that the Son of Man should be glorified"), Jesus uses the analogy of a seed kernel that disappears in the ground before sprouting: "A grain of wheat remains a solitary grain unless it falls into the ground and dies; but if it dies, it brings a rich harvest."[5] Saint Paul uses the same analogy in response to questions about the raising of the dead: "The seed you sow does not come to life unless it has first died."[6] Such statements express a deep awareness that new life, the birth and fruitfulness of a new identity, arise out of the death of what has preceded it.

The apparent "dying," the disappearance of a seed in the dark ground prior to its emergence as a fruit-bearing grain, is being used as a metaphor for the disappearance or "dying" of the old ego. The transformed personality can live and thrive only if the previous personality has "died." This is also the meaning of Meister Eckhart's saying that the Kingdom of God (which symbolizes the transformed, enlightened state of consciousness) is "for none but those who are thoroughly dead".[7] Both physical dying and psychological "dying" are valued because they lead to a better state, a transformed and more enlightened state. Similarly, there is an ancient tradition that dying leads to liberation and wisdom. Thus we hear Socrates say that "true philosophers," those who love wisdom, "make dying their profession, and to them of all men death is least alarming."[8]

A positive, less fearful attitude toward death is the necessary preparation for a transformed state of heightened aliveness. Furthermore, a reduction of fear of death is a consequence of undergoing metaphoric, or psychological, "dying." Thus it is not surprising that in folklore and mythology all over the world, the moral of many stories is that death must be treated with respect and honor.[9] Most societies prohibit verbal insult or physical assault of dying or dead individuals (except in the case of conquered enemies, who may be dishonored). Ancient funeral practices, such as the three-day wake, bespeak the respect, and even awe, with which those who undertake the final passage are regarded.

Many a mythic hero or heroine, including Gilgamesh, Inanna, Odysseus, the Grail knights, and the Mayan twins, undertake dangerous journeys into the underworld land of the dead in order to fathom the secrets of death and life. Such journeys pay homage to the power and mystery of death. In the Indian wisdom literature, the best-known journey of this kind is that of the youth Naciketas, told in the Katha Upanishad. The story is that Naciketas, as a result of a quarrel with his father, waits for three days and nights in the land of Yama, Lord of Death, and thereby earns the right to ask three favors of this mighty god. Perhaps the three-day journey to death is a metaphor for a mortal illness, which takes individuals out of their usual state, into a "near-death" experience from which they return with greater knowledge.

In any event, according to the legend, Naciketas asks first to be able to restore his broken relationship with his father. His second favor is to learn how to practice the fire ritual (which takes place "in the secret place of the heart"), so that he can, through this ritual, establish his awareness of and relationship with the higher realms. The third favor he asks—which the god Yama is most reluctant to grant—is to know the mystery of life and death and the true nature of being. "Tell us about that which they doubt, O Death, what there is in the great passing-on. This boon which penetrates the mystery, no other than that does Naciketas choose." Yama then proceeds to instruct Naciketas in a long philosophical and yogic discourse, ending with, "The inner Self [*Atman*] abides always in the heart. . . . One should draw [him] out, as one may the wind from the reed. Him one should know as the pure, the immortal."[10]

The young man on the LSD-induced death experience quoted earlier was, in a way, reexperiencing the ancient legend of Naciketas, when he obtained "unshakable knowledge of [his] own identity" after consciously stepping across the "threshold of death." The Katha Upanishad ends with the words: "Then Naciketas, having gained this knowledge declared by Death and the whole rule of Yoga, attained *Brahman* and became freed from passion and from death. And so may any other who knows this in regard to the Self."[11] Self-knowledge is the ultimate favor and reward given to those who confront their own death. In such an experience, the self that I thought I was dies, and my true Self is revealed and recognized. Such an experience may be devastating, but it is certainly humbling, and potentially ecstatic and liberating.

Acknowledgment and respect for the value and significance of death are also found in the mystery cults of ancient times. Many of these contained, at their core, a ritual reenactment of a death-rebirth myth—such as those of Osiris and Isis, Tammuz and Ishtar, Demeter and Persephone, Cybele and Attis, and of Dionysus, Orpheus, and many others. In these mythic rituals, one's own personal death and rebirth were symbolically equated with that of the god, and this in turn was patterned after the cyclic death and rebirth of vegetative life.[12]

Many of the descriptions of the ultimate state of consciousness, to be attained on the disciplined path of self-transcendence and transformation, are indicative of a kind of ego annihilation, a total dying of the self and all its normal identifications. The Buddhist goal of *nirvana* is "extinction," a "passing away" of the flames of desire and attachment. The Islamic Sufi's ultimate state of *fana* is likewise a "dissolution," a merging of individual identity into union with universal beingness. In a magnificent poem by Rumi, the great thirteenth-century Persian poet-sage our dying is seen as a repeated phase in a cosmic evolutionary process:

> I died a mineral, and became a plant.
> I died a plant, and rose an animal.
> I died an animal and I was a man.
> Why should I fear? When was I less by dying?
> Yet once more I shall die as man.[13]

The poem tells us that we have died many deaths—as humans and in those life forms that preceded the human. Death, therefore, is not to be feared but welcomed and embraced. As Rumi says, "O let me not exist"—for this "passing on" signals the ultimate realization, the return to the divine inner Source.

The Taoist philosopher Chuang Tsu has given us a wonderful portrait of the sage who has attained to this level of wisdom and freedom, though practicing the *tao*.

> The true man of old knew nothing of loving life and hating death. When he was born, he felt no elation. When he entered death, there was no sorrow. Carefree he went. Carefree he came. That was all. He did not forget his beginning and did not seek his end. He accepted what he was given with delight, and when it was gone, he gave it no more thought."[14]

Every time something *ends* in us, it dies: thus we experience thousands of little deaths each day, each hour. Thoughts arise, die, arise again; images form, dissolve, form again; feelings well up from within, crest and recede, to emerge again later. Insofar as we are identified with these thoughts, images, and feelings, *we* die, are reborn, redie, are reborn, continuously. Rumi said that "every instant you are dying and returning." The German theologian and mystic Johannes Tauler spoke of the great value of such daily dying: "A man might die a thousand deaths in one day and find a joyful life corresponding to each of them."[15] Anyone who has ever had the experience of letting go of some craving or attachment and has felt the sudden lift, the ecstatic freedom that comes from this, will know the truth of these statements.

Tauler goes on to speak of the special value of consciously dying "to a scornful word, . . . to some inclination, acting or not acting against [one's] own will, in love or grief, in word or act, in going or staying." In other words, inclinations, impulses, desires, wishes, judgments—all these are born and die within the psyche. Gurdjieff's statement on the importance of consciously dying, intentionally letting go of false identifications, is characteristically forceful and vivid:

> A man must die, that is, he must free himself from a thousand petty attachments and identifications. . . . He is attached to everything in his life, attached to his imagination, attached to his stupidity, attached even to his sufferings, possibly to his sufferings more than to anything else. . . . Attachments to things, identifications with things, keep alive a thousand useless I's in a man. These I's must die in order that the big I may be born. But how can they be made to die? They do not want to die. It is at this point that the possibility of awakening comes to the rescue. To awaken means to realize one's nothingness.[16]

So we are dealing with intentional psychological dying, with consciously letting go, or releasing, or dissolving identity complexes—those clusters of thoughts, feelings, perceptions, impulses, in which we have invested psychic energy and identity. Such intentional dying of self-concept or self-image was practiced in ritual form in the mystery schools where the symbolic enactment of a death-rebirth myth facilitated the personal "dying" of the initiate or aspirant.

Similarly, in shamanic cultures, the preparatory training of the shaman-healer typically involved either an "illness" or a "wounding," both primarily internal and symbolic, but frequently accompanied by psychosomatic and physical manifestations. During this shamanic experience the shaman would let go of all his or her old attachments: a more or less total "dying" to the old way of living was called for. Sometimes the older shaman, while instructing the apprentice, would symbolically "kill" the apprentice. This was then followed by a restoration, or reconstitution, often aided by an animal ally or spirit, into a new, more power-filled form, endowed with healing and magical abilities.[17]

In alchemy, the process of *mortificatio*, which literally means "killing" or "dead-making," was the process of consciously and intentionally "working on" the reduction of ego attachments and impulses. This was done through symbolic meditations and visualizations that emphasized, in Edinger's words, "darkness, defeat, torture, mutilation, death and rotting," these images leading in turn to positive ones of growth, regeneration, fruiting, ripening, and rebirth.[18] We shall return to the theme of *mortificatio* again below.

Nearness to Death as Transformative Experience

The metaphor of death as a teacher and liberator, as the beginning of a new way of being and as the stimulus to knowledge of God, is found in all the great spiritual traditions of humankind, in Eastern and Western mysticism, yoga, shamanism, and alchemy. Confirmation of this view has come from three different groups of people: those who have almost died, but returned; those who have experienced the death of a close relative; and those who are approaching death slowly in a terminal illness. All three situations can be triggers for far-reaching and profound changes in consciousness and personality. Nearness to death is what they have in common, whether it is one's own death or that of another.

(1) One who has been touched by the awesome hand of death inevitably has afterward a far different understanding of the meaning of life. In the past two decades, psychological research on the experiences of people who have come close to dying but have returned has been pursued and reported by Russell Noyes, Karlis Osis, Raymond Moody, Kenneth Ring, and others. Due to this work, the notion of "near death" as a profound altered state of consciousness has gained some degree of acceptance. While it is possible to treat these accounts as purely subjective phenomena, with no real validity, what is striking is the unanimity of the reports and the profound changes in worldview and spiritual values that occur with these "near-death experiences" (NDEs).[19]

The experiences typically include sensations of being outside the body, sometimes looking down or back upon the physical body; feelings of a definite transition, sometimes experienced as crossing a boundary or threshold, or sometimes as passing through a dark, enclosed space, such as a tunnel or cave; after this transition, people usually report feelings of peace, unity, serenity, ecstasy, timelessness. These are feelings comparable to those of mystical visions and shamanic journeys. Frequently, people report seeing dead relatives beckoning to them from a region of light, or they see spirit beings, made of pure light. The return to everyday reality is often accompanied by a profound sense of loss and regret and by the insistence that the experience is incommunicable. Individuals feel they have been granted a preview of what death is actually like, and that this preview is a potent catalyst for changing one's life.

In some accounts people report perceptual changes comparable to those found in psychedelic or spontaneous illuminative experiences. One incident was told to me by the woman to whom it happened. As a college student she was out sailing with a friend. Both were inexperienced sailors and got caught in a storm. After initial panic, the woman thought that this was the end; she already saw the obituary notices. Suddenly a profoundly peaceful mood descended over her, and the spray from the waves crashing over the boat, sparkled with rainbow-colored jewelled droplets. A state of timeless serenity filled her until she and her companion were at length rescued.

In their book *Beyond Death,* Stanislav and Christina Grof have shown how much the experiential accounts of near-death experiences resemble the myths, ritual texts, paintings, and sculptures, found all over the world, that relate to after-death journeys. Because of this similarity, some anthropologists and psychologists have suggested that these ancient myths and images are accounts of such altered-state experiences, couched in the familiar symbolism of a particular culture. If true, this suggests that such near-death visions have been known for ages and have been incorporated into the religious values and practices of many cultures.

Another feature of the typical NDE, which also has its mythic analogy, is what has been called the "life review." For some, though not all, near-death survivors, in bare seconds of "real" time, a movielike panorama of their lives unfolds before their eyes. A striking example was reported to me secondhand: a man with a group of friends had taken a high dose of LSD and was on a city rooftop at night. When he stepped off a three-foot-high boxlike structure on the roof, he thought in the dark that he had stepped off the edge of the roof and would surely now die. In the split second before his foot landed on the roof, three feet below, he experienced the whole classic life review played out before his astonished eyes.

Such life-review visions may be the experiential basis for the metaphor of the judgment scene found in many after-death myths, where the good and bad deeds of one's life are assessed and weighed. Esoteric philosophy teaches that after death there is a review of lessons learned and mistakes made in this life. Variations on this theme abound in every culture. In Egyptian myth the heart of the deceased is weighed in a scale against the Truth Feather of the goddess Maat. In Tibetan Buddhism, it is taught that the death god Yama holds a mirror up to the just deceased, in which they can see all their deeds and intentions.

If life review experience, or even only a detached mood of objective reflection on one's life, is a fact common in near-death experiences, it may explain why people who have had these experiences often choose to practice some kind of meditative or spiritual discipline afterward. These tend to be central, life-changing experiences, much as LSD has been for many, or as their first space walk is for astronauts. Almost dying is clearly a very powerful awakener, a turning point or conversion.

(2) Equally powerful as a catalyst to realization and transformative development, can be the encounter with death through the death of a relative, loved one, friend, or child. My personal estimate is that experiencing the death of a loved relative is probably the most prevalent trigger for profound spiritual transformation. When someone you love dies, it is as if a part of you dies as well.

Even the death of an individual we do not know personally but who we idealized or regarded highly can be the trigger for a profound altered state—as those who still remember vividly the stunning impact of John Kennedy's assassination can attest. The perceptual encounter with a transcendent archetype of this kind—the death of the leader or king—leaves images in the mind that seem like etchings in burnished copper. Many people remember every sensory detail of that day with unforgettable clarity.

In recent years, a number of individuals and organizations have devoted themselves to exploring more humane and enlightened ways of relating to dying people. In our culture the approach to death is dominated by anxiety, embarrassment, and denial. Elizabeth Kubler-Ross, Ram Dass, Stephen Levine, and others have made contributions to our knowledge of how to "work with the dying," or, rather, how to just be, and perhaps meditate, with the dying. Levine writes: "You relate to one who is ill the same way you relate to any being. With openness. With an honoring of the truth we all share. Work to dissolve the separateness that keeps one lost in duality. Become one with the other. No help, just being. See the conditioned illusion. Break that ancient clinging. Allow both of you to die."[20]

In the work of these individuals, and in organized efforts such as the hospice movement and the Shanti project, we see a renewal of ancient ways of helping people come to terms with death, both those dying and the survivors.[21] The surviving relatives often have greater psychological difficulties in coming to terms with death than does the dying person.

(3) In situations involving terminal illness, a person approaches the final transition gradually (as opposed to the sudden, and unexpected confrontation that occurs in the near-death experience) and has the opportunity to resolve old conflicts, complete unfinished business, release fears and attachments to past images of self and others. This is the vast potential of dying slowly; but unless there is support for such an intention from family, friend, or guide, it would be hard for the dying person to maintain this conscious attitude. Someone needs to be there to help the person through the shoals of resistance, anger, fear, and other sharp-edged emotions. Often the guide need do no more than be there with an attitude of open, truthful, and aware support.

This modern work on the humane preparation for dying has involved the reexamination of ancient religious texts. The practices and rites of the ancient Egyptians, as collected in their *Book of the Dead*, have become the objects of renewed interest; and their beliefs concerning the after-death state and reincarnation are now being presented in serious, if fictionalized, accounts by such writers as Joan Grant, Elizabeth Haich, and Isha Schwaller de Lubicz.[22] In medieval Europe there were tracts known under the general title of *Ars Moriendi* (*The Craft of Dying*), written as manuals for those who attended the dying. Tibetan Buddhists encoded their visions and records of after-death consciousness in a profound document known as the *Bardo Thodol,* subtitled *The Book of Liberation Through Hearing on the After-Death Planes,* which contains the most central doctrines of Vajrayana Buddhism. In this text, the person attending the dying is instructed to speak the words of guidance into the ear of the departing traveler.

Over and over again, the text emphasizes the importance of practicing the meditations, the yogic disciplines, before one dies, in order to be better prepared for this
most difficult passage.

This *Bardo Thodol* (also known as the Tibetan Book of the Dead) was
adapted by Timothy Leary, Ralph Metzner (the present author) and Richard
Alpert (later Ram Dass), as a manual for people taking high-dose LSD trips.[23]
We had observed that the essential features of this map of after-death visions
could easily be identified in psychedelic experiences. Instead of "death," these
trips had "ego death"; instead of "peaceful and wrathful deities," they had
heavenly and hellish visions corresponding to the person's own religious background; and instead of "rebirth," they had "reentry," or return to the world of
ordinary, familiar identity in a transformed and renewed condition, if the experience was successful.

LSD psychotherapy has also been found to be extremely valuable for people
with terminal cancer, in work done by Walter Pahnke, Stanislav Grof, and
others.[24] The experience with LSD often enabled cancer patients to transcend
their pain-wracked bodies, and become attuned to a level of reality and consciousness that included the physical, although experienced in the context of a more
comprehensive, more unitive, timeless, love-filled, and pain-dissolving awareness.

In experiences with LSD or without, it is possible for people who are dying
to attain this kind of transcendence of the physical in a way that alleviates much
of the usual pain and fear accompanying death. One might well ask whether this
is not the natural, true way of dying, designed for us by God and/or Nature. This
is exactly the question posed by the biologist-philosopher Lewis Thomas:

> Could it be that the sensations associated with dying are the manifestation of
> a physiological mechanism? Is there, in fact, such a thing as the "process"
> of dying? It does not seem unreasonable to me, considering the meticulously
> designed, orderly mechanisms at work in all other important events of living.
> It is not unlikely that there is a pivotal moment at some stage in the body's
> reaction to injury or disease, maybe in aging as well, when the organism
> concedes it is finished and the time for dying is at hand, and at this moment
> the events that lead to death are launched, as a coordinated mechanism.
> Functions are then shut off, in sequence, irreversibly, and while this is going
> on, a neural mechanism, held ready for this occasion, is switched on."[25]

Thomas proposes that such a mechanism, possibly involving endorphins, the
body's own pain-reducing chemicals, could be responsible for the often calm,
detached, painless, even illuminative experiences of individuals who are dying. If
this is true, a healing transformation is "built in" to the very process of coming
nearer and nearer to death.

Dying, in this very organic view, is not just the ending of life or the cessation
of vital processes. It is, rather, an active process, almost a kind of physiological
unwinding, a progressive withdrawing from the world of external sense objects.

Emotional "Deadening"

In the introduction, I suggested that there are "regressive" and "progressive" transformations. We can sink into deeper sleep and unconsciousness, as well as become more awake and aware. We can find ourselves in states where we are more bound, more trapped, as well as states that bring us toward liberation. In states of pathological psychic disorganization, the parts of the psyche are more fragmented and disjointed than is usual. At this other end of the spectrum of states of consciousness, we encounter, in terms of the present metaphor, states of greater "deadness" than are a normal aspect of conditioned existence. Such emotional deadness is the opposite of "aliveness" and vitality; in its clinical forms it is known as depression, rigid defensiveness, or catatonia.[26]

We would do well to study these states: by gaining some understanding of how they come about, we may also understand more about how the transition from death into new life takes place. Just as recognition of the shadow, or dark, aspect of our nature is a necessary precondition for wholeness, so is recognition of the dead and dying parts of our psyche a necessary precondition for true aliveness. This is the realm that Freud described with his notion of *thanatos,* the "death urge." Also in this realm is the alchemical operation of mortificatio, "dead-making," which is conscious and intentional transformational work with these forces of psychological dissolution. In madness and certain forms of psychic disorder we may experience deadness as a lowered, contracted awareness, a "deadening" or numbing of one's sense of life. This is a cold and joyless death-in-life, very different from the life-enhancing, high-spirited attitude of the liberated master, who is also a "dead man in life."

Many psychotics sense themselves to be dead or in the process of being killed or destroyed, as the work of R. D. Laing, John Perry, and others has demonstrated. Robert Lifton describes the concept of the "dead self" as analogous to Laing's "false self." And Laing has written of the schizophrenic's "desire to be dead, desire for non-being"; he attributes this "state of death-in-life" to "primary guilt of having no right to life in the first place, and hence being entitled only to a dead life."[27] Schizophrenics' eyes are often said to look "dead."

Lifton, who has done research with survivors of Hiroshima, compares the schizophrenic's deadness with the kind of "psychic numbing" found in survivors of nuclear catastrophe or concentration camps. Just as the motionless postures of the catatonic may represent the ultimate defense against overwhelming impulses toward annihilation of self and world; so the robotlike deadness of catastrophe survivors may be their sole remaining response to the threat of total destruction. It must be emphasized that such "death-in-life" states, unlike those of the mystic, the yogi, or the shamanic initiate, are not intentional or voluntary and often are not followed by rebirth and renewal, except when the schizophrenic is able to complete the transformation process.

Feelings of deadness, of psychic and sensory numbing, are also found in other, milder forms of psychological disorder. As Lifton points out, in "reactive depression," which is the mourning we do for the loss of a loved one, people often express the feeling that a part of them has died and that they "killed" the other person in some way.

> In character disorders, and in the related phenomena of psychosomatic disorders, . . . there are life-long patterns of deadening or numbing of various parts of the psyche. This numbing may involve moral sensitivity or interpersonal capacities. . . . Turning to hysteria, the "psychic anaesthesia" emphasized in early literature suggests the centrality of stasis, deadening or numbing.[28]

Following earlier theories of Otto Rank and Ernest Becker, Lifton proposed that death anxiety, or fear of death, is a central, unacknowledged motive of human life. Fear of death, for these authors, is the hidden underside of human beings' ubiquitous quests for immortality.[29] In his works *Denial of Death* and *Escape from Evil,* Becker extended the work of Rank, Wilhelm Reich, and Norman O. Brown to argue that the repressed fear of death is at the root of much of man's evil behavior: we destroy another in order to symbolically stave off our own fear of destruction. On the collective scale, the exploitation of this fear of death underlies the most dreadful phenomena of tyranny, oppression of the masses, war, totalitarianism, and genocide.

To overcome the destructive, numbing effects of the denial and fear of death, we must, as always in conscious transformation, first recognize and acknowledge death and turn it into our friend and ally; into a happily anticipated final journey. Such an acceptance and affirmation of dying is not a morbid "death wish" but, rather, a deeply and joyously felt awareness of the transcendent continuity of life. I had the good fortune to see this kind of awareness when I had a meeting with an old Mongolian Buddhist lama, who chuckled and smiled happily whenever the topic of his impending death came up in the conversation —and he was the one who kept bringing it up.

When Sigmund Freud was sixty-three, two years before he discovered the first signs of cancer in his body, he put forward, in his book *Beyond the Pleasure Principle,* the most startling and controversial of his many innovative theories: —the coexistence in all life of a death drive (*thanatos*) as well as a life drive (*eros*). It has been suggested that there is a connection between Freud's formulation of the theory and the cancerous processes going on in his body at the time.[30] His own experience, his own awareness of the death process, provided the impulse and basis for his discoveries and interpretations. In alchemical terms one could say he was practicing *mortificatio,* by working with the symbols and images of death.

However, Freud's theory of *thanatos* has been often criticized and is not generally accepted by his followers.[31] As a result, the insights that led Freud to postulate a death urge and the old master's vision, with its mythic and mystic overtones, has been largely ignored. Freud wanted to explain the enormous destructiveness of human behavior, which he had vividly experienced in the First World War, as well as the manifestations of sadism and masochism he saw in his patients.[32] He felt that the life drives and death drives, *eros* and *thanatos*, are primordial biological principles, the first tending toward unification and organization, the second toward separation and disorganization.

On the ego level the personal manifestations of these two drives are sexual libido for *eros* and violent aggression for *thanatos*. We experience them in our dreams and fantasies as well as in our outward behavior; we embody them in our own personal symbols and myths. At the physiological level, as Freud pointed out, we experience them in the complementary coexistence of anabolic ("building up") and catabolic ("breaking down") processes occurring in our bodies. Another physiological metaphor for the dual process, used by the Tibetan Buddhists, is breathing: when we breathe in, we are expressing eros, building strength, inspiring, vivifying; when we breathe out, we are expiring, letting go in a kind of dying. The aim of *thanatos*, as Freud said, is to reduce tension, to break down, to return to the quiescence of the inorganic world. "Everything living dies from causes within itself, and returns to the inorganic; . . . the inanimate was there before the animate."[33]

The value of such analogies and formulations, which Freud himself admitted were highly speculative, lies in their insight into life as a complementary duality composed of life and death principles, an idea that is found in virtually every major spiritual and religious tradition, in the writings of the mystics, and in the death-rebirth mythologies of cultures all over the world. This unitary vision of life as a creative interweaving of two complementary strands or processes that vary in relative potency at different stages of our life—and are subject to influences that may distort and deviate their natural expression—has the potential for transforming consciousness in a most radical fashion: death is no longer to be feared and denied as painful and horrible, but can be accepted as a natural and inevitable counterpoint to the ordering, life-enhancing processes of *eros*.

As we focus awareness on death, we may find, as Freud did, that there is a perfectly natural dying (*thanatos*) going on in us all the time, that complements and balances the life-affirming energy of *eros*. Conscious focussing on the processes of dying, and the associated symbolic imagery of death, for the purpose of transformation is, I believe, one of the psychological meanings of the alchemical operation of *mortificatio*.

Alchemical Mortificatio

If we allow that cells have consciousness and identity, and that it is possible for human beings to increase their awareness of the body wisdom residing at the cellular level, then awareness of cellular birthing and dying may well be another experiential basis for subconscious feelings of an everchanging balance of life forces and death forces. We know that from two to three million of our cells die each second, while equal numbers are being born. At this level, then, there is no possibility of attachment to the individual life form. Cells live out their life span in periods ranging from several days to several months, and within seven years or so, all of our cells have died and have been replaced. Yet we have retained our life, beyond all of these countless lives and deaths.

In Greek myth, Thanatos, the god of death, was seen in some literature as a black-robed, sword-wielding figure, comparable to the Grim Reaper of European folklore. In this guise he is the personification of death as fearful and evil. However, the more common perception of Thanatos was as a winged spirit who lived with his twin brother Hypnos, the god of sleep. As such, he is a very different figure, an angel of death who aids the dying on their final journey. Merciful and benign, he guides us in the great river crossing. He is familiar to us from our nightly meetings with his twin, sleep. How effortlessly we drift off and release our hold on the physical form each night! Can we be similarly calm and composed when we make the final transition? And can we be equally calm when we have to "die" to some object of our affection and attachment?

Although I do not claim to have completely transcended or transformed my fear of death, I have had experiences in altered states of consciousness that have convinced me of the validity of this benign interpretation of death. I have come to understand that the alchemical operation of *mortificatio* is actually the conscious and intentional contemplation of death-related symbols and images, and the meditation on natural processes that are analogous to dying. The following shift in awareness occurred to me during a session involving the process known as rebirthing, in which one is guided, through special methods of breathing, to recall and release early traumatic memories. A memory of physical pain would "surface," as it were, from lower depths of unconsciousness, be reexperienced, and then released into the stream of present awareness. At that moment, the whole complex of thoughts, feelings, and sensations associated with that memory died; and to the extent that "I," a part of me, was *in* that memory complex (the part that said, "This painful thing happened to *me"*), that part, that little ego, died. As it died, in a micromoment "I" went through the fear, pain, anger, grief, and finally release that we go through when we die. This, then, was practice dying —providing practice in letting go and releasing attachments.

We feel mortified when our pride or vanity has been wounded, and we try as soon as possible to recover from the blow to our ego and the perceived humiliation and shame. In the alchemical transformational practice of *mortificatio,* on the other hand, such death blows to the ego are not avoided and may even be cultivated, because they bring about liberation from attachments. Edward Edinger has pointed out how often alchemical *mortificatio* is associated with symbols of the conscious ego: the "king" dies, the "sun" dies, the "lion" dies, and so forth. The kingly ego undergoes "darkness, defeat, torture, mutilation, death, and rotting," which is Edinger's summary of *mortificatio.* It is also the *nigredo,* the blackness, and *putrefactio,* which is decomposition, decay, disease, and rotting.[34] Out of the decaying matter comes new life; out of darkness comes light; out of death comes rebirth; out of defeat comes triumph. "Where is death's sting, where grave thy victory?"

There are distinct parallels to *mortificatio* practices in other traditions of spiritual transformation. Buddhist monks are taught to overcome desire by contemplating the body of a young woman as a worm-filled corpse or a skeleton. Hindu renunciates wander homeless, foodless, naked, and with ashes on their head, to express their detachment from all sensory-physical concerns. Christian ascetics meditate on the passion of Christ and the suffering of the martyrs, expressing their union with Christ through this identification (referred to as "the imitation of Christ"). The eleventh-century Persian Sufi Khurquani said, "Thou must die daily a thousand deaths and come to life again, that thou mayest win the life immortal."[35]

Although many partial "little deaths" are possible and valuable, when the whole ego-personality "dies," everything changes. The old self-image, the one we acquired from our parents and from society, which is symbolized by the old king in alchemy, by the dragon, or by the rotting blackness—all these have to be "killed," that is, rendered completely lifeless within us, so that they have no more power, no more of our life energy invested in them. The new personality, the new sense of identity that results from the transformational work, is symbolized by the reborn child.

The new being that arises and grows after the death of the old self is called by the alchemists "the philosopher's son (or daughter)," the *filius philosophorum.* In Chinese Taoist alchemy, the term used was "foetus of immortality."[36] As Jung writes, "The alchemists assert that death is at once the conception of the *filius philosophorum.*"[37] The "philosopher's child" is called this because it is the offspring, or result, of philosophical work (the alchemical *opus*). This work of the philosophers (who are, in the literal meaning of the term, "lovers of wisdom") is the practice of daily dying, as Socrates had said. From the intentional, conscious "dying," involving the release of past identifications, a new and wiser kind of being arises and grows in us.

One could say that through these images the alchemists showed that they regarded the processes of physical, organic death as an appropriate analogy for the ending of old self-images, beliefs, and emotional patterns. Similarly, they felt that new birth, or rebirth, was the appropriate metaphor for the new, completely changed persona, the newly developed way of perceiving the world.

The New Birth and the Eternal Child

The process of psychologically dying while one is still alive is followed by a psychological rebirth, or renewal. In the words of Ramana Maharshi, "He who finds his way to the core of the Self, whence arise all levels of the I, all spheres of the world, he who finds his way home to his first source with the question 'whence am I' is born and reborn. Know that whoever is so born is the wisest of the wise—each moment of his life he is born anew."[38]

This rebirth phase of the transformation may be experienced in several different ways. (a) First, there is the idea of a resurrection, a restoring to life of a personality that has died. (b) Alternatively, rebirth is seen as the replacement of the small self by another, greater Self or Spirit. (c) Third, it is said that one who has died, whether actually or metaphorically, lives afterward in a different world, a different state. (d) In the fourth variant, the new being is actually imagined as a child: this is the archetype of the radiant, divine, or eternal child, which, as Jung points out, symbolizes "the potential future."[39]

(a) The idea of resurrection, the restoration to life of an adult body that has died, is described in many mythic and shamanic tales: Osiris is put together again by Isis; the twins Hunter and Jaguar of the Popul Vuh reassemble themselves after being dismembered; shamans who have "died" may be reconstituted by their power animal or ally. Many modern practitioners of shamanic work recount how they were "cut up," "pulverized," "burned," "eviscerated," or otherwise "killed," then reconstructed by their animal helper.[40] For example, one man reported how his animal, a "horse," stood over his lifeless "corpse" and passed its huge nostrils gently all over his body, "breathing" life back into him. While, from a sceptical point of view, we could dismiss all this as the deluded fantasy of an overactive imagination, we would still have to account for the fact that this man, like others, felt better and healthier after this experience.

In the New Testament, the story of Lazarus, as well as that of Jesus himself, exemplifies this kind of physical resurrection. To a lesser degree, the modern accounts of near-death experience (NDE) coincide with this kind of pattern. In the case of Jesus, the resurrection was into a nonphysical, "spiritual" body that yet resembled the physical in all significant respects, even to having the wounds that the physical body had suffered. The closest most of us come to this kind of experience is in suffering a near-fatal illness and then recovering—the body appears to be fully restored to health. A common feature in all these accounts, when the individual is intentionally pursuing a death-rebirth transformation, is that the new body is better than the old; it is stronger, healthier, and lighter.

(b) Another aspect of this rebirth and renewal experience is that the little self is overshadowed or replaced by the Great Self, the personal-physical ego replaced by the transpersonal Spirit, the mortal by the Immortal. Meister Eckhart says, in this experience "the soul . . . is dead to self and alive to God." A Sufi saint wrote, "thy being dies away, and His person covers they person." Or, in the words of the Gospel of John, "No one can enter the Kingdom of God without being born from water and Spirit. That which is born of the flesh is flesh, that which is born of the Spirit is spirit."[41] People in such states feel their own ego concern and interests fade into insignificance or nothingness in the face of the awesome power and light of the Great Self, the god within, the "diamond essence," the *Atman*.

The encounter with the Self can be an overwhelming and annihilating self-confrontation, as was pointed out by C. G. Jung. In his essay "Concerning Rebirth," Jung wrote that

> He who is truly and hopelessly little will always drag the revelation of the greater down the level of his littleness, and will never understand that the day of judgment for his littleness has dawned. But the man who is inwardly great will know that the long-expected friend of his soul, the immortal one, has now really come, "to lead captivity captive"; that is, to seize hold of him by whom this immortal had always been confined and held prisoner, and to make his life flow into that greater life—a moment of deadliest peril![42]

As this quotation makes clear, the deadly danger exists for those identified with the small self, the personal ego. Not all encounters with Self, however, need be traumatic or even painful. There is, after all, the vast literature of mysticism that sings in rapturous tones of ecstatic union with the divine, of dyings that are peaceful and blissful, of unitive experiences that have the character of a nuptial or are likened to dissolving in an oceanic feeling of oneness.

(c) Some accounts of death-rebirth experiences emphasize the new quality of awareness and perception that comes into existence afterward. It is as if we had entered a new world in which everything looks and feels different, and a kind of pristine, shining radiance suffuses everything we perceive. Mental and emotional responses to what is perceived are also new; there is a quality of joy and spontaneity and an outpouring of affection and enthusiasm. In an anonymous medieval Hermetic treatise we read, "The resurrection is the revelation of what is, and the transformation of things, the transition [*metabole*] into newness. For imperishability descends upon the perishable; the light flows down upon the darkness, swallowing it up."[43] Here we find the metaphor of the newly born paralleling the metaphor of vision with the veils removed, the doors of perception having been cleansed. The mystics say that after the death-rebirth revelation, everything is seen with love and wisdom, from the perspective of the infinite and eternal *(sub specie aeternitatis)*.

(d) The biblical admonition that "except ye become as children, ye cannot enter the Kingdom of Heaven" follows naturally from the teaching that one needs to die before entering the blessed, enlightened state of this Kingdom. Here the death-rebirth metaphor leads us to the archetype of the divine child, the *puer aeternus.* While most discussions by Jungians of the *puer* or *puella* focus on the shadow side of this archetype and on its clinical manifestations in flighty, immature "playboys" or "babies," these represent only a limited interpretation of this powerful image. Chinese and Western alchemists spoke of the fetus of immortality, the philosophers' child that is born as a consequence of the inner conjunction of male and female. The idea of the eternal child, who comes into manifestation after a conscious "death" experience is connected to the numerous myths, which play a central role in most religions, of the birth of a god in human form. The Indian legends of the boy Krishna and the Christian legends of the infant Jesus are only the best-known examples.

Jung, in his essay on "The Psychology of the Child Archetype," pointed out several of the significant features or meanings of this profound symbol. He described it as an anticipation of the synthesis of conscious and unconscious, as a symbol of wholeness, or the Self. The child-god or child-hero always has an unusual, miraculous birth or a virgin conception—which corresponds to the "psychic genesis" of the new being. The child image represents a link to the past, to our childhood, as well as a link to the future, as it anticipates a "nascent state of consciousness." The "golden child" or "eternal youth" is androgynous, because he/she represents the perfect union of opposites. Only the old self, the ordinary ego, identifies itself as male or female—and this self has now died. The "child" is both beginning and end, "an initial and a terminal creature," because the wholeness that it symbolizes is "older and younger than consciousness, enfolding it in time and space."[44]

The divine child is invincible. He/she overcomes dangerous enemies in infancy: one of the images of the boy Krishna shows him trampling a giant serpent underfoot in a dance—a metaphor for the overcoming of reptilian instinctual aggressiveness. An example from Greek mythology is the story of the baby Herakles, who strangled a serpent that attacked him in his crib. The Child has all the power of a god, since it is a god: it is the Immortal One that replaces the mortal personality that has "died." Here, too, we find the notion of the divine child as representing the triumph over death. Christ demonstrated the power to resurrect—himself as well as another (Lazarus)—and many other divine heroes and yogic adepts of high degree have demonstrated similar powers, as documented particularly in Eastern mystical literature. While such powers might seem remote to the average person, the myths and images that convey them show potentials; they reveal what humans *can* attain.

In the Russian Orthodox liturgy, the triumph over death is expressed in the following words: "Christ is risen from the dead, trampling down death by death, and upon those in the tomb bestowing life." I suggest that this imagery refers to the change that occurs in the psyche as the healing, transformative power of the intentional dying is experienced. The unconscious death tendencies *(thanatos),* which function to oppose the body's life-preserving tendencies *(eros)* through disease and other destructive operations, are gradually reduced; or rather, brought into balance. One of my teachers referred to "pockets of death" within our nature, that are opened up and dissolved by enlightened awareness, thus bringing about the death of death. As we consciously accept dying and "dying," the process provides spiritual nourishment. Shakespeare expresses this idea in one of the sonnets:

> So shalt thou feed on death,
> That feeds on men,
> And death once dead, there's
> No more dying then.

In the nontheistic Chinese Taoist tradition, the archetype of the eternal child is also known and treasured. The newborn child is still connected to the Tao, to the source of its life and its arising, and this is why we should emulate it. As Chuang Tsu says: "Can you be like a newborn child? The baby cries all day and yet his voice never becomes hoarse. That is because he has not lost nature's harmony."[45] Characteristically, the Taoists emphasize the practical value, in terms of health and well-being, of attunement to the awareness of the infant.

For the individual in a process of transformation, the imagery and mythology of the eternal child fosters a positive and life-affirming attitude: we are encouraged to confront and transform our fear of death, to embrace the process of "dying" as liberating and as bringing wisdom. We thus come to know that out of the turmoil and darkness of dying comes the sparkling vitality of the newborn self. This new self is connected to the eternal source of all life, that source from which we all derive, the divine essence within. It is hence aptly named "the eternal child."

10

Unfolding the Tree of Our Life

Beloved, gaze in thine own heart,
The holy tree is growing there,
From joy the holy branches start,
And all the trembling leaves they bear.

—WILLIAM BUTLER YEATS

The tree has been one of mankind's most ancient and universal symbols, appearing in myth, ritual, legend, shamanic initiation, sacred literature, art, and poetry, as well as in the dreams and visions of seekers and seers, both ancient and contemporary. The manifold branching form of the tree has symbolized protection, shade, nourishment, shelter, fertility, birth, regeneration, stability, and continuity. The seemingly miraculous, ever-renewing growth of the tree, from seed kernel to flowering or fruit-laden giant, has been seen as a metaphor for the process of human life itself in its growth, development, extension, and unfolding. In relation to transformation, the tree symbolizes the ascent of the mind, or awareness, from the "earth" of matter-nature-body to the "sky-heaven" of spirit-god-consciousness. Like trees, we are "rooted in darkness and crowned with light": our being is grounded in the unconscious darkness of matter, grows and extends itself throughout life, and reaches upward into the "higher" realms of consciousness. The tree stands as the preeminent symbol of growth, renewal, and transformation.

Besides its symbolic or philosophical meanings, the tree has a personal emotional significance for many individuals. Most people have very positive feelings and associations connected with trees. In talks and workshops I have asked people to remember a tree that was significant to them in growing up: almost universally, people have tree memories that they cherish. Perhaps there was a tree that they hugely enjoyed climbing and looking out from; a tree whose height, strength, color, and solidity they admired; a tree that sheltered them from the sun's heat or from the rain; or a tree whose delicious apples they gathered. Exceptions do exist, of course: for one man, the image of the tree reminded him of being forced by his father to cut down a switch for a beating; for another, there was a tree from which he fell and suffered painful injuries. But by and large, the image of the tree, whether actual and remembered, or imagined, is so powerful and numinous that we are clearly dealing with an archetype, in the Jungian sense.[1]

In connection with trees, some people have had experiences of emotional transformation that are so vivid that the idea of communication with trees or the spirits of trees seems very natural to them. I can recall that when I was in the throes of intense grief over the death of my son, I walked under the dome-shaped canopy of a willow tree and felt a kind of comforting embrace enveloping me, offering solace. Another example is given in Victor Frankl's book on his experiences in a concentration camp. When he asked a mortally ill young woman in the camp how she was able to be so cheerful and positive even though she knew she was dying, she told him about a small tree outside her window that she was able to talk to. "This tree is the only friend I have in my loneliness," she said. Asked if the tree replied to her, she answered, "Yes, it says 'I am here, I am here, I am life, eternal life.' "[2] The mythology, literature, poetry, and art of all cultures abound with stories and images of communication and emotional bonding between humans and trees. In shamanic practice, trees and other plants can be "helpers" in healing and therapeutic work.

The unfolding and growth of a tree is a metaphor for the unfolding and growth of an individual, physically, psychologically, and spiritually. It is a metaphor for a process in time, a life in progress. We sense our "roots" in the past, and our "crown" is our full future potential. As Jung states, "If a mandala may be described as a symbol of the Self in cross-section, then the tree would represent a profile view of it: the self depicted as a process of growth."[3] We explore this metaphor, and the experiential meanings of "seed," "roots," "trunk," "branches," "leaves," and "fruit."

The tree is one of a number of symbols of ascent, a theme that has already been discussed from the point of view of its role in shamanic "flight" and upper world journeys. "Climbing the tree" is metaphorically analogous to climbing the mountain, the pillar, the tower, the pyramid, or the ladder—all are journeys "upward" in consciousness, to higher states of being. The tree, mountain, pillar, tower, pyramid, ladder, or staff represents the axis of travel, the interdimensional axis that connects ego with Self (in the Jungian terminology). Moving "up" and "down" along this axis is equivalent to changing one's state and level of consciousness. There is also the associated metaphor, from ancient Egypt, of "straightening the pillar"—which symbolizes straightening the axis, so that soul or consciousness can unobstructedly leave the body, or transcend the physical level.

The tree that is climbed in shamanic and mythic lore is not only the individual's axis that links ego to Self, the personal to the transpersonal. In accord with the Hermetic principle of macro-micro correspondence—"as above, so below"—the individual's axis and the world's axis (the *axis mundi*) are aligned or connected. There is a world tree, a world mountain, a world axis, which allows the shamanic or mystic traveler to move through the realms of being and consciousness that exist on the planetary and cosmic level. The image of a world tree axis also exists in a fascinating variant, that of the inverted tree, known in Hinduism and in the Jewish Kabbalah.

The tree of life, along with its counterpart, the tree of knowledge, plays a central role in the biblical account of the creation and genesis of humanity. There are two trees in the Garden of Eden, one giving immortal life, the other giving knowledge of duality and opposites. Western civilization has evidenced an ambivalent relationship to these two principles since its beginnings. The European alchemists turned their explorations to this dual tree, which they called the philosophers' tree *(arbor philosophorum),* as well as the tree of truth or of wisdom. They sought for it *inside,* because they understood that for the transformation of consciousness to take place, one had to seek for and know this inner tree.

The Tree as a Symbol of Self-Unfoldment

The vision of man as a tree and of the world as a tree is a unitary vision in which all objects, events, processes, and structures are seen as interrelated, ramifying from a center, the axis or trunk of the tree. The historical origin of any process can always be traced to a single seed, whether we are speaking of a tree, a human life, the life of a group, of a culture, of the whole world; or the course of a self-transformation. In comparing the seed to the fully grown tree, we are considering a process of unfolding in time, as Jung stated. We can think of each one of us as a tree, or as having a tree, that started from seed and grows and develops, each year adding another "ring."

Seen this way, a tree becomes a symbolic journal, a record of a journey of an individual's growth through time. Psychologists have even used tree drawings as a way of assessing a person's own internal, largely unconscious perception of the stage they have reached in their development. Jung, for example, collected many paintings of trees by patients; these paintings reflected the particular phase and characteristics of their individuation process. The exercize of drawing this basic symbol appears to allow other parts of the mind (perhaps older parts of the brain) to express some inner knowing not normally accessible to rational intelligence.[4]

When people are asked to draw a tree, it is as if they are drawing a portrait of their life in process, in both its natural and spiritual aspects. In classes and workshops, I have guided structured imagination exercises based on this theme of the unfolding of the tree of our life. The results of this process, which may involve drawing, painting, or movement, are always highly revealing to the individual. The symbolic meanings that people discover in the tree and its parts —seed, roots, trunk, branches, leaves, fruit—are also remarkably consistent.

Seed. What, then, is the meaning of the seed of our tree? Each man and woman, each plant and animal, grows from a single seed, as do all forms of life and all growing processes. In a manner that has always impressed the student of nature's ways as nothing short of miraculous, the potential of the entire tree is somehow present in the tiny seed: as the potential of the fully developed adult human being is present in the fertilized ovum. Some clairvoyants claim to "see" the entire form of a tree in the seed kernel. In the germ cell of the human embryo, coded into the DNA coil, is packed the genetic information necessary to make a human organism. This is our material link to our parents and ancestors.

Everything that we later become, develop, express, or create is present here, in potential only, in the seed, in conception. To tune into this seed-consciousness is a process metaphorically equivalent to the journey back to the source, to our point of origin. Remember the famous Zen koan, "What was your original face before you were born or conceived?" By seeing and holding the original face in mind, we may be able to come to a better appreciation of the wonder and complexity of our existence.

If the tree of our natural human life begins with the biological seed, fertilized in the moment of conception, the treelike process of self-transformation must also begin with a "seed." This seed has been variously called a spiritual seed, or *bindu* in Sanskrit yoga terminology; the seed of enlightenment; or the seed of God. This seed is the initial idea, the *conception* that transformation is possible. It is the awakening impulse, the illuminating word or compassionate gesture of a teacher or master that initiates the process of inner growth. For example, in a Buddhist Tantric text we read,

> From the seed of pure compassion
> Planted in the field of man
> Grows the Wish-Fulfilling Tree
> Of the openness of Being.[5]

The Sanskrit term *bindu* is used in both Hindu and Buddhist Tantric yoga teachings to refer to the concentrated source seed, a kind of subtle psycho-physiological essence, the point of origin from which the processes of self unfold. The *bindu* is usually represented pictorially in the center of a mandala, which represents the whole, unified field of consciousness. The *bindu* is the center from which the process of self-transformation is initiated, from which the intrinsic divine nature is manifested. Meister Eckhart expressed it in the following beautiful analogy: "The seed of God is in us . . . it will thrive and grow up to God, whose seed it is; accordingly its fruit will be God-nature. Pear seeds grow into pear trees, nut seeds grow into nut trees, and God seeds into God."[6]

Roots. The roots of the tree symbolically represent the roots of our life in the genealogical sense: the parents, who provided the genetic base for the physical body; the grandparents; and other more distant ancestors—familial, cultural, ethnic, and racial. Tracing our roots all the way back, we come eventually to Adam and Eve, the first ancestors, the original human parents. Our true ancestry goes much further back, however, as shamanic and native cultures know well. We have animal ancestors, evolutionary forebears, earlier branches on the tree of earthly life, branches from which we ourselves branched out—going all the way back through the evolution of species.

It is not uncommon, in such imaginative explorations, to experience another kind of "roots": the past incarnations that have preceded us individually. This appears to be quite a different strand than the ancestral one. Each of the "lives," with its joys and sorrows, has left imprints or traces, what Indian philosophers call *samskaras,* in our psyche. Thus the "roots" of our tree are the residues of our past history on this earth, in this lifetime and perhaps in others. In the process of spiritual self-transformation, tracing one's roots would be analogous to the metaphor of returning to the origin by retracing one's steps. This is the place within from which we originated, and it is the place from which, like trees, we draw strength and nourishment.

An interesting commentary on and example of transformative tree symbolism was shown to me in a series of about a dozen drawings of trees done by a woman in her forties. This woman left a marriage of twenty years and three teenage children to move away and start living in a lesbian relationship. All her tree drawings showed exposed roots—they were hovering in the air. This clearly portrayed her feeling of "uprootedness," of not having firm boundaries or a foundation for the changes she was making. In Jungian terms, we would say that the "roots" are our links to the creative unconscious, from which we draw up the sap of inspiration and insight.

Trunk. The trunk of the tree is the evolving development of our psyche and our identity through life. The coming up through the ground, into the air and light, corresponds, in a plant or tree, to the moment of birth for animals and humans: for both, it is the first contact with breath and with light. Just as a tree grows in a spiraling fashion, each year adding a ring to the expanding trunk, so do we grow in recurring cycles. Each year's experiences add *samskaras,* memory traces, to the field of our psyche, which to varying degrees leave physical imprints in nerve synapse connections, muscles, blood vessels, tissues, sinews, and bones. The physical form, as the natural philosophers such as Paracelsus well understood and as modern psychologists following the pioneering work of Reich have rediscovered, develops over time into a visible record of the individual's inner state, patterns of mood, or disposition.

As an example of how the interior mental image of a tree trunk might reveal and be related to characteristics of the psyche, consider again tree drawings used as projective tests by psychologists. In such drawings, characteristics of the bark of the tree are seen as indicative of an individual's sense of his or her periphery, the "skin" of their persona, as it were. Feelings of needing a tough or rough exterior manner might be expressed in rough, thick bark; or feelings of being exposed and vulnerable to penetration, may be expressed in bark that looks faint and thin. It has even been observed that people drawing trees will indicate a physical abnormality of some kind, resulting from injury or accident, at a height on the tree corresponding to the age at which the injury or accident occurred.

The painter Paul Klee compared the artist to a tree, in language that applies equally well to anyone engaged in a process of self-transformation.

> From the roots the sap rises into the artist, flows through him and his eyes. He is the trunk of the tree. Seized and moved by the force of the current, he directs his vision into his work. Visible on all sides, the crown of the tree unfolds in space and time. . . . And so with the work. . . . In his appointed place in the tree trunk, he gathers what rises from the depths and passes it on. He neither serves nor commands, but only acts as a go-between. His position is humble.[7]

Here the tree is a metaphor of the creative artistic process and of the process of expression, of bringing out something from within. The individual is the medium, the bridge, the "trunk," that connects the matrix of the creative unconscious to the light of full expression.

Branches. The branches of the tree represent our self-extensions and relationships: the qualities, traits, characteristics, skills, and abilities we have developed, which serve to relate us to the world and to other people. With our branches we reach out, we extend ourselves; we make contact; we communicate and interact, both physically, socially, and interpersonally. A person's branching structure may be profuse, varied, and rich in associated meanings; or it may be sparse and simple, reflecting the relative simplicity of his or her personality structure and relationships.

The "branches," then, are our major "parts." Trees standing together seem to be relating and communicating through their branches. We can examine each of our "branches" and determine whether they are flowering and producing fruit or whether they have ceased to grow and have atrophied. A couple I know described to me a (physical) tree pruning operation they undertook in their yard. This event became metaphorical and psychological when they started to imagine that the dead branches they were pruning were the "dead" parts of their relationship that they desired to get rid of or change.

Leaves and flowers. The leaves and flowers of the tree are the thoughts and images of our mind: as the health and beauty of the leaves and flowers are a function of the nourishing sap rising up from below under the influence of light and warmth, so, we may suggest, the health and vitality of our thoughts and images are a function of how unobstructed their connectedness is to the instinctual nature "below," and of the mental and emotional acceptance and support they receive from "outside"—from other people and the world. The association of leaves and petals with the realm of ideas is also implicit in the Indian yoga symbolism of the "thousand-petaled lotus" *chakra* at the top of the head.

In art therapy, using tree-drawings, depressed individuals will sometimes draw bare, or even dead, trees, thereby reflecting an inner feeling of noncreative barrenness or spiritual impoverishment. Normally and naturally, ideas and concepts seem to arise, flourish, and drop out of our minds in much the same way as leaves grow, change colors, and drop off a tree. Here is another way in which both trees and humans practice "dying daily": it is good for us to remember and learn again and again that the little death of some idea of ours, of some project, plan, or vision, is not at all equivalent to the death of our identity. The tree in nature and the tree of the mind both have valuable lessons of nonattachment to teach us.

Fruits. The fruits of the tree represent the creative products that we bring forth, the results and output of our growing, self-extending activity in the world. They are the "fruits of our actions," by which we are known. They contribute to the nourishment, welfare, and delight of our fellow human beings and of all living creatures. The creative impulses begin deep inside the unconscious parts of the psyche; they then expand and develop and are eventually brought forth. "The apples in my mind are ripening," my eight-year-old son remarked one day to his grandmother apropos of nothing in particular. He was expressing a warm and exuberant mood.

Since the evolutionary function of fruit is that of a carrier of seed that will propagate the species, perhaps one of the functions of creative expression (symbolic fruit) is to carry the seed of enlightenment, the seed of growth and spirituality, to an environment that is receptive to these "seeds." Art, in other words, can be an inspiration to spiritual development and transformation: not only does it describe the process, it can stimulate and facilitate it. A Buddhist text refers to "the perfect tree of unitary mind," whose "flower, compassion, bears the fruit of being-with-others."[8] We are led thus to the conclusion that the life of an individual can be, and often is, described metaphorically as the growth and flowering of a tree. Artists and creative people, who "put out" a great deal of creative energy, are involved in externalizing something. They might correspond to flowering trees.

There is also the "tree" that represents the process of self-transformation and guides this process in its natural channels. The upward-rising growth of this tree seems to connect to the idea of "high" states, visionary states, flying, spirituality, and ascent to God. The poet Rilke, in the first of his inspired *Sonnets to Orpheus,* explored this theme of the tree of transcendence. Orpheus is the divine musician empowered to play the sacred inner sounds that cause all creatures to cease their conflicts. This mysterious subtle sound, which evokes, "calls forth," profound change, seems to "grow" in the ear.[9]

There rose a tree. O pure transcendence!
O Orpheus singing. O tall tree in the ear!

And all was silent. Yet even in the silence
There was new beginning, beckoning, change.

Climbing the Tree, Straightening the Pillar

Stories of shamans and mythic heroes climbing trees are found in native cultures all over the world. In many of the shamanic societies, particularly in central and northern Asia, the shaman describes an ascent of a tree in a dream or in a vision; this ascent leads to his or her obtaining a leaf or fruit for healing or divination.[10] The wood of the particular tree seen in the vision is used to make the shaman's drum; this links the tree to the drumbeat that serves to induce the trance, or "journey." Hallucinogenic mushrooms, such as *Amanita muscaria,* which grow in association with birch trees in Siberia, may also have been used by some shamans as part of their initiation or practice, according to R. Gordon Wasson.[11] "Climbing the tree" is a variant of the initiatory altered-state journey, in which the shamanic practitioner explores other realms of consciousness. "Tree climbing" is a type of upper world journey and thus parallels magical flight and other ascensional metaphors (climbing the mountain, pillar, ladder, and so on).

The tree that is climbed in shamanism is variously said to have nine, twelve, sixteen, or (most often) seven notches or branches on which the vision seeker ascends. These "branches," which parallel the rungs of the ladder, the steps of the ziggurat pyramid, or the layers of cloud, symbolize the levels or planes of consciousness through which the shaman ascends—the various "heavens" of his or her culture's cosmology. The Altaic Siberian shaman sings:

I have climbed a step, . . .
I have reached a plane, . . .
I have broken through the second ground,
I have climbed the second level.
See, the ground lies in splinters.[12]

This notion of levels that are separated by branches or planes is consistent with the idea, already discussed, of veils, borders, or gaps, between levels of consciousness.

The tree, then, is something like an axis that connects the different levels or dimensions. It is analogous to the axis that connects ego and Self in Jung's teaching. The ascent of the tree is a vision-seeking inner journey, undertaken while the physical body lies in a trance or coma, though the shaman may continue to speak or sing. Like other mystical, shamanic, or mythic voyages, it has three main parts: the *departure* from the everyday plane of reality, and ascent to "higher" planes; the *arrival* at the top, crown, or summit, where a healing leaf or other substance is given or a vision is offered; a *return,* the descent back to the ordinary world.

Shamanic mythology describes the tree that is climbed as a world tree, heaven tree, or cosmic tree, at the top of which may live a ruling deity. This parallels the idea of the axis mundi, the world axis, and the Mount Meru, the central mountain of the Indian tradition. These inner explorers are saying that the individual axis is aligned with the world axis, the microcosmic tree with the macrocosmic. As Eliade states,

> By climbing up the seven or nine notches of the ceremonial birch tree, or simply by drumming, the shaman sets out on his journey to heaven, but he can only obtain that rupture of the cosmic planes which makes his ascension possible or enables him to fly ecstatically through the heavens because he is thought to be already at the very centre of the world.[13]

The individual and the world are linked by a relationship of micro-macro correspondence, by analogy or co-incidence. By going to my center, my central axis, or inner tree, I can also experience the central axis, pole, or pillar of the world—the cosmic hub, the navel of the world (*omphalos*).

In many cultures, in addition to this ritual ascent of the cosmic tree, there are myths that account for human birth as a descent, a coming down the tree, a traveling from higher realms to the physical world. In Sumatra, for example, there is the myth of *djambu baros,* the heaven tree, which has leaves of different personal qualities on it. The individual soul picks several of these leaves as it descends to Earth for incarnation. In other Asiatic societies, the souls of unborn children perch on the branches of the cosmic trees—and shamans go there to find them, if necessary.

In pre-Christian Hawaiian mythology, when a person dies he or she comes to a tree, one-half of which is dead and brittle while the other is alive and green. Around the tree young children are playing; they instruct the deceased to ascend the tree on the dead side and then re-descend on the living side. This and similar myths point to the idea that the soul's initiatory ascent, at death and in special trance states (climbing the tree), is somehow a reversal of the descent into form, the birth into Earth (descending the tree).

The myth of Osiris as a metaphor for Spirit being first imprisoned and then released, as well as scattered, also has a profound connection with the tree of life motif. We remember that in the story as told by the Greek historian Plutarch, Osiris is tricked by his evil brother Set and locked in an intricately carved wooden coffer, which is thrown into a river; floating down the river, the coffer eventually comes to land, where a tree grows through and around it; finally the tree, with the god still in it, becomes the wooden framework of the house of a local king.

I propose the following interpretation of this mystic metaphor: Spirit, symbolized by Osiris, becomes enveloped, on the way "down" into material incarnation, in four stages of form, or body. The wooden chest, with its intricately carved design, probably represents the mental body, or, in Vedantist terms, the "sheath"; the flowing river is the astral or emotional body; the tree symbolizes the etheric or perceptual body, which is connected to the treelike sensory nervous system; and the house represents the physical body, where we live most of the time. Thus, according to this myth, there is something akin to a tree inside and throughout the human psyche and nervous system.

This tree inside the human psyche and body is represented in Egyptian sacred temple art: we find there the frequent portrayal of a secret ritual referred to as the "straightening of the *djed* pillar." This pillar looks like a tree trunk with its branches cut off—which makes it look like a human vertebral column as well. Sometimes two human figures (presumably priests) are shown pushing and pulling the pillar into an upright position. Sometimes ceremonial cloths are offered to or draped over the *djed;* the face or headdress of Osiris may also be painted on the pillar. In some depictions, the head of the god is mounted on the top of the pillar.

Erich Neumann has pointed out that the *djed* pillar was composed of two segments: an upper segment, corresponding to a treetop and to the neck and head of Osiris; and a lower segment, corresponding to the trunk and base of a tree and to the back and sacrum of Osiris. When a person died a small golden *djed* replica was placed around his neck, and the following prayer was uttered: "Rise up, O Osiris, thou hast thy backbone. O still Heart, thou has the ligatures of the neck and head. Place thyself upon thy base."[14]

The straightening of the *djed* pillar, which is an alignment of the upper and lower segments, seems to symbolize the union and integration of the generative with the cerebral, the physical with the spiritual, the "lower" with the "higher." Straightening the physical vertebral axis is itself a healing process, as those who have been "Rolfed" or have had their back straightened can confirm. "Straightening the *djed* pillar" is, moreover, a metaphor for the aligning of the interdimensional axis, through which the "lower" world of personality and physical body can be connected with the "higher" world of spirit and consciousness.

Within this framework of belief, placing the miniature *djed* on the dying person's heart center was believed to facilitate the "straightening of the pillar" and thus the final release of the soul from the body at the moment of death. The resurrection of Osiris is depicted in the Egyptian Book of the Dead as the Horus-Sun, who is the son of Osiris, rising out of the *djed* pillar, which is placed between the two mountains of sunset (the past) and sunrise (the future). As Neumann says, "the *djed* is therefore the material body that gives rise to the sun soul."[15]

The pillar, like the tree, symbolizes the physical body—specifically the vertebral-cerebro-spinal axis of the body—as well as symbolizing the energy-center axis that connects us with the subtler, "higher" dimensions of our being. In the Indian teachings of Tantra yoga and Hatha yoga, the vertical alignment, or straightening, of this double axis is regarded as essential to the processes of meditation and transformation. It provides the basis for the alignment of the "inner bodies" and for the "upward" and "downward" movement of awareness through the levels of our being.

Some colloquial expressions in current American usage appear to reflect the idea of an axis of some kind in our psyche—an axis that can be changed. For example, we may tell ourselves or another to "straighten up," to "straighten your act," or to "be straightforward"; these all refer to desirable psychological conditions or changes. By contrast, when we wish to refer to an unpleasant state, one that should be changed or corrected, we might speak of a "distorted attitude" or "twisted mentality." More temporarily, we could get "bent out of shape" by receiving some insult or offense; or someone could abruptly "be beside himself" with rage or another emotional shock. The latter expression in particular seems to imply that we can become "split" vertically, dissociated as well as misaligned.

The World Tree and the Inverted Tree

As already described, the individual tree that the vision seeker ascends is, in shamanic mythology, equated with the world tree, the world axis. The world axis is in the world, as the individual axis is in the body. And even though the world has the form of a rotating sphere and the human body has quite a different shape, they both have a central vertical axis. This is an example of the principle of macro-micro correspondence; or, isomorphism between person and world. Furthermore there is an axis on the physical plane, and there is the interdimensional axis that links the physical with the higher or subtler dimensions—all these are connotations of the tree symbol.

Thus because the tree-climbing visionary is able to ascend the world tree, not just the individual tree, great visions that affect all of humanity have been recorded by such seers. This is how Black Elk, the great visionary elder of the Oglala Sioux Indians, recorded his vision of the cosmic tree:

> Then I was standing on the highest mountain of them all, and round about
> me was the whole hoop of the world. . . . I was seeing in a sacred manner
> the shapes of all things in the spirit. . . . And I saw the sacred hoop of my
> people was one of the many hoops that made one circle, wide as daylight and
> as starlight, and in the center grew one mighty flowering tree to shelter all
> the children of one mother and father. And I saw that it was holy.[16]

Here the world tree is seen as the unifying center from which all forms of life on the Earth, all humans of different races, all animals, plants, and elements, branch out: all of creation is held together through this *axis mundi.*

Another vision of the world tree, from Hippolytus, bishop of Rome in the third century, is strikingly similar to that of the American Indian holy man:

> This tree, wide as the heavens itself, has grown up into heaven from the earth.
> It is an immortal growth and towers between heaven and earth. It is the

fulcrum of all things and the place where they are all at rest. It is the
foundation of the round world, the center of the cosmos. In it all the diversi-
ties in our human nature are transformed into a unity.[17]

This kind of vision is not at all limited to saints or sages: "ordinary" individuals
have had similar experiences, perhaps without recognizing their archetypal lin-
eage. The image of the world tree, when "seen" or "climbed" in an exalted state,
allows individuals to experience their connectedness to the family or tribe, to the
culture or society, to all of humanity, and to the whole of nature.

The cosmic tree is often associated with a circular or spherical form, or a
mandala, which is basically a circle in a square; or it can be associated with a
square-based pyramid or a mountain, such as the Indo-Tibetan Mount Meru.
Perhaps prophets and seers of native cultures, ancient or contemporary, could
perceive the spherical form of the planet Earth in their visions, even without the
benefit of scientific information. Thus, one meaning of the "world tree" is that
it is literally the axis of the globe. In some mythologies it is called the "pole" and
is seen as extending or attaching to the sun or to the North Star. In ancient
Chinese Taoism, it was called *t'ai chi t'u,* "the great ridge-pole" or "supreme
beginning." It was regarded as the hub that lets the *yang* and the *yin* appear in
cyclic alternation.

A similar duality of the tree symbolism is found in Navaho sacred art, where
there are sand paintings that depict the "giant corn plant." In the stalk of this
giant corn plant is the "pollen path" or "blessing way": this is shown as the
central axis of the corn plant; a male zigzag lightning stroke is shown descending
on the right, and a female curved rainbow descends on the left. This parallels the
left-female/right-male polarity of many other traditions. At the top of the tree
is a blue bird, symbolizing transcendence and the release of free inspiration and
insight.

Eagles and other birds are found in association with the top of the tree in
many cultures. These birds are regarded as the observers and messengers of the
gods; for the individual they symbolize insight, wisdom, and transcendence
(flying). The other animal most frequently associated with the tree of life is the
serpent or dragon, which is usually associated with the base, or root, of the tree.
Kundalini yoga has the image of a serpent coiled around the "root *chakra,* from
which it rises in serpentine motion to the crown *chakra.*" For the individual, the
serpent symbolizes generation, regeneration, and the instinctual knowledge associated with the reptilian. Among mammals, the deer and the horse in particular
have been found in association with the tree of life.[18]

The most elaborate symbolism of the World Tree is found in the ancient
Scandinavian myth of Yggdrasil, the giant tree called "steed of Odin," which
is the world. Its roots descend into Hel, the underworld, where the dead reside,
as well as the frost giants; and where the gods sit in council by Urd, the Well

of Fate. A giant serpent is coiled around the tree's roots, gnawing at them constantly. The trunk of the giant ash tree ascends through Midgard, the middle world of human beings and animals and plants. The branches reach upward to a crown that is Asgard, the heavenly abode of the gods, where Odin resides, with his all-seeing eagle. In one central legend, Odin voluntarily hung himself from the tree Yggdrasil for nine days and nights, in order to obtain wisdom and prophetic vision. This image of the self-sacrificing god, trapped or fixated in the physical world, parallels the images of Osiris in the coffer tree and Christ on the cross.

The Nordic myth of *Ragnarök,* the "twilight of the gods," is that the Earth trembles as the tree shakes, and the roots come loose from the constant gnawing of the serpent, which symbolizes the destructive forces of time, entropy, decay, and degeneration. The great tree, however, continues, ever renewing itself and nourishing the life of animals and humans.

This kind of end-of-the-world vision, of a world falling apart and becoming uprooted, can occur in the course of a transformative process, as is shown in the following account (by a thirty-five-year old man) of an LSD experience, which also included interior yogic energy work:

> I felt as though deep-seated, very old complexes were being loosened, released, and discharged into open awareness, in a manner that felt like the uprooting of deeply tangled root systems. As these sick and decaying roots were being pulled up, analogously to a kind of weeding-out process, I felt my body shaking, going through miniconvulsions. Since my awareness and my sense of identity were "in" my body, it felt like the whole environment—my whole "world," in fact—was shaking and convulsing. I felt that in this upheaval, a whole era in my life and in the life of the world was coming to an end. The rule of the old gods was ending.

This experience suggests one possible psychological basis for the myth of the twilight of the gods: it represents the ending and dying of the old religious values and beliefs, including beliefs about the stability and continuity of the world. In archetypal mythology this dying is followed by a renewal and rebirth.

A fascinating variant of the cosmic tree symbolism occurs in the ancient Indian Vedas and Upanishads and in the Jewish mystical Kabbalah. In both of these traditions, the tree is described as having its roots above, in heaven, in the Infinite, and extending its branches downward into the world of sense objects and matter.

> With the root above and the branches below stands this ancient fig tree. That indeed is the pure; that is *Brahman.* That, indeed, is called immortal. In it all the worlds rest. (From the *Katho Upanishad)*[19]

> Now the Tree of Life extends from above downwards, and is the sun which illuminates all. (From the *Book of Zohar)*[20]

This symbolism of the inverted tree emphasizes that the true origin, root, and source of our life is Spirit, both individual and cosmic—in the *Atman-Brahman* or the *Ain Soph,* the Infinite and Eternal. The downward-extending branches are our sense perceptions and emotional desires, through which we become attached to terrestrial Nature. In India, the banyan tree, which sends down long aerial branches that form new roots in the ground, became a paramount symbol of the power of sense-based attachments. The idea that our source or origin is "above," in the "higher" world, agrees with previously mentioned myths describing birth as a descent from the world tree.

The Kabbalistic Tree of Life is pictured as an array of three vertical axes, with ten circles aligned on them: these represent the *sephirah,* the emanations, or divine powers, that bring cosmic life energy from God down into the world. The tree diagram is also applied to the human psychic constitution; and when it is laid over the human body, we have a close analog to the Indian *chakra* system. The Indian system, instead of having three parallel axes, has one central channel *(sushumna)* and two serpentine side channels, one solar-right and one lunar-left. (These are retained in the Greek *caduceus* staff, with two coiling serpents, that became the emblem for the art of healing.) The Kabbalistic analogy with the yogic *chakra* system is seen further in the fact that the topmost *sephiroth* on the central axis, which is situated at the crown of the head in the human body, is known as *Kether* (Crown); this is also the place of the "thousand-petaled lotus," or crown *chakra,* in Indian yoga.

We can see that the idea of an inverted tree, rooted "above," representing the human body and consciousness situated in this world, is a natural and meaningful elaboration of the basic themes behind the tree of life symbolism. In the Kabbalah, as in yoga, there exists a subtle and sophisticated psychology and technology for the transformation of human consciousness—and the tree or axis symbolism is central to both of these systems.

The Tree of Life and the Tree of Truth

The tree of life, of course, plays a major role in the Hebrew Old Testament, as well as in the Christian New Testament. In the Book of Genesis account, two trees stand in the center of the Garden of Eden, and four rivers flow out from the center. In the vision of the Book of Revelation, the "river of the water of life, sparkling as crystal," flows from the throne of God; a tree of life stands on either side of it, bearing twelve kinds of fruit and having leaves "for the healing of nations."

Other ancient cultures also have the image of two trees that play a central role in myths of the origin of humanity. Instead of the Judaeo-Christian tree of the knowledge of good and evil, certain myths have a tree of wisdom or a tree of truth. The focus on the dualism of moral judgment that has literally "bedeviled" Judaeo-Christian civilization is expressed in the original emphasis on "knowledge of good and evil." In other ancient religions, particularly those that worshipped the Great Goddess, the tree, the serpent, and the woman were regarded quite differently: it was through them that men were taught the mysteries of death, regeneration, and longevity. Only in the biblical account is the tree taboo and the serpent the instigator of sin.

It has long been widely accepted that two or more different accounts are interwoven in Genesis. Recent researches by feminist scholars have suggested that the earlier account is that of a Tree-Serpent-Goddess mystery religion, such as those of Isis, Astarte, and Ishtar; and that the popularly accepted version, which regards the woman as succumbing to the temptation of the serpent, then in turn leading the man into sin, is a priestly overlay, imposed in order to support the newly emerged patriarchal, male-dominant monotheism.[21] The fragments that remain of the original story suggest that the tree of life had to do with healing and longevity, and the tree of knowledge with wisdom. The serpent is the one who initiates the woman into evolutionary knowledge, the knowledge of survival and regeneration.

According to the Book of Genesis, God forbids Adam and Eve to eat of the tree of knowledge, because "on the day that you eat from it, you will surely die." The serpent, however, tells Eve that "of course you will not die . . . your eyes will be opened and you will be as gods, knowing both good and evil." Thus, the fruit of the tree of knowledge causes Eve and Adam to awaken, to open their eyes, to gain awareness and insight into their true nature. The serpent, it turns out, is right—at least in part: Adam and Eve do not die from the fruit, but they do become aware of their sexuality, experience shame, and are subsequently expelled from Eden.

God is apparently concerned that they might now "take from the Tree of Life also, and live forever."[22] This strange statement, attributed to God, supports the connection of the tree of life with ancient mysteries of regeneration and longevity. (The very long lives of the biblical patriarchs, including Adam, who reportedly lived 930 years, also support this notion.)

After Adam and Eve depart from the Garden of Eden, they have to gain their bread "by the sweat of [their] brow," instead of being able to eat the abundant fruit of the garden effortlessly. In other words, they have to learn to survive in the physical world. Likewise they are told that they are now mortal: "dust you are and to dust you shall return." So the descent, or departure, from Eden is like the descent into physical incarnation, down from the spiritual level of being-consciousness that is called Eden (or Paradise, or the Garden, or Heaven, or the Pure Land). A text by the fourteenth-century Arabic alchemical philosopher Abul Kasim gives the esoteric interpretation:

> The prime matter . . . of the elixir is taken from a single tree which grows in the lands of the West. . . . This is the tree of which whosoever eats, men and *jinn* [spirits] obey him. It is also the tree of which Adam (peace be upon

him) was forbidden to eat, and when he ate thereof he was transformed from
his angelic form to his human form."[23]

Some authors have suggested that the tree of life represents the central
vertical axis, with its energy centers and branching channels, that allows us to
connect with the higher, spiritual realms within. This would explain the reference
to Adam's "angelic form" and the idea that by eating of this tree, Adam and Eve
would "become like gods." The fruit of this tree is the divine energy essence,
referred to in other traditions as the nectar and ambrosia of the gods, the divine
soma juice, or the *amrita,* the "drink of immortality."

According to this view, which to me has a great deal of plausibility, the tree
of knowledge, or of truth, corresponds to the cerebrospinal and sensory nervous
system; this is clearly a treelike branching structure, the function of which is to
give us knowledge of the physical world of matter and of how to survive in Nature
—that is, what is good to eat and what is not. Each human being, following in
the footsteps of Adam and Eve, descends into physical bodily incarnation from
the higher, spiritual plane, and in doing so is plunged necessarily into the realm
of dualities and of mortality. This is not, however, a punishment for disobeying
God's word; it is, rather, the inevitable consequence of the decision to descend
into physical, human form.

"Eating the fruit" of the tree of knowledge is a metaphor for experiencing
sensations and sense objects, in all their attractiveness. Sense perception is inherently linked with dualistic judgments—of what is pleasurable and what painful;
what is nourishing and "good" to eat and what is toxic and therefore to be rejected
as "bad," or "evil." Especially potent among the objects of the senses are of course
sexual stimuli, which awaken the sex centers in the reptilian layers of the brain.
The wisdom of the serpent includes, among other things, the "knowing" of
sexuality, of reproduction and species survival.

Jesus Christ spoke of the serpentine wisdom initiation when he counseled
his disciples to "be gentle as doves and wise as serpents." According to Christian
tradition, Christ was the "second Adam," who completed the cycle begun by the
first Adam. The first Adam committed the "original sin," which brought us into
mortality and separation from God; Christ, the second Adam, brings redemption,
rebirth, and union with God. In developing these parallels further, we see that
Christ's cross was identified with the original tree in the Garden. The legend of
the Holy Rood arose: according to this legend some wood from the tree of life
was taken out of Eden and many generations later was used to make the cross
of the crucifixion.

Christ is nailed to the cross (symbolically equivalent to the tree), as Odin
is hung on the tree and as Osiris is encased in the coffer-tree: these are all
representations of the god, of Spirit, becoming attached, transfixed, and identified
with the material world. Like these great Spirits, we are all, through the structure

of the human nervous system itself (the "tree"), caught in the crucifix of dual opposites—good and bad, pleasure and pain, craving and aversion. Each of these myths also points to the release from bondage, the resurrection, the overcoming of pain, death, and the limitations of the physical world.

The world tree, cosmic tree, or tree of life, also plays a central role in other world religions. In the legend of the historical Buddha, it is told that he sat under a *bodhi* (wisdom) tree, until he attained *nirvana* and realized complete enlightenment. It was said that the cobra king came and spread his hood over Buddha's head to protect him against heat and rain—an image that echoes again the ancient serpent-tree connection. In the famous Night Journey of Muhammad, the prophet descended into hell, where he found the infernal thorn tree, planted for the torment of the wicked; when he ascended to paradise, he found at the center of it the miraculous tuba tree, hung with rubies, sapphires, and emeralds. This jewel-bedecked tree is a theme echoed in alchemy.

The association of the tree of life with the processes of spiritual transformation and initiation—found in the mythic-sacred traditions of shamanism and of ancient Egypt, Mesopotamia, Scandinavia, and India, as well as in the world religions of Judaism, Buddhism, Islam, and Christianity—is continued and developed in the Hermetic-alchemical philosophy. Because the alchemists were concerned with Nature as a living, divinely infused interrelated totality and with the transmutation and spiritualization of matter, their use of the tree symbol plays some interesting variations on the orthodox Judeo-Christian version.

There are alchemical drawings that depict the tree of life with Hermes Trismegistos, the sage and master, standing beneath it, instead of Adam and Eve; this Hermes is shown both as old man *(senex)* and as youth *(puer)*. Here the symbolism points to the regenerative potency of the tree. Another alchemical text offers the following recipe for transformation: "Take the tree and place in it a man of great age. The old man does not cease to eat of the fruit of that tree, until he becomes a youth."[24] In other words, by tapping into our inner tree of life and eating its fruit, we can overcome or reverse the processes of aging and dying. Elsewhere, the fruit of the tree is likened to *manna,* the bread of life, and to the healing *panacea,* the divine tincture of immortality.

In George Ripley's *Scrowle,* an alchemical text extensively quoted by Jung, there is a picture of a tree with a serpent, which is half woman *(Melusina),* coming down; a male figure is climbing up the tree to meet her halfway. This is in striking contrast, as Jung points out, to the biblical story of Adam and Eve, who are led into error through the tree and try to hide themselves. It is more consonant with the idea, found in ancient Goddess religions, where the serpent-woman was revered and worshipped as the guardian and teacher of sacred natural wisdom.

Sometimes the tree in alchemy is described as being "in the sea" and likened to a tree of branching coral. I suggest here that the "tree in the sea" refers to the vegetative (autonomic) nervous system—which is embedded in the fluid matrix of blood vessels and lymphatic and endocrine systems. These three systems together constitute what alchemists called "our inner sea," the continuum of fluids within our organism. Here, alchemical symbolism communicates experiential physiology: organic processes and structures that were observed by the alchemical experimenters to be taking place in the "retort" of the human body.

The notion that the tree is physical, in and of the nature of the physical body, esoterically connected to the vegetative and sensory-motor nervous systems, is hinted at in a mysterious verse from a poem by William Blake:

> The Gods of the earth and sea
> Sought thro' Nature to find this tree;
> But their search was all in vain:
> There grows one in the Human Brain.[25]

There is also an interesting drawing by Blake of a figure he had seen in a vision; the figure, he said, taught him painting. It is a strange androgynous-looking face, with wide-set eyes and a kind of tree form growing between the eyes, up over the forehead. These visions and experiences of Blake are clearly of an alchemical nature and suggest that one meaning of the tree of knowledge is that it consists of our brain and nervous system.

In dreams, meditations, or visions, people not infrequently envision a tree-like structure in their head or branches coming out of their head; Jung, in his essay on "The Philosophical Tree," reproduced a number of paintings of trees done by patients, many of which showed a tree emerging out of the woman's head; this is an image also found in alchemical graphics.[26] It is suggestive of a tree of mind or of ideas; and is congruent with the expression "to explore the ramifications (literally, the "branchings") of an idea."

Another alchemical inner-tree vision occurred in an altered state of consciousness induced by the empathogenic substance MDMA. A forty-year-old woman described her experience as follows:[27]

> Strong sense that my head is expanding . . . feel like there's a small tree in my head. R [the guide] must see the tree. I am a tree and he sees it. Tree in my head expands . . . branches in my head and arm; torso becomes trunk; legs and feet become roots . . . combination of old roots and new branches . . . I'm attempting to integrate the old and the new.

One gets a strong sense here of the tree image as an integrative psychic structure, a thought form or symbol that can hold the many diverse parts and aspects of the psyche, including ideas, feelings, perceptions, and sensations, in a unitive form or pattern.

For the alchemists, then, the tree of knowledge has little to do with the making of judgments—separating good and bad; it is more a symbol for inner "seeing," for insight into the inner structure of things, for seeing how everything hangs together. To them, and to those who follow their work today, the tree symbol is a vast reservoir of imagery and psychic energy. The "tree of the philosophers" is, to the alchemist, the axis of the transformational work, the unfolding *opus*. I find it highly significant that the Old English root word for "tree" and for "truth" is the same; it is *treow*. Perhaps this means that you are "straight" as a tree when you speak the truth.

From an elemental point of view, the alchemists' tree of truth and transformation is both watery and fiery: watery through its connection to fluids, to the humors and hormones, the emotional nature; and fiery through its expression of electrical life energy, vitality, and regenerative potency. Typically, the dual nature, as fire and water, was also portrayed in alchemical art as the sun-moon tree; sun was always above on the right of the tree, moon usually above on the left.

Alchemical experimenters, students of the art of transmutation of matter, observed the operations in their retorts—in both the outer and the inner retort (read "body")—the way a clairvoyant seer might observe a crystal ball or a geomantic pattern of lines. In the visions and images seen, they were advised to watch for the appearance of the tree in the retort and to contemplate its growth. The vision of the tree was considered a highly desirable and auspicious sign.

Instead of bearing conventional fruit, alchemical or vision trees are apt to be hung with many jewels and precious metals. These symbolize the gems of understanding and insight we have discovered, the pearls of wisdom we have been fortunate enough to find and express creatively. Hence, the seeming hyperbole of praise often showered on the tree in alchemical literature. A text attributed to the Jewish Gnostic adept Simon Magus, who was a contemporary of Jesus and the disciples, states, "Of all things which are both concealed and manifested, . . . the supercelestial fire is the treasure house, as it were, a great tree . . . from which all things are nourished."[28]

This is none other than the great, multidimensional tree of life energy and wisdom, the prime foundation and axis of our physical and spiritual life. This is indeed the tree of life and of truth, whose roots are nourished in the soil of our "earth," the physical ground of our being, the awakening darkness of matter; and whose crown reaches up to the heights and absorbs into itself the radiating energy essence of light, awareness and Spirit.

Notes and References

Introduction

1. Andrew Greeley and William McCready, "Are We a Nation of Mystics?" *New York Times Magazine,* 16 January 1975. A follow-up study was reported by L. Eugene Thomas and Pamela Cooper: "Incidence and Psychological Correlates of Intense Spiritual Experiences," *Journal of Transpersonal Psychology,* 12, no. 1 (1980). These authors found the same overall percentages of reported spiritual experiences but noted that there were great differences in the kinds of experiences. They also showed that having such spiritual experiences was correlated with indices of psychological flexibility, and not with anxiety or psychopathology.

2. Of the many recent works on this theme, the following are representative: O. W. Markley et al., *Changing Images of Man;* Marilyn Ferguson, *The Aquarian Conspiracy;* Alvin Toffler, *The Third Wave;* and Fritjof Capra, *The Turning Point.*

3. Sri Aurobindo: "In the previous stages of evolution Nature's first care and effort had to be directed toward a change in physical organization, for only so could there be a change of consciousness. . . . But in man a reversal is possible, indeed inevitable; for it is through his consciousness, through its transmutation and no longer through a new bodily organism . . . that evolution can and must be affected" (Satprem, *Sri Aurobindo, or The Adventure of Consciousness,* p. 316).

Erich Jantsch: "Evolution, or order of process, is more than just a paradigm for the biological domain; it is a view of how a totality that hangs together in all of its interactive processes moves. This dynamic totality spans a vast spectrum from subatomic processes to social and further on to noetic (mental and psychic) processes" (in *Evolution and Consciousness: Human Systems in Transition,* ed. Erich Jantsch and Conrad H. Waddington, p. 9).

Other books that present a comprehensive evolutionary theory, including prebiological processes, the total planet, and the spiritual dimensions, are Pierre Teilhard de Chardin's *The Phenomenon of Man;* Arthur Young's *The Reflexive Universe;* and Peter Russell's *The Global Brain.*

4. Lama Anagarika Govinda, from *Foundations of Tibetan Mysticism:* "Completeness can only be established within ourselves through a thorough transformation of our personality . . . a transformation of the *skandhas,* i.e., a change or reversal *(pravritti)* of the very foundations of our existence" (p. 82). Govinda goes on to spell out how, for example, perception of form *(rupa-skandha),* is transformed into transcendent awareness of emptiness *(sunyata).* In each case, a previously ego-centered, limited mode of functioning changes into a relational, interdependent, interconnected mode.

5. Michael Murphy and Rhea White, *The Psychic Side of Sports.* Another work, based on personal experience, that describes and discusses the potential for physical transformation is *The Mind of the Cells,* by Satprem. This book, whose subtitle is *Willed Mutation of Our Species,* presents the experience of Sri Aurobindo's associate The Mother.

6. Freud's analogy of the oceanic unconscious and Reich's idea of the character armor are scattered widely throughout their writings. Jung's night-sky metaphor is perhaps less well-known. In his essay "On the Nature of the Psyche" *(The Structure and Dynamics of the Psyche),* he writes, "We would do well to think of ego-consciousness as being surrounded by a multitude of little luminosities" (p. 190); further, referring with obvious affinity to Paracelsus' views, he says, "He beholds the darksome psyche as a star-strewn night-sky, whose planets and fixed constellations represent the archetypes in all their luminosity and numinosity" (p. 195).

7. George Lakoff and Mark Johnson, *Metaphors We Live By.* The authors, trained in linguistics and philosophy, do not say much about the psychological aspects of metaphors. They do, however, include in their discussion some speculations about what they call the experiential basis of metaphors. "We feel that no metaphor can ever be comprehended or even adequately represented independently of its experiential basis" (p. 19).

It is interesting that psychologists studying artistic development in children have become convinced of the importance of metaphoric processes in the life of the individual. Howard Gardner, in *Art, Mind, and Brain,* writes, "We can discern metaphor in the very first forms of learning, in which the child searches out commonalities in objects or situations known to be different, and then proceeds to behave in a similar fashion toward comparable elements" (p. 166).

Classic discussions of metaphor, from a literary point of view, may be found in *Metaphor and Reality,* by Philip Wheelwright. He writes: "What really matters in a metaphor is the psychic depth at which the things of the world, whether actual or fancied, are transmuted by the cool heat of the imagination. The transmutative process that is involved may be described as semantic motion; the idea of which is implicit in the very word 'metaphor,' since the motion (phora) that the word connotes is a semantic motion —the double imaginative act of outreaching and combining that essentially marks the metaphoric process" (p. 72)

Of the numerous other applications of metaphoric thinking in psychology, we might mention here only (1) the use of metaphors in psychotherapy, as described, for example, in David Gordon's *Therapeutic Metaphors,* and (2) the use of metaphors in learning and problem solving, as developed by Synectics (see W. J. Gordon, *The Metaphorical Way of Learning and Knowing).*

8. Evelyn Underhill, *Mysticism.* p. 79.

9. In her 1984 doctoral dissertation at the California Institute of Integral Studies ("Goddesses and Gods as Vehicles for Self-development: An Application of Jungian Theory in a Group Process"), Sandra Lewis showed that a group process in which men and women worked imaginatively with the myths of Greek gods and goddesses had a significant effect on their perception of their own identity.

Notes and References

10. Two useful general reference books on symbolism are *Symbolism: The Universal Language,* by J. C. Cooper, and *A Dictionary of Symbols,* by J. E. Cirlot. Funk and Wagnall's *Standard Dictionary of Folklore, Mythology, and Legend* is an invaluable source for the cross-cultural exploration of symbols.

11. *The Structure and Dynamics of the Psyche,* pp. 336, 409.

12. Buckminster Fuller, *Synergetics.* In his inimitable style, Fuller says, "Omnidirectional consideration as generalized conceptual pattern integrity requires an inherently regenerative nucleus of conceptual observation reference" (p. 613).

13. William James, *Varieties of Religious Experience,* p. 157.

14. Mircea Eliade, *Ordeal by Labyrinth,* p. 154.

15. William James, *op. cit.,* p. 319; Evelyn Underhill, *Mysticism,* p. 81.

16. C. G. Jung, "Concerning Rebirth," in *The Archetypes and the Collective Unconscious.*

17. R. Gordon Wasson, Carl A. P. Ruck, and Albert Hofmann, *The Road to Eleusis. Unveiling the Secret of the Mysteries.*

18. A. K. Coomaraswamy, "On Being in One's Right Mind," in *Selected Papers,* ed. Roger Lipsey. The author writes: "Metanoia is a transformation of one's whole being, from human thinking to divine understanding . . . and the birth of a new man." This important essay has been reprinted in *Re-Vision* 5, no. 2, (fall 1982).

19. Ken Wilber, *The Atman Project.* Wilber says he is extending the stages of development, as laid out in Western child psychology, to the transpersonal realms described in Asian psychologies. One could argue that he is describing transpersonal development on the basis of an analogy with child development, or using child development as a metaphor for transpersonal development.

20. William Bridges, *Transitions, Making Sense of Life's Changes.*

21. Satprem, *Sri Aurobindo, or The Adventure of Consciousness,* p. 316.

22. Adolf Portmann, "Metamorphosis in Animals: The Transformation of the Individual and the Type," in *Man and Transformation,* Papers from the Eranos Yearbooks, 5. "The concept of metamorphosis employed by Goethe and still used by comparative morphology: the divergent forms successively embodying a fundamental type or blueprint. . . . All theories of evolution deal with such metamorphoses, and accordingly seek to determine how one fundamental type develops from another" (pp. 297–325).

23. Julian Huxley, "On Psychometabolism," *Journal of Neuropsychiatry* 3, no. 1 (August 1962); also in *Psychedelic Review* 2 (fall 1963).

24. Evelyn Underhill, *op. cit.,* p. 179. Using the imagery of liberation that we discuss in chapter 3, Underhill adds, "the deeper mind stirs uneasily in its prison, and its emergence is but the last of many efforts to escape."

25. Cognitive psychologists have concerned themselves with this distinction of lasting v. temporary changes by differentiating "states" from "traits." For example, a widely used test designed by Charles Spielberger measures "state anxiety," the current level of anxiety; and "trait anxiety," the relatively stable tendency to be anxious. William James concerned himself with the same issue by asking the question whether a conversion experience, or a religious experience, though positive in itself, would necessarily lead to the development of "saintliness," i.e., enduring personality traits with similar qualities.

26. Descriptions of the miraculous features of the Buddha's "body of transformation" *(nirmanakaya)* abound in the Buddhist literature. One early text, quoted by Govinda in *Foundations of Tibetan Mysticism,* refers to the Lord's form, "adorned with eighty minor signs and thirty-two major signs of a great man, . . . full of splendor and virtue, incomparable and fully awakened" (p. 216). Another text describes with great wealth of detail the many kinds of multicolored radiance issuing from the body of the Teacher.

The description of the Taoist sage, who corresponds, in the Western tradition, to the hermit "hiding his light," is found in verse 15 of the *Tao Te Ching.* "Tentative, as if fording a river in winter / Hesitant, as if in fear of his neighbors / Formal, like a guest / Falling apart, like thawing ice / Thick, like an uncarved block / Empty, like a valley / Obscure, like muddy water. Who can be muddy and yet, settling, slowly become clear?"

27. Under the category diminution of personality, Jung discusses the primitive's "loss of soul" and Janet's term *abaissement du niveau mental:* "It is a slackening of the tensity of consciousness, which might be compared to a low barometric reading. . . . The tonus has given way, and this is felt subjectively as listlessness, moroseness, and depression." This can occur as a result of fatigue, illness, violent emotions, shock, and, modern psychologists would add, stress. Elsewhere in the same essay, "Concerning Rebirth," Jung writes of changes of internal structure that are neither enlargement nor diminution. Possession is an example, which is "identity of the ego-personality with a complex." Identification with the persona, the social mask; with the inferior, unconscious function; with anima or animus; with deceased ancestors; or with a group or a cult hero are all listed by Jung as examples of this kind of transformation (C. G. Jung, *op. cit.,* pp. 120–128).

28. Jung, in the essay cited above, describes "transcendence of life" experiences, either induced by ritual or occurring "in the form of a spontaneous, ecstatic, or visionary experience." These are experiences "in which the spectator becomes involved though his nature is not necessarily changed. . . . These more aesthetic forms of experience must be carefully distinguished from those which indubitably involve a change of one's nature."

Ken Wilber, in his writings on transpersonal developmental theory, seems to confuse the two processes. Developmental transformation, for him, is a series of transcending movements of consciousness, from lower to higher levels. For example, in *A Sociable God* he writes, "As we turn to transformative or vertical development, . . . in order for an individual to transform to the next higher level, he or she has, in effect, to accept the death of the present level of adaptation. . . . It is only when the self is strong enough to die to that level that it can transcend that level, that is, transform to the next higher level of phase-specific truth, food, manna" (p. 53).

Sri Aurobindo, in his writings, distinguishes between transcendence as ascent, and transformation as ascent followed by descent: "one rises to higher and higher levels of consciousness, but at the same time one brings down their power not only into mind and life, but in the end even into the body." This is also, I believe, the significance of the mysterious passage in the Hermetic "Emerald Tablet": "It rises from the earth to the heavens, and again descends to the earth, and receives the power of things superior and inferior. By this means thou shalt have the glory of the world."

29. *Chuang Tsu: Inner Chapters,* trans. Gia-Fu Feng and Jane English, p. 136.

CHAPTER 1   Awakening from the Dreams of Reality

1.   From an unpublished account by James Mahood, California Institute of Integral Studies; quoted by permission.

2.   "The Gospel of Truth" is one of the newly discovered Gnostic texts, published in *The Nag Hammadi Library* (ed. James M. Robinson). The "nightmare parable" reads, in part, as follows:

> They were sunk in sleep and found themselves in disturbing dreams. Either there is a place to which they are fleeing, or, without strength they come from having chased after others, or they are involved in striking blows, or they are receiving blows themselves, or they have fallen from high places, or they take off into the air though they do not even have wings. . . . When those who are going through all these things wake up, they see nothing, they who are in the midst of all these disturbances, for they are nothing. . . . They leave them behind like a dream in the night. (p. 43)

Other excellent discussions of Gnostic thought are found in Elaine Pagels' *The Gnostic Gospels:* and in Jacques Lacarrière's *The Gnostics.* The passage quoted from the latter work continues: "Hermes is one of their favorite gods, because he is the personification of 'The Wide Awake,' the god to whom Homer attributed the power 'to awaken, with his golden wand, the eyes of those who sleep.' . . . There is a quest for an asceticism and a specific power: to the ability to keep one's eyes open, to refuse sleep, to awaken to a true consciousness of oneself." (pp. 22–23).

3.   The Diamond Sutra and The Heart Sutra are published, in translation by Edward Conze, in *Buddhist Wisdom Books.*

4.   Nagarjuna's commentary is quoted in the work cited above (note 3) pp. 68–70.

5.   Selections from Gregory of Nyssa's writings are published in a volume entitled *From Glory to Glory.* The passage on Angelic Vigilance is found on p. 243.

6.   An excellent brief introduction to modern sleep and dream research is *Some Must Watch While Some Must Sleep,* by William Dement.

7.   The association of awakening with "up" and of going to sleep with "down" seems to hold in several different languages, although there are some interesting variations. This would provide a fascinating study in linguistics, illustrating both the pervasiveness of metaphor and some aspects of the structure of human consciousness. In German, one says *einschlafen,* literally "to sleep inward," and *aufwachen,* literally "to awaken open." Here we have an associated metaphor of closing within, and opening outward. In French one says *s'endormir,* literally "to sleep inward" (comparable to the German expression); and

se reveiller, literally "to reveal oneself"—again the notion of closing and opening. The last expression we shall encounter again in the next chapter, in connection with the symbolism of veils and reveiling (revelation).

8.   A large amount of interesting work has been published in recent years about lucid dreaming. Stephen LaBerge has done research on learning to enter voluntarily and control lucid dreaming; see his book *Lucid Dreaming*. Some useful books are *Creative Dreaming,* by Patricia Garfield; *Dream Reality,* by James Donahoe; and *Living Your Dreams,* by Gayle Delaney. There are several dream research networks, with their own journals and newsletters. A newsletter written by leading consciousness researcher Charles Tart has recently published enormously interesting material on how to learn and use lucid dreaming (*The Open Mind,* P.O. Box 371, El Cerrito, CA 94530).

9.   In Castaneda's books, lucid, consciously controlled dreaming is referred to as *dreaming,* or "dreaming," and several techniques are described for learning to become lucid in a dream, such as looking at one's own hand in the dream. Flying dreams play a major role in many shamanic cultures and are analogous to what are called "upper world journeys," i.e., altered states of consciousness in which one appears to be moving upward. Mircea Eliade, in his book *Shamanism,* writes: "The shaman's instruction often takes place in dreams. It is in dreams that the pure sacred life is entered and direct relations with the gods, spirits, and ancestral souls are re-established. It is in dreams that historical time is abolished and the mythical time regained—which allows the future shaman to witness the beginnings of the world, . . . the primordial mythic revelations" (p. 103).

10.   Tibetan dream yoga teachings and practices are described in W. Y. Evans-Wentz's *Tibetan Yoga and Secret Doctrines* and are also referred to in Patricia Garfield's book *Creative Dreaming.* Evans-Wentz writes: "As a result of these methods, the yogin enjoys as vivid consciousness in the dream-state as in the waking state. . . . Thereby the content of the dream-state is found to be quite the same as that of the waking state, in that it is wholly phenomenal, and therefore, illusory" (p. 216 n.). Mutual dreams, which present the strongest challenge to the conventional view of reality, are described and discussed in *Dream Reality,* by James Donahoe.

11.   A very useful collection of articles on kundalini was published as *Kundalini, Evolution, and Enlightenment* (ed. John White). In this work, Swami Rama quotes the eminent nineteenth-century authority on the Indian Tantras, Sir John Woodroffe: "When kundalini sleeps in the muladhara, man is awake to the world; when she awakes to unite, and does unite, with the supreme consciousness which is Shiva, then consciousness is asleep to the world and is one with the Light of all things" (p. 33). The kundalini energy is always conceived of as female, the Mother, Shakti, full of enormous power; and she is said to unite with her consort Shiva, in the crown center, who represents pure consciousness, without energy or power.

12.   Daniel Goleman, *Varieties of Meditative Experience,* p. 116.

13.   The clearest exposition of Gurdjieff's ideas regarding the sleeplike characteristics of ordinary consciousness are in P. D. Ouspensky's *In Search of the Miraculous,* especially pp. 142–145. Gurjieff says: "man can be a self-conscious being. Such he is created and such he is born. But he is born among sleeping people, and, of course, he falls asleep among them just at the very time when he should have begun to be conscious of himself."

14.　The passage from Saint Teresa is quoted from William James' *Varieties of Religious Experience* (p. 314); the one by Ramakrishna is from *The Gospel of Sri Ramakrishna,* p. 257.

15.　Studies of the physiological and psychological changes occurring in meditation have demonstrated two quite different kinds of responses, depending on the type of meditation, which correspond to the distinction made here. The book *Altered States of Consciousness* (ed. Charles Tart) contains the accounts of these studies. In one study of Indian yogis, it was observed that when they were absorbed in deep meditation *(samadhi),* their brain-wave recordings did not show the usual kind of response to outer stimuli, such as lights, sounds, and so on. In other words, they had become oblivious to the external world; they had transcended it. A different study used Zen meditators and noted that habituation—which is the normal diminishing of brain response to outer stimuli—did *not* occur. This suggests that while meditating, these meditators were not absorbed but rather more alert and attentive to all kinds of stimuli than normally. Several interesting reviews of current meditation research have appeared: one is by G. Boals, "Toward Cognitive Reconceptualization of Meditation," *Journal of Transpersonal Psychology* 10, no. 2 (1978): 143–182; another, by D. H. Shapiro, "Meditation as an Altered State of Consciousness," *Journal of Transpersonal Psychology* 15, no. 1, (1983): 61–81.

16.　The story of Black Elk is told in John Neihardt's *Black Elk Speaks,* pp. 271–272.

17.　Gopi Krishna's account of his kundalini experiences is in his book *Kundalini: The Evolutionary Energy in Man.*

18.　1 Corinthians 15:51–52. In the New English Bible, the word *sleep* has been replaced with *die;* which omits the metaphor of sleep and simply conveys the straightforward idea that we are totally changed at the moment of death.

19.　The quotation from D. T. Suzuki is from his essay on "The Awakening of a New Consciousness in Zen," in *Man and Transformation* (ed. Joseph Campbell).

CHAPTER 2　Uncovering the Veils of Illusion

1.　*The Life and Teachings of Naropa,* trans. Herbert V. Guenther, p. 63.

2.　William James, *Varieties of Religious Experience,* p. 183.

3.　From the *Visuddimagga,* by Buddhaghosa; quoted by Edward Conze in *Buddhist Wisdom Books,* p. 68. The concept of avidya plays a central role in both Hindu and Buddhist philosophy, paralleling the centrality of the notion of the unconscious in Western depth psychology. In the Sankhya-Yoga philosophy, for instance, avidya is the first and most important of the five "afflictions," or "impairments" *(kleshas),* that condition consciousness. The main difference is that according to Western psychology, the unconscious is the source of neurotic and psychotic complexes and symptoms, whereas in the Asian teachings, all human beings are blinded or afflicted by avidya: it is our blindness to the spiritual realities of our existence.

4. Quotation from "The Cloud of Unknowing," in Evelyn Underhill's *Mysticism,* p. 350.

5. William James, *op. cit.,* p. 129.

6. Edward Conze, *Buddhist Wisdom Books,* pp. 93–95. There are said to be three kinds of "thought coverings": those that stem from wrong actions in the past; those that arise from the defilements, such as hate, greed, and so on; and those that arise from false beliefs about the nature of reality. The phrase "the unobstructed universe" is from the book of the same title by Stewart Edward White.

7. From the *Atma Bodha* of Shankaracharya, translated by Ramamurti Mishra as *Self Analysis and Self Knowledge,* no. 63.

8. Eliot Deutsch's *Advaita Vedanta* is an excellent discussion of the Vedanta philosophy.

> "In the writings of Shankara . . . the terms *maya* and *avidya* come to be used interchangeably, with avidya actually taking precedence over maya in the explanation of bondage and freedom. When asked "what is the cause of our bondage, of our not realizing Brahman?" the answer most frequently given is avidya, ignorance. And in describing the process of avidya, Shankara introduces one of his most significant and interesting notions, that of *adhyasa,* which means "superimposition." (p. 33)

9. Gopi Krishna, *Kundalini: The Evolutionary Energy in Man,* p. 207.

10. Fritjof Capra, *The Tao of Physics,* p. 68. David Bohm, one of the leading exponents of the "New Physics," uses the cloud symbolism to explain the same point in his book *Wholeness and the Implicate Order:*

> The atom is, in many ways, seen to behave as much like a wave as a particle. It can perhaps best be regarded as a poorly defined cloud, dependent for its particular form on the whole environment, including the observing instrument. . . . Both observer and observed are merging and interpenetrating aspects of one whole reality, which is indivisible and unanalysable. (p. 9)

11. Edward Conze, *op. cit.,* p. 81.

12. Account of meditation experience, from author's files of clients and students.

13. Fritjof Capra, *op. cit.,* p. 222.

14. Plato's well-known cave parable is found in book 7 of *The Republic.*

15. William James, *op. cit.,* p. 298.

16. William James, *op. cit.,* p. 129.

17. Jung's views on the functions and his theory of types are given in his *Psychological Types* and in *Lectures on Jung's Typology,* by Marie-Louise von Franz and James Hillman. An alternative view of the functions, which does not assume that they are arranged in pairs of opposites, is presented in the paper "Toward a Reformulation of the Typology of Functions," by Ralph Metzner, Cecil Burney, and Arden Mahlberg. *Journal of Analytical Psychology* (1981): 26, 33–47. This model seems to accord better with the empirical evidence on the distribution and arrangement of the functions, as measured by personality inventories.

18. The research by Bernard Aaronson on hypnotic alterations of perception is reported in his paper "Mystic and Schizophreniform States and the Experience of Depth," in *Journal for the Scientific Study of Religion* 6, 1967, no. 2. An excellent discussion of the theme of three kinds of vision, as found in medieval Scholastic philosophy and as applied in modern transpersonal psychology, is in Ken Wilber's *Eye to Eye*, pp. 1–37.

19. These famous lines of Blake are in his *The Marriage of Heaven and Hell*. The following line reads; "For man has closed himself up, till he sees all things thro' narrow chinks of his cavern."

20. Reich's theories on the muscular armor, and on the character armor, which he termed "functionally equivalent," are explained in several of his writings, most notably in *Character Analysis*. The passage by Eckhart is quoted by Aldous Huxley, *The Perennial Philosophy*, p. 162.

21. Shunryu Suzuki, *Zen Mind, Beginner's Mind*, p. 80. In his commentary on this saying, Suzuki, who was Zen master of the San Francisco Zen Center, said: "When your life is always a part of your surroundings, . . . then there is no problem. When you start to wander about in some delusion which is something apart from yourself, then your surroundings are not real anymore, and your mind is not real anymore. If you yourself are deluded, then your surroundings are also a misty, foggy delusion" (p. 82). Again we note that symbolism of fog and mist as obscurations of perception.

22. William James, *op. cit.*, p. 296–297.

23. The powerful myth of the descent of the goddess, Inanna or Ishtar into the underworld has recently been brought out in a new translation by Diane Wolkstein and Samuel Noah Kramer, *Inanna: Queen of Heaven and Earth*. Discussions of the symbolism and psychological meaning of the myth are found in *The Descent to the Goddess*, by Sylvia Brinton Perera, and in *The Time Falling Bodies Take to Light*, by William Irwin Thompson. Concerning the relation of Inanna's seven garments and the chakras, Thompson says, "If indeed the seven laws are the seven chakras, then the untying of knots which bind the physical body to the subtle would remove the etheric and astral body to wander in hell in the out-of-the-body state" (p. 178). In other words, Inanna/Ishtar's descent and the unveiling of the chakras can be regarded as a metaphoric description of an initiatory experience, which involves stripping the chakras of obstructions (ornaments), and an altered state of confrontation with disease and death, followed by rebirth.

24. R. A. Nicholson, *The Mystics of Islam*, p. 15.

25. *Meister Eckhart*, trans. Raymond B. Blakney, p. 77. The complete passage reads, "That to which the soul inclines tends always to become like a cover or hood; but in being lifted up, the soul is made naked before the idea of God, for God's getting; the image of God is unveiled and free in the open soul of the aristocrat." In a related passage (p. 221),

Eckhart writes, "I say that intelligence draws aside the veil and perceives God naked, stripped of goodness, or of being, or of any name."

CHAPTER 3   From Captivity to Liberation

1.   The Swiss psychoanalyst Alice Miller wrote a book, *The Prisoners of Childhood,* that was subsequently reissued under the title *The Drama of the Gifted Child.* In this book she eloquently demonstrates how the unspoken expectations of parents create a subtle yet powerful set of limits and inhibitions for the child, especially the sensitive gifted child. *Man in the Trap,* by Ellsworth Baker, is an exposition of Reich's theories.

2.   Plato's cave parable and the passages cited here are from books 6 and 7 of *The Republic.*

3.   Shankara's *Atma Bodha,* translated as *Self Analysis and Self Knowledge,* by Shri Ramamurti Mishra), sutra 49. In Sanskrit, *moksha,* or *mukti,* is the process or state of liberation, and *jivan-mukta* (from *jivan,* "living") is one who is "freed while living," i.e., a liberated being. "Being-consciousness-joy" (or bliss), *sat-chit-ananda,* is the Vedanta term for the kind of consciousness of someone who has attained enlightenment or liberation.

4.   Jacques Lacarrière, *The Gnostics;* Evelyn Underhill, *Mysticism.* In Saint John's symbolism, the body is the prison for the soul, which knows nothing except what it can see through the windows of its cells, which are the senses.

5.   H. V. Guenther, *The Life and Teachings of Naropa,* pp. 25–26.

6.   The Harvard Prison Project, as it was called, was written up as a technical research report in a paper by Timothy Leary, Ralph Metzner, et al., "A New Behavior Change Project Using Psilocybin," in *Psychotherapy: Theory, Research, and Practice* 2, no. 2 (1965): 61–72. It is also described, less formally, in Leary's autobiographical *Flashbacks,* chapter 11.

7.   John Milton, *Samson Agonistes,* l. 40.

8.   From "The Dove and the Darkness in Ancient Byzantine Mysticism," by Jean Danielou, in *Man and Transformation,* ed. Joseph Campbell, p. 282.

9.   Wilhelm Reich, *The Function of the Orgasm,* pp. 206–207. See also his *Character Analysis.*

10.   Alexander Lowen, *Bioenergetics,* pp. 183ff. Other useful books on body "reading," or diagnosis from body structure, influenced by Reich's work, are Ken Dychtwald's *Bodymind;* Hector Prestera and Ron Kurtz's *The Body Reveals;* and Stanley Keleman's *Somatic Reality.*

11.   Don Johnson, *The Protean Body,* pp. 20–21. Johnson's most recent work, not as closely based on the work of Ida Rolf, is called *Body.*

12.   T. S. Eliot, from "Burnt Norton" (l. 80), in *Four Quartets.*

13. From an unpublished account by Alan Levin; used by permission.

14. Robert Monroe, *Journeys out of the Body.* The parapsychology research on out-of-body experiences (OOBEs, as they are called) is well summarized and reviewed in *Psi. Scientific Studies of the Psychic Realm,* by Charles Tart.

15. Shirley MacLaine, *Out on a Limb,* p. 329.

16. Stanislav Grof, *Realms of the Human Unconscious,* pp. 116–121. Grof's theories and findings on the importance of the birth experience, which, as he says, sets up "perinatal matrices" for the experiencing of subsequent life-and-death traumas, was anticipated to some extent by Otto Rank, one of Freud's closest disciples.

17. The phrase "the imprisoned splendor" is from Robert Browning's poem "Paracelsus." It was also used as the title of an important book on mysticism by Raynor Johnson, which synthesizes findings from the natural sciences, psychical research, and classical mysticism.

18. My interpretation of the Osiris myth, though independently arrived at, is similar to the one put forward by William Irwin Thompson in *The Time Falling Bodies Take to Light.* "When we come to the coffin that has become embedded in a tree, we are, as any student of yoga would recognize, clearly in the realm of the esoteric physiology of the central nervous system" (pp. 218ff.).

19. Katho Upanishad, 2.3.15; and Mundaka Upanishad, 2.2.9.

20. Mircea Eliade, "The God Who Binds and the Symbolism of Knots," in *Images and Symbols,* p. 112.

21. The "double-bind theory of schizophrenia" was first enunciated by Gregory Bateson and is described in several of his books and articles, including *Steps Toward an Ecology of Mind* and *Mind and Nature.*

22. See the essay by Eliade cited above, in note 20. The *Fata* were the Roman goddesses of fate who enunciated the word, or decrees, of Jupiter; *fata* means literally "that which has been spoken." The Moirae were the Greek goddesses of fate: Clotho, the spinner of the thread of life; Lachesis, the one who determined its length; and Atropos, the one who cut it at the end. The Norns are the Scandinavian goddesses of fate, sometimes called "Past," "Present," and "Future." They all seem to resemble the threefold goddess of Celtic mythology and the three fairy godmothers of many folktales.

23. P. D. Ouspensky, *In Search of the Miraculous,* p. 30.

CHAPTER 4   Purification by Inner Fire

1. Agni Yoga, or Light-fire Yoga, as taught in the School of Actualism, is described in my books *Maps of Consciousness* and *Know Your Type.* The Actualism fire yoga teachings, which were "brought through," or "channeled," by Russell Schofield, the founder of the school, are quite unrelated to the Agni Yoga teachings formulated by the

Russian painter-philosopher Nicholas Roerich, who traveled in the East and in America extensively during the 1920s and wrote a number of books on the subject.

2. *The Rig Veda,* an anthology selected and translated by Wendy Doniger O'Flaherty, pp. 99–117. See also Satprem, *Sri Aurobindo,* pp. 322–327.

3. See Mircea Eliade's *History of Religious Ideas,* 1, pp. 187–214.

4. Of the enormous literature on the mythology and iconography of Shiva, I mention only three books: *Shiva and Dionysus,* by Alain Danielou; *Asceticism and Eroticism in the Mythology of Siva,* by Wendy O'Flaherty; and *The Presence of Siva,* by Stella Kramrisch.

5. Daniel 10:6.

6. Psalms 68:2.

7. Luke 12:29; Matthew 3:11; Gospel of Thomas, no. 82.

8. Extensive discussions of alchemy in general and of the symbolism of fire in particular can be found in C. G. Jung's *Alchemical Studies* and *Mysterium Coniunctionis.* In addition, there is a chapter on alchemy in my *Maps of Consciousness.* The alchemical texts "Glory of the World" and "The Sophic Hydrolith," from which several quotations are drawn, are found in the collection called *The Hermetic Museum* (ed. A. E. Waite). The original was published in Frankfurt in 1678.

9. An excellent introduction to Taoist mysticism is the book *Tao: An Eastern Philosophy of Time and Change,* by Philip Rawson and Laszlo Legeza. An extraordinary compilation of dragon lore from all over the world is Francis Huxley's *Dragon.*

10. The passage cited is from Boehme's work Clavis *(The Key),* first published in 1624; translation by the author.

11. An outstanding compilation of art and literature on the theme of hell and paradise is *Visions of Heaven and Hell,* by Richard Cavendish. Another book that contains much valuable material on these themes is *Beyond Death,* by Stanislav and Christina Grof.

12. Aldous Huxley's *Heaven and Hell* was first published in 1956 and issued together with *The Doors of Perception.* Huxley says: "The Inferno is psychologically true. Many of its pains are experienced by schizophrenics, and by those who have taken mescalin or lysergic acid under unfavorable conditions" (p. 109). Interesting personal accounts of schizophrenic experiences, which illustrate the points made here, have been collected in the book *Exploring Madness: Experience, Theory, and Research,* ed. James Fadiman and Donald Kewman. This book includes an extract from *One Flew Over the Cuckoo's Nest,* by Ken Kesey, an outstanding and vivid fictionalized inside view of mental illness.

13. Stanislav Grof, *Realms of the Human Unconscious,* p. 131.

14. For a discussion of the role of suffering and sacrifice in shamanic cultures, see Joan Halifax's *Shaman: The Wounded Healer.*

15. The *Treatise of Purgatory* is quoted from Evelyn Underhill's *Mysticism*. The passage continues: "The more it is consumed, the more they [the souls] respond to God their true Sun. Their happiness increases as the rust falls off and lays them open to the divine way" (p. 204).

16. From *Supersensual Life,* quoted in *Treasury of Traditional Wisdom,* ed. Whitall Perry.

17. See note 8 above.

18. Account from the author's files; used by permission.

19. A brilliant and insightful series of papers on the alchemical processes in psychotherapy has been written by the Jungian analyst Edward Edinger. These papers were published in the journal *Quadrant* in the following issues: summer 1978, winter 1978, summer 1979, spring 1981. These papers explore many aspects of and variations on the alchemical themes and images, which we have touched on only briefly in the present work.

20. J. Krishnamurti, *The Flame of Attention.*

21. Lee Sannella, *Kundalini: Psychosis or Transcendence.* A volume edited by John White, *Kundalini, Evolution, and Enlightenment,* contains experiential accounts of kundalini phenomena, as well as extracts from the Indian literature and from modern research studies.

22. Itzhak Bentov, *Stalking the Wild Pendulum.* Bentov's proposed model for what he calls the "physio-kundalini syndrome" is also presented in Sannella's work, *op. cit.*

23. Gopi Krishna, *Kundalini: The Evolutionary Energy in Man.*

24. For Aurobindo's views on Agni and for Actualism, see the references cited in notes 1 and 2 above.

25. Taoist yoga principles and practices are detailed in *The Secret of the Golden Flower,* ed. and trans. by Richard Wilhelm, with commentary by C. G. Jung; and in *Awaken Healing Energy Through the Tao,* by Mantak Chia.

26. The Actualism Agni Yoga experience recounted is from the author's files; used by permission.

27. From "The Glory of the World," in *The Hermetic Museum* (ed. A. E. Waite).

28. From *The Poems of Saint John of the Cross,* trans. J. F. Nims; and from *The Treatise on Purgatory,* cited in Evelyn Underhill's *Mysticism,* p. 221.

29. The extract from Richard Rolle is cited in *Silent Fire,* ed. Walter H. Capps and Wendy M. Wright. Rolle's reference to "we exiles" touches on the metaphor of alienation and homecoming, discussed in chapter 8.

30. Sri Aurobindo, *The Life Divine,* p. 907.

31. The picture of the wolf and the king is one of a series of alchemical emblems, published in 1617 under the title *Atalanta Fugiens (The Fleeing Atalanta)* by the alchemist Michael Mainer. This series is reproduced in Maitreya Three (Berkeley, Calif.: Shambhala, 1972). The wolf picture also is reproduced in my *Maps of Consciousness* and in *Alchemy,* by Allison Coudert.

CHAPTER 5   From Darkness to Light

1. Ken Wilber, *Eye to Eye,* pp. 2–4.

2. Modern research on subtle energy phenomena is summarized and discussed in a number of different works: *Rainbows of Life,* by Mikol Davis and Earle Lane; *Galaxies of Life,* edited by Stanley Krippner and Daniel Rubin; *In Search of Healing Energy,* by Mary Coddington; *Orgone, Reich, and Eros,* by Edward Mann; *The Fields of Life,* by Harold S. Burr; *Future Science,* edited by John White and Stanley Krippner; and *Break-through to Creativity,* by Shafica Karagulla. The last of these is a particularly careful and impressive collection of first-person accounts by "sensitives," i.e., clairvoyants and psychics.

3. The experience of the German traveler with Ramana Maharshi is quoted in Lama Govinda's *Foundations of Tibetan Mysticism* (p. 164). All the biographies of Ramakrishna mention the luminescence phenomena, as reported by eyewitnesses. Several other similar enlightenment transfigurations are described in Mircea Eliade's essay "Experiences of the Mystic Light." This excellent compilation of materials from many sources is found in his book *The Two and the One.*

4. Matthew 17:2–10; Mark 9:2–10.

5. *Meister Eckhart,* ed. Raymond Blakney, p. 104.

6. From Arthur Young's highly original and insightful formulation of the role of light in physics, presented in his book *The Reflexive Universe.* Another contribution that combines scientific analysis and revelatory experience of a very high order is Walter Russell's *The Secret of Light,* a work unfortunately much less known and appreciated than it deserves to be.

7. Brihadaranyaka Upanishad 4.3.7. The quotation from Shankara is from his *Atma Bodha,* in R. S. Mishra, *Self Analysis and Self Knowledge* (no. 4).

8. Quoted in Fritz Meier, "The Transformation of Man in Mystical Islam," in *Man and Transformation,* ed. Joseph Campbell.

9. See C. G. Jung's essay "Paracelsus as a Spiritual Phenomenon," in *Alchemical Studies.*

10. E. Swedenborg, *Heaven and Hell,* no. 130.

11. *The Tibetan Book of the Dead,* trans. Francesca Freemantle and Chogyam Trungpa, p. 37.

12. From the Buddhist Dighanikaya and the Lalitavistara, cited in Mircea Eliade, *op. cit.*

13. *The Tibetan Book of the Dead,* trans. Francesca Freemantle and Chogyam Trungpa, p. 43.

14. The New Testament passages are 2 Thessalonians 5:5 and Matthew 6:22. Gospel of Thomas, no. 24.

15. Saint Augustine, *Confessions;* Quoted in Evelyn Underhill, *Mysticism,* p. 250.

16. C. G. Jung, "On the Nature of the Psyche," in *The Structure and Dynamics of the Psyche,* p. 190.

17. Gerhard Dorn, in C. G. Jung, *op. cit.,* p. 192.

18. The following are excellent surveys of the current state of psychological knowledge about creativity: Silvano Arieti, *Creativity: The Magic Synthesis;* C. W. Taylor and F. Barron, eds., *Scientific Creativity: Its Recognition and Development;* and Arthur Koestler, *The Act of Creation.*

19. Franz Hartmann, *Jacob Boehme: Life and Doctrines,* p. 50.

20. Rig Veda, II, 27.

21. See Evelyn Underhill, *Mysticism,* chapter 9, pp. 380–412.

22. I owe the suggestion that this would be a more accurate phrase to Salvador Arrien and Angeles Arrien.

23. R. M. Bucke, *Cosmic Consciousness,* p. 8.

24. Sri Aurobindo, *The Life Divine,* p. 944.

25. R. S. Mishra, *op. cit.,* no. 67; Chandogya Upanishad, 3.13.7.

26. Saint Teresa, in Evelyn Underhill, *Mysticism,* p. 78.

27. G. R. S. Mead, *The Doctrine of the Subtle Body in the Western Tradition,* p. 59.

28. Eckhart, *op. cit.,* p. 104.

29. Yogananda Paramahansa, *Autobiography of a Yogi,* p. 166–168.

CHAPTER 6   From Fragmentation to Wholeness

1. From the author's files; used by permission.

2. Quoted in Aldous Huxley, *The Perennial Philosophy,* p. 96.

3. William James, *Varieties of Religious Experience,* p. 143.

4. Roberto Assagioli, *Psychosynthesis,* p. 75. The analogy of the Self as an orchestra with its conductor is suggested by John O. Beahrs, in his book *Unity and Multiplicity.*

5. For a description and discussion of the humoral and other earlier somatically based typologies of personality, see my *Know Your Type*, chapter 2. See also Robert J. Campbell, *Psychiatric Dictionary*, under "type."

6. Georg Groddeck, *The Book of the It*, p. xiv.

7. P. D. Ouspensky, *In Search of the Miraculous*, p. 59.

8. David Bohm, *Wholeness and the Implicate Order*, p. 7.

9. Robert J. Campbell, *Psychiatric Dictionary*, p. 458.

10. There are many reference books on the concepts and methods of "holistic" health and healing; a good one is Kenneth Pelletier's *Mind as Healer, Mind as Slayer*. Some researchers have proposed that desynchronization of the body's physiological cycles—a kind of temporal fragmentation—plays a significant role in physical and psychosomatic illnesses. Evidence supporting this thesis is presented in Gay Luce's book *Body Time*.

11. Numerous examples of shamanic dismemberment visions are cited in Mircea Eliade's monumental study *Shamanism: Archaic Techniques of Ecstasy*, especially in chapter 2. The extraordinary experiences of Australian aboriginal medicine men are vividly recounted in A. P. Elkin's *Aboriginal Men of High Degree*. The case for the similarity between shamanic initiations and psychotic experiences was first made by Julian Silverman in an article on "Shamanism and Acute Schizophrenia" (*American Anthropologist* 69 [1967]: 1).

12. W. Y. Evans-Wentz, *Tibetan Yoga and Secret Doctrines*, pp. 277–333.

13. T. S. Anantha Murthy, *Life and Teachings of Sri Sai Baba of Shirdi*.

14. Ezekiel 37:1–14.

15. The mystery cults apparently involved an elaboration and collectivization of earlier individual priestly initiations. Tests for the initiates, consisting of a sequence of experiences, were staged; for outside members of the public, they were instructive ritual dramas, akin to later morality plays. Initiates and observers were sworn to secrecy, to maintain a "closed mouth" (Greek *mustes*). The purpose of keeping the secret was to ensure that the meaning and power of the initiation ceremonies would not be diluted or distorted by misinterpretation. Those who had eyes to see and ears to hear would understand the deeper meanings of the rituals, in terms of their own interior process. Others would simply see and hear the mythic story presented in dramatic form and perhaps be partially awakened by the images and symbols. So when the initiates heard again the familiar story of Osiris being cut up by his evil brother Set, it presumably reminded and prepared them for purposeful, intentional experiences of dismemberment. An outstanding introduction to these ancient Mediterranean traditions is the book *Mystery Religions in the Ancient World*, by Joscelyn Godwin. There is also a volume in the Eranos Yearbooks no. 2, published in the Bollingen Series, by Pantheon Books, which is devoted to *The Mysteries*.

16. For interesting discussions of "remembering" and "recollection," see Evelyn Underhill's *Mysticism* and P. D. Ouspensky's *In Search of the Miraculous.* For the Islamic equivalent (termed *dhikr*), see R. A. Nicholson's *The Mystics of Islam.*

17. Walter Otto, *Dionysus: Myth and Cult,* p. 136.

18. Erich Neumann, *The Origins and History of Consciousness,* p. 61. Historians of comparative religion have pointed to the striking parallels between the Dionysos story and other Near Eastern cults in which the son or lover of the Mother Goddess is either killed or mutilated, as part of fertility rituals (Dumuzi and Inanna, Tammuz and Ishtar, Attis and Cybele).

19. I am indebted to Edward Edinger's brilliant elucidation of the psychological meanings of the *separatio* complex, in his paper "Psychotherapy and Alchemy VII: Separatio," *Quadrant* 14, no. 1 (1981).

20. For more extended discussion of the alchemical elements and the process of their integration, see the chapter on alchemy in my *Maps of Consciousness;* see also my essay "Alchemy and Personal Transformation," in *Laughing Man Magazine,* 2, no. 4. (1980).

21. C. G. Jung *Alchemical Studies,* p. 68; and *Mysterium Conjunctionis,* p. 353.

22. S. Grof, *Realms of the Human Unconscious,* pp. 123–137.

23. The tract *Splendor Solis,* attributed to an undoubtedly pseudonymous Salomon Trismosin, exists as an illustrated manuscript, dated 1582, in the British Museum; it was published in an undated edition by Kegan Paul, Trench, Trubner and Co. of London. In 1981 it was reissued, in a new translation in a limited edition, as part of the Magnum Opus Hermetic Sourceworks series (Edinburgh; ed. Adam McLean). Jung cites and comments on this text extensively in his alchemical works.

24. Erich Neumann, *op. cit.,* p. 228.

25. *Meister Eckhart,* ed. R. B. Blakney, p. 173.

26. The statement by Origen is quoted by Jung in *Mysterium Conjunctionis,* p. 8n; the other lines are in *The Gospel According to Thomas,* p. 35. A parallel saying is found in Luke 11:34.

27. The passage by Walt Whitman is from his "Specimen Days and Collect," published in 1882; quoted by William James in *Varieties of Religious Experience,* p. 304n.

CHAPTER 7   Journey to the Place of Vision and Power

1. The three paths in Hinduism leading to liberation or enlightenment are *jnana marga,* the path of knowledge, in which the seeker seeks direct insight into reality; *bhakti marga,* the path of devotion, in which the disciple surrenders to the guru and the deity; and *karma marga,* in which one becomes unattached to the fruits of one's actions. The quotation is from the *Brihad-aranyaka Upanishad,* 4.4.8.

2. John 14:6; Matthew 25:14.

3. See Fritz Meier's essay, "The Transformation of Man in Mystical Islam," in *Man and Transformation,* ed. Joseph Campbell, p. 47.

4. *The Sacred Pipe: Black Elk's Account of the Seven Rites of the Oglala Sioux,* recorded and edited by Joseph Epes Brown, pp. 58–59.

5. Mircea Eliade, *Shamanism: Archaic Techniques of Ecstasy,* p. 182.

6. R. D. Laing, *The Politics of Experience,* pp. 68–69.

7. Muhyiddin Ibn 'Arabi, *Journey to the Lord of Power,* p. 27.

8. *The Epic of Gilgamesh,* trans. N. K. Sandars, p. 94.

9. The Theravada school of Buddhism, which is the oldest, speaks of three kinds of saints, or three stages on the mystic path: those who have "entered the stream," those who are "once returning," and the "never-returning Holy Ones" *(arhats).* Mahayana Buddhists argue that this mystic path is a kind of escape, a release (nirvana) from the pangs of worldly existence, and that the real work of the Buddhist is to return for the sake of all other as-yet-unenlightened beings.

10. These journal entries, here and below, are quoted by permission from an unpublished autobiographical work by Marilee Stark.

11. The practice of "walkabout," known among several of the Australian aboriginal tribes, is described in various ethnographic sources; it was also the subject of a prize-winning Australian film with the same title, by Nicholas Roeg. The "year walk" is a practice that Basques living in the Pyrenees and elsewhere enter into during their adolescence, as a way of learning to see, relate to nature, and overcome fear. The initiate spends a year walking in solitude in the wilderness. I am indebted to Angeles Arrien, Basque anthropologist and folklorist, for providing information about this practice.

12. See Edward Bernbaum, *The Way to Shambhala,* for an interesting discussion of this idea and the myths surrounding it.

13. Joseph Campbell, *The Hero with a Thousand Faces,* p. 58. Other interesting discussions of the threshold theme in mythology and shamanism are found in Joseph Henderson's *Thresholds of Initiation,* and in Stephen Larsen's *The Shaman's Doorway.*

14. Marilee Stark; see note 10 above.

15. Hildegard von Bingen, *Quellen des Heils (Sources of Salvation),* pp. 15–16. My translation. The image of the exile, in the last line of the quoted passage, is the subject of chapter 8, "Returning to the Source."

16. *Selected Poems of Rainer Maria Rilke,* trans. Robert Bly, p. 177.

17. Walt Whitman, *Leaves of Grass,* p. 80.

18. *The Kabir Book,* versions by Robert Bly, p. 17.

19. *Zen Flesh, Zen Bones,* comp. Paul Reps, p. 88.

20.   For an account of "lower world journeys" in traditional shamanism and in contemporary individuals learning the ancient methods, see Michael Harner, *The Way of the Shaman,* pp. 20–39. It is interesting to compare the shamanic experience of going "downward" in the altered state with the almost universal experience of downward movement when falling asleep. In the shamanic journey, one travels downward but stays awake. There are some similarities of this approach with what some have called the "waking dream" method in psychotherapy. See the book *Waking Dreams,* by Mary Watkins, for details on this approach.

21.   Jonah 2:5–6.

22.   Joan Halifax. *Shaman: The Wounded Healer,* p. 18.

23.   A beautiful new poetic version of the myths of Inanna has been done by Diane Wolkstein and Samuel Noah Kramer: *Inanna: Queen of Heaven and Earth.* An in-depth discussion from a Jungian point of view is found in *Descent to the Goddess,* by Sylvia Brinton Perera, which also focuses on the question of what aspect of the feminine psyche is represented by the death goddess Ereshkigal. The interpretation of the stripping of the ornaments at the seven gates, in terms of the yogic chakras, is based on this ritualistic element in the story: at the first gate, she must remove her crown (crown center); at the next, her earrings (brain center); at the third, her necklace (throat center); then her breast ornaments (heart center); then ornaments from hands and feet; then her abdominal girdle (abdominal center); and finally her pelvic girdle (generative or root center).

24.   For a review of parapsychology research on remote viewing and out-of-body experiences, see *Psi. Scientific Studies of the Psychic Realm,* by Charles Tart.

25.   Quoted in "The Dove and the Darkness in Ancient Byzantine Mysticism," by Jean Danielou, in *Man and Transformation, op. cit.,* pp. 277–278.

26.   *Selected Poems of Rainer Maria Rilke,* trans. Robert Bly, p. 13.

27.   Mircea Eliade, *Shamanism: Archaic Techniques of Ecstasy,* p. 191.

28.   *Tibet's Great Yogi Milarepa,* trans. and ed. W. Y. Evans-Wentz, p. 212.

29.   Maitri Upanishad, 6.22.

30.   Psalms: 104.

31.   Quoted in *Treasury of Traditional Wisdom,* ed. Whitall Perry, p. 948.

32.   In chapter 4, on purification, I mentioned H. A. Murray's hypothesis of an "Icarus Complex," which combines interest in fire, *ascensionism,* and urethral-phallic eroticism. This complex, according to Murray, may be an immature form of the "solar complex," and it includes ambition, craving for immortality, and tendencies toward messianic enthusiasm. In Jung's psychology, it parallels the concept of ego-inflation. See *Endeavors in Psychology: Selections from the Personology of Henry A. Murray,* ed. Edwin S. Shneidman, pp. 535–556.

33. René Daumal, *Mount Analogue,* p. 156.

34. Farid ud-Din Attar, *The Conference of the Birds,* p. 131. The symbolism of the valleys to be traversed on the mystic's journey appears also in the writings of the nineteenth-century Persian founder of the Baha'i religion, Baha'Ullah *(The Seven Valleys* and *The Four Valleys),* as well as in the recorded talks and teachings of the nineteenth-century Indian saint Ramakrishna. One account is given in *The Face of Silence,* by Dhan Gopal Mukerji.

35. Job 12:24.

36. Hosea 2:16–17.

37. Hildegard von Bingen, *op. cit.,* pp. 18–19.

CHAPTER 8   Returning to the Source

1. J. M. Cohen and J-F. Phipps, *The Common Experience,* p. 158.

2. From the author's files; used by permission.

3. T. S. Eliot, from "Little Gidding," one of the poems in *Four Quartets.*

4. D. T. Suzuki, "The Awakening of a New Consciousness in Zen," in *Man and Transformation,* ed. Joseph Campbell, p. 196.

5. *Zen Flesh, Zen Bones: A Collection of Zen and Pre-Zen Writings,* compiled by Paul Reps, p. 103.

6. *People Magazine,* December 1982, p. 71.

7. Walter Kaufmann, "The Inevitability of Alienation," introductory essay in *Alienation,* by Richard Schacht, pp. xv–lviii.

8. Walter Kaufmann, *op. cit.,* p.lv.

9. Ephesians 4:18.

10. Richard Rolle, from *The Fire of Love (Incendium Amoris),* quoted in *Treasury of Traditional Wisdom,* ed. Whitall Perry, p. 458. The passage of Hildegard von Bingen's is from her text *Scivias;* it is translated by the author from the German version in *Quellen des Heils,* p. 16.

11. *The Nag Hammadi Library,* ed. James M. Robinson, p. 443.

12. Jacques Lacarrière, *The Gnostics,* pp. 26–29.

13. Philo Judaeus, "On the Confusion of Tongues," in *Treasury of Traditional Wisdom,* ed. Whitall Perry, p. 365.

14. For discussions of *pravritti* and *nivritti,* see *The Language of the Gods,* by Judith M. Tyberg, pp. 31–32, and *The Yoga of the Bhagavat Gita,* by Sri Krishna Prem, especially chapter 16.

15. *Hsin Hsin Ming: Verses on the Faith-Mind,* by Sengtsan, Third Zen Patriarch, trans. Richard B. Clarke.

16. For etymologies of *evolution* and *involution,* see *Origins,* by Eric Partridge, under "voluble."

17. David Bohm, "The Enfolding-Unfolding Universe," interview by Renée Weber, in *Revision,* 1, no. 3/4 summer/fall 1978, p. 24. Somewhat parallel to the concept of explicate order is J. G. Fichte's concept of *Entäusserung,* "externalization." Schacht, in his *Alienation* (p. 22), writes that in Fichte's view, "The phenomenal world (the "object") is produced by spirit (the "subject"). It is brought forth by spirit out of itself, and is set out by spirit over against itself, as something that is now external to it. Fichte characterizes this process as an *Entäusserung* on the part of spirit—an externalization and detachment of something of its own."

18. Arthur Young, *The Reflexive Universe,* p. 164.

19. *Sri Aurobindo, or the Adventure of Consciousness,* by Satprem, p. 301. At another place in the same work, Aurobindo is quoted: "We speak of the evolution of Life in Matter, the evolution of Mind in Matter; but evolution is a word which merely states the phenomenon without explaining it. For there seems to be no reason why Life should evolve out of material elements or Mind out of living form, unless we accept . . . that Life is already involved in Matter and Mind in Life because in essence Matter is a veiled form of Life, Life a form of veiled consciousness" (p. 304).

20. *Allogenes,* in *The Nag Hammadi Library,* ed. James M. Robinson, p. 449.

21. Several versions of the Zen ox-herding pictures and commentaries exist. The ones drawn on here are in; *Zen Flesh, Zen Bones,* compiled by Paul Reps, pp. 130–155; in *Coming Home,* by Lex Hixon, pp. 77–107; and in *The Hero: Myth/Image/Symbol,* ed. Dorothy Norman, pp. 180–191.

22. William Bridges, "The Odyssey and the Myth of the Homeward Journey," in *Consciousness and Culture* 1, no. 1 (1977): 99–112.

23. C. G. Jung quotes the alchemist Kalid: "And Hermes said to his father: Father, I am afraid of the enemy in my house. And he said: my son, take a Corascene dog and an Armenian bitch, join them together, and they will beget a dog of a celestial hue. . . . He will guard your friend, and he will guard you from your enemy, and he will help you wherever you may be, always being with you, in this world and in the next" (*The Psychology of the Transference,* p. 86n). The process is also reminiscent of shamanic practices involving an animal ally.

24. The parable of the prodigal son is in Luke 15:11–32; the Syrian "Hymn of the Robe of Glory" is in *The Wisdom of the Serpent,* ed. Joseph L. Henderson and Maud Oakes, pp. 153–160; a version called "Hymn of the Soul," extracted from The Acts of Thomas, is given in *The King's Son,* ed. Robert Cecil. This book, which is an anthology of writings on "Traditional Psychologies and Contemporary Thought on Man," includes a whole section entitled "Steps on the Road Home."

25. The Navaho prayer given in extract here, or versions similar to it, may have been published in several places; this particular version was found by the author many years ago, on a trip through the Southwest, in a newspaper article on Navaho myth and religion.

CHAPTER 9   On Dying and Being Reborn

1. William Bridges, *Transitions.*

2. Paul Reps, comp., *Zen Flesh, Zen Bones.*

3. The LSD experience is cited with permission from an unpublished account by John Prendergast.

4. C. G. Jung, "Concerning Rebirth," in *The Archetypes and the Collective Unconscious* p. 115.

5. John 12:23–24 (New English Bible).

6. 1 Corinthians 15:36 (New English Bible).

7. Meister Eckhart, in Whitall Perry, ed., *Treasury of Traditional Wisdom,* p. 208.

8. Plato, *The Phaedo;* quoted in Edward Edinger's paper "Psychotherapy and Alchemy VI: *Mortificatio,*" in *Quadrant* 14, no. 1 (spring 1981): 36. Edinger's article is one of a series published in *Quadrant* on alchemical themes. My debt to Edinger's outstanding work on the amplification of these images is obviously great.

9. An interesting compilation of European folklore on the figure of Death is Edgar Herzog's *Psyche and Death.*

10. Katha Upanisnad, in S. Radhakrishnan, ed. and trans., *The Principal Upanishads,* p. 607.

11. *Ibid.,* p. 648.

12. For an excellent account of the ancient mystery religions, see *Mystery Religions in the Ancient World,* by Joscelyn Godwin. This book describes the cults of Mithras and Aion, Cybele and Attis, Isis and Serapis, and Dionysus, Orpheus, and Hercules.

13. *Rumi: Poet and Mystic,* trans. R. A. Nicholson, p. 103.

14. *Chuang Tsu: Inner Chapters,* trans. Gia-Fu Feng and Jane English, p. 114.

15. Quoted in *Mysticism,* by Evelyn Underhill, p. 217.

16. P. D. Ouspensky, *In Search of the Miraculous,* p. 218.

17. For account of shamanic "killing" rituals see Mircea Eliade's *Shamanism* and A. P. Elkin's *Aboriginal Men of High Degree.*

18. Edinger, Edward, *op. cit.* (see note 8 above), p. 25.

19. R. A. Moody's book is *Life after Death;* Karlis Osis' is *Deathbed Observations by Physicians and Nurses;* Kenneth Ring's is *Life at Death.* Kenneth Ring's latest work is *Heading Toward Omega* (1984). In it, Ring makes the startling claim, based on the reports of survivors, that "near-death experiences may be part of an evolutionary thrust toward higher consciousness for all humanity. . . . They may foreshadow the birth of a new planetary consciousness as we head toward Omega, the final goal of human evolution." (from the jacket)

20. Stephen Levine, *Who Dies,* p. 157. Levine founded, with Ram Dass, the Dying Project, which conducts seminars for the terminally ill and their families, in which attitudes toward death are examined and transformed. Levine's book *Who Dies,* subtitled *An Investigation of Conscious Living and Conscious Dying,* is a profound and moving description of this work, with many meditation and guided imagery sequences given for self-work.

21. The hospice movement encourages home care of the terminally ill and provides back-up services as an alternative to costly and impersonal hospital care. The Shanti Project offers workshops and training experiences in a variety of humanistic processes for aging and ill elders.

22. Joan Grant's most powerful and vivid story is *Winged Pharaoh,* one of three she wrote about different periods in Egyptian history; they contain detailed accounts of death-rebirth and other initiations and trainings. Joan Grant claimed to remember these as "far-memories" of past incarnations. The work by Elizabeth Haich, *Initiation,* is also based on past life recall. Of the several books describing the theories and research of the Egyptologist and esoteric philosopher R. A. Schwaller de Lubicz, *Her-Bak: Egyptian Initiate*, by Isha Schwaller de Lubicz, gives a good account of mythic initiatory training.

23. The W. Y. Evans-Wentz version of *the Tibetan Book of the Dead* (1960) is the one used by Leary, Metzner, and Alpert to prepare their adaptation, *The Psychedelic Experience* (1964). Since then, a new translation by Francesca Freemantle and Chogyam Trungpa, *The Tibetan Book of the Dead* (1975), has appeared. In-depth scholarly commentaries on the text are provided in D. I. Lauf's *Secret Doctrines of the Tibetan Books of the Dead* (1977). Other works on the Indian and Buddhist views of death and the afterlife are: *Death and Beyond in Eastern Perspective,* by John Y. Lee, and Swami Nikhilananda's *Man in Search of Immortality.*

24. The work by Walter Pahnke, Grof, and others on LSD psychotherapy with cancer patients is described in *The Human Encounter with Death,* by Stanislav Grof and Joan Halifax.

25. Lewis Thomas, who is the author of such classics of "natural philosophy" as *The Lives of a Cell* and *Late Night Thoughts on Listening to Mahler's Ninth Symphony,* wrote the passage quoted in the article "A Meliorist View of Disease and Dying," published in *Journal for Medicine and Philosophy* 1, no. 3 (1976).

26. "Catatonia" is characterized by "plastic immobility of the limbs, stupor, negativism, and mutism" *(American Heritage Dictionary).* Literally, the term means "lower," or "downward" *(cata-),* "tone," "tonicity," or "tonus." Catatonia could thus be said to be a condition of lowered psychic tonus.

27. R. J. Lifton, *The Life of the Self,* especially pp. 43–45. See also R. D. Laing, *The Divided Self.*

28. R. J. Lifton, *op. cit.,* p. 44.

29. Otto Rank, who was one of Freud's most brilliant students, made fear of death one of two central motives in human nature (the other being fear of life). In his book *Beyond Psychology,* he proposed that throughout history, human beings have pursued immortality in various ways: through the creation of "other world" religious beliefs (the "historic" solution); through identification with heroes who conquered monsters (the "heroic" solution); through idealized love relationships (the "romantic" solution); or through the accumulation of objects (the "philistine" solution). Rank's own preferred, and hoped-for, solution was the "creative" one: achieving immortality through works of art.

30. David Bakan, *The Duality of Human Existence,* pp. 157–158. In this book, Bakan quotes from a letter Freud wrote to a friend after he discovered he had cancer: "From that time on the thought of death has not left me, and sometimes I have the impression that seven of my internal organs are fighting to have the honor of bringing my life to an end." One could argue that the awareness of death processes going on in the body is probably quite common. The crucial question to look at, considered in connection to healing transformation, is, 'What is my attitude toward these processes?' Is it fear, repugnance, avoidance; or is it acceptance, affirmation, release?

31. In part, the resistance to Freud's ideas may be explained by errors in the English translation of some of Freud's terms, as Bruno Bettelheim has recently argued in his book *Freud and Man's Soul.* The German word translated as "instinct" was *Trieb,* which would be much better rendered as "drive" or "urge." The notion of a "death instinct" has a kind of inherent implausibility that "death drive" or "death urge" do not. Apart from this semantic confusion, it would seem that the well-known fear and denial mechanisms with regard to death have played a role in the nonacceptance of Freud's ideas.

32. Freud's theory was that sadism represented a splitoff death drive that had "entered the service of the sexual function." Cruelty and violence toward others were seen as the death drive projected outward via the muscular system. The basic, original function of the death drive was, according to Freud, a natural complement to eros.

33. Sigmund Freud, *Beyond the Pleasure Principle,* p. 47.

34. An interesting elaboration and amplification of the theme of *putrefactio* is offered in a paper by Michael Flanagin, "Putrefactio: Death and Decay in the Alchemical Imagination," published in *Transcendence and Transformation: Writings from the California Institute of Integral Studies,* ed. Vern Haddick.

35. Whitall Perry, ed., *Treasury of Traditional Wisdom,* pp. 203–244.

36. For discussions of Chinese Taoist alchemy, see *The Secret of the Golden Flower,* ed. and trans. Richard Wilhelm, and *The Forge and the Crucible,* by Mircea Eliade.

37. C. G. Jung, *The Psychology of the Transference,* p. 102. It can be stated that *conjunctio* is the alchemical operation that corresponds to eros; and *mortificatio* the alchemical operation associated with thanatos.

38. See *The Spiritual Teachings of Ramana Maharshi,* with a foreword by C. G. Jung.

39. C. G. Jung, "The Psychology of the Child Archetype," in *The Archetypes and the Collective Unconscious,* p. 164. Jung continues: "In the psychology of the individual, the 'child' paves the way for a future change of personality. In the individuation process, it anticipates the figure that comes from the synthesis of conscious and unconscious elements in the personality. It is therefore a symbol which unites the opposites; a mediator, bringer of healing, that is, one who makes whole."

40. The reader is referred also to the accounts of modern shamanic journey experiences in Michael Harner's *The Way of the Shaman.*

41. The quote from Eckhart is in Raymond B. Blakney (trans.), *Meister Eckhart.* The Islamic Sufi quoted is Najm ad-din al Kubra, from "The Transformation of Man in Mystical Islam," by Fritz Meier, in *Man and Transformation,* ed. Joseph Campbell. The New Testament quote is John 3:3. A parallel passage is 1 Corinthians 15:44: "It is sown a natural body, it is raised a spiritual body. There is a natural body, and there is a spiritual body."

42. C. G. Jung, "Concerning Rebirth," in *The Archetypes and the Collective Unconscious,* p. 121. Edinger, in his writings and talks on the encounter with the Self, has emphasized, somewhat one-sidedly it seems to me, the overwhelming, shattering kinds of Self-confrontation, as symbolized in the story of Job. See his *Creation of Consciousness.*

43. The "Treatise of the Resurrection," quoted in Evelyn Underhill's *Mysticism.*

44. C. G. Jung, "The Psychology of the Child Archetype," *op. cit.,* pp. 151–181.

45. *Chuang Tsu: Inner Chapters,* trans. Gia-Fu Feng and Jane English.

CHAPTER 10   Unfolding the Tree of Our Life

1. C. G. Jung's important essay on "The Philosophical Tree," originally published in 1954, appears in *Alchemical Studies* 13. An earlier version of the present chapter was published as "The Tree as a Symbol of Self-Unfoldment," in *The American Theosophist* 69, no. 10 (fall 1981).

2. Victor Frankl, *Man's Search for Meaning,* p. 37.

3. C. G. Jung, *op. cit.,* p. 253.

4. The tree paintings of Jung's patients are presented and analyzed in the above-mentioned essay on the philosophers' tree. In psychological assessment by "projective drawing," drawings of persons, houses, trees, and animals are frequently used. There is a "House-Tree-Person" projective drawing test. In my own practice I have found it useful to have the person draw all three objects on a single sheet: interesting insights can be gained by noting the arrangement on the page and the relative sizes of the three elements. It is generally agreed that the house represents the individual's feelings about home and family; the person represents their self-image; and the tree represents their instinctual *and* spiritual nature. A very detailed and comprehensive extension of tree drawings as projective test devices is presented in a book by Karen Bolander, *Tree Drawings.*

5.   H. V. Guenther, *The Tantric View of Life,* p. 120.

6.   *Meister Eckhart,* trans. Raymond B. Blakney, p. 75.

7.   From a lecture by Paul Klee, published in 1924 under the title *On Modern Art.* Quoted in *The Tree of Life,* by Roger Cook, p. 31. This book is an excellent compendium of art and symbolism related to the theme of this chapter.

8.   H. V. Guenther, *op. cit.,* p. 119.

9.   My version of the sonnet differs slightly, both from the version by M. D. Herter Norton (*Sonnets to Orpheus,* by Rainer Maria Rilke) and that by Robert Bly, in *Selected Poems of Rainer Maria Rilke.*

10.   Mircea Eliade, *Shamanism,* chapter 4, pp. 110–144, and chapter 8, pp. 259–287.

11.   See R. Gordon Wasson, *SOMA: Divine Mushroom of Immortality,* and Peter T. Furst, *Hallucinogens and Culture.*

12.   Quoted in Roger Cook, *op. cit.,* p. 37.

13.   Mircea Eliade, *Images and Symbols,* p. 46.

14.   Erich Neumann, *The Origins and History of Consciousness,* pp. 230, 232. Additional information and interpretation concerning the Egyptian *djed* pillar can be found in Wallis Budge's *Egyptian Religion,* in *Her-Bak: Egyptian Initiate,* by Isha Schwaller de Lubicz, and in *The Time Falling Bodies Take to Light,* by William Irwin Thompson.

15.   *Ibid.,* p. 234.

16.   John G. Neihardt, *Black Elk Speaks,* p. 43.

17.   Roger Cook, *op. cit.,* p. 21. Cook quotes this passage from an essay by Hugo Rahner, "The Christian Mystery and the Pagan Mysteries," in *The Mysteries,* ed. Joseph Campbell (Eranos Yearbooks, vol. 2), where it is actually attributed to Pseudo-Chrysostom, not to Hippolytus (p. 386).

18.   In the Yggdrasil myth there are deer that eat the leaves of the world tree, and the deer-tree association is widespread in shamanism. The snake at the base of the tree and the bird at the top also form an extremely ancient image pattern, as has been shown by Marija Gimbutas' work on the Snake and Bird Goddess in the myth and iconography of Europe, going as far back as the sixth millennium B.C. (Marija Gimbutas, *The Goddesses and Gods of Old Europe*). The horse is linked with the tree-complex, both in Scandinavia (*Yggdrasil* means "steed of Odin") and in Vedic India, where Agni, the god of fire and transformation, is said to hide in the *ashwattha* tree for a year, in the form of a horse. The

horse symbolizes the power of the shamanic initiate to travel, to move through the world zones.

19. Katho Upanishad, 2.3.1.

20. Roger Cook, *op. cit.,* p. 18.

21. Persuasive reexaminations of the Bible in the light of the evidence for earlier Mother Goddess religions are offered in *When God Was a Woman,* by Merlin Stone, and in *Behind the Sex of God,* by Carol Ochs. I am indebted to Elaine Pagels for drawing my attention to the parallel between these views of *Genesis,* and certain Gnostic texts, particularly the Jewish *Life of Adam and Eve* and the *Gospel of Phillip.*

22. Genesis 3:22 (New English Bible). The symbolic equation of tree and cross in the legend of the Holy Rood is discussed in Alan Watts's *Myth and Ritual Christianity.*

23. C. G. Jung, *Psychology and Alchemy,* p. 438.

24. From the "Turba Philosophorum," in C. G. Jung, *Alchemical Studies,* p. 305.

25. Milton Klonsky, *William Blake: The Seer and His Visions,* p. 122. The title of this poem, one of Blake's *Songs of Experience,* is "The Human Abstract."

26. C. G. Jung, "The Philosophical Tree," *op. cit.* (see note 1 above). On the basis of the alchemical art, Jung concluded that for women, the tree was most often imagined as emerging out of the head, and it represented a tree of the mind; for men, the tree is more often shown emerging out the loins, a tree of generation.

27. Experiential account from the author's files; quoted with permission.

28. C. G. Jung, *Alchemical Studies,* p. 310. The tree as made of fire, which fits with the idea of the tree being related to the nervous system, is also found in the Indian traditions. See A. K. Coomaraswamy, "The Inverted Tree," in *Selected Papers of A. K. Coomaraswamy,* ed. Roger Lipsey. "The Tree is a fiery pillar as seen from below, a solar pillar as from above . . . it is a Tree of Light" (p. 387).

Bibliography

IBU 'ARABI, MUHYIDDIN.   *Journey to the Land of Power: A Sufi Manual on Retreat.* Translated by Rabia Terri Harris. New York: Inner Traditions International, 1981.

ARIETI, SILVANO.   *Creativity: The Magic Synthesis.* New York: Basic Books, 1980.

ASSAGIOLI, ROBERTO.   *Psychosynthesis.* New York: Viking Press, 1971.

ATTAR, FARID UD-DIN.   *The Conference of the Birds.* Boulder, Colo.: Shambhala, 1971.

AUGUSTINE, SAINT.   *Saint Augustine: Confessions.* Edited by R. S. Pine-Coffin. New York: Penguin Books, 1961.

AUROBINDO, SRI.   *The Life Divine.* 2 vols. Pondicherry: Sri Aurobindo Ashram, 1977.

BAHA' ULLAH.   *The Seven Valleys and the Four Valleys.* Wilmette, Ill.: Baha'i Publishing Trust, 1975.

BAKAN, DAVID.   *The Duality of Human Existence.* Chicago: Rand McNally, 1966.

BAKER, ELSWORTH.   *Man in the Trap.* New York: Macmillan, 1980.

BATESON, GREGORY.   *Mind and Nature.* New York: E. P. Dutton, 1979.

————.   *Steps Toward an Ecology of Mind.* New York: Ballantine, 1972.

BEAHRS, JOHN O.   *Unity and Multiplicity: Multilevel Consciousness of Self in Hypnosis, Psychiatric Disorder and Mental Health.* New York: Brunner/Mazel, 1982.

BENTOV, ITZHAK.   *Stalking the Wild Pendulum.* New York: E. P. Dutton, 1977.

BERNBAUM, EDWIN.   *The Way to Sambhala.* Garden City, N.Y.: Doubleday, Anchor Books, 1980.

BETTELHEIM, BRUNO.   *Freud and Man's Soul.* New York: Alfred A. Knopf, 1983.

THE *BHAGAVADGITA.*   Translated by S. Radhakrishnan. New York: Harper Torchbooks, 1973.

BINGEN, HILDEGARD VON.   *Quellen des Heils* [*Sources of Salvation*]. Salzburg: Otto Mueller Verlag, 1982.

————.   *Wisse die Wege* [*Scivias-Know the Ways*]. Salzburg: Otto Mueller Verlag, 1954.

BLAKE, WILLIAM.   *The Marriage of Heaven and Hell.* Coral Gables, Fla.: University of Miami Press, 1968.

BOEHME, JACOB. *The Forty Questions of the Soul and the Clavis.* Translated by John Sparrow. London: J. M. Watkins, 1911.

BOHM, DAVID. *Wholeness and the Implicate Order.* London: Routledge and Kegan Paul, 1980.

BOLANDER, KAREN. *Tree Drawings.* New York: Basic Books, 1977.

BOYD, JAMES W. *Satan and Mara: Christian and Buddhist Symbols of Evil.* Leiden: Brill, 1975.

BRIDGES, WILLIAM. *Transitions: Making Sense of Life's Changes.* Menlo Park, Calif.: Addison-Wesley Publishing Co., 1980.

BROWN, JOSEPH EPES, ed. *The Sacred Pipe: Black Elk's Account of the Seven Rites of the Oglala Sioux.* New York: Viking Press, 1953.

BUCKE, R. M. *Cosmic Consciousness.* New York: E. P. Dutton, 1901.

BUDGE, WALLIS. *Egyptian Religion.* New York: Bell Publishing Co., University Books, 1959.

BURR, HAROLD S. *The Fields of Life.* New York: Ballantine Books, 1972.

CAMPBELL, JOSEPH. *The Hero with a Thousand Faces.* Cleveland, Ohio: World Publishing Co., 1956.

———. *The Way of the Animal Powers.* San Francisco: Harper and Row, 1983.

CAMPBELL, JOSEPH, ed. *Man and Transformation.* Eranos Yearbooks, vol. 5; Bollingen Series, no. 30. Princeton, N.J.: Princeton University Press, 1964.

———. *The Mysteries.* Eranos Yearbooks, vol. 2; Bollingen Series, No. 30. Princeton, N.J.: Princeton University Press, 1978.

CAPPS, WALTER H., and WENDY M. WRIGHT, eds. *Silent Fire.* San Francisco: Harper and Row, 1978.

CAPRA, FRITJOF. *The Tao of Physics.* Boulder, Colo.: Shambhala, 1983. 2d ed.

———. *The Turning Point.* New York: Simon and Shuster, 1982.

CAVENDISH, RICHARD. *Visions of Heaven and Hell.* New York: Crown Publishers, 1977.

CECIL, ROBERT, ed. *The Kings Son: Readings in the Contemporary Psychologies and Contemporary Thoughts of Man.* London: Octagon Press, 1981.

CHIA, MANTAK. *Awaken Healing Energy Through the Tao.* New York: Taoist Esoteric Yoga Foundation, 1981.

CHUANG TSU. *Inner Chapters.* Translated by Gia-Fu Feng and Jane English. New York: Random House, 1974.

CIRLOT, J. E.   *A Dictionary of Symbols.* New York: Philosophical Library, 1962.

CLARK, KENNETH.   *Animals and Men: Their Relationship as Reflected in Western Art from Prehistory to the Present.* New York: William Morrow, 1977.

CODDINGTON, MARY.   *In Search of Healing Energy.* New York: Destiny Books, 1983.

COHEN, J. M., and J-F. PHIPPS.   *The Common Experience.* Los Angeles: J. P. Tarcher, 1979.

COUDERT, ALLISON.   *Alchemy.* Boulder, Colo.: Shambhala, 1980.

CONZE, EDWARD.   *Buddhist Wisdom Books.* San Francisco: Harper and Row, 1958.

COOK, ROGER.   *The Tree of Life. Image for the Cosmos.* New York: Avon Books, 1974.

COOMARASWAMY, A. K.   *Hinduism and Buddhism.* Westport, Conn.: Greenwood Press, 1971.

———.   *Selected Papers of A. K. Coomaraswamy.* Vol. 1, *Traditional Art and Symbolism.* Vol. 2, *Metaphysics.* Edited by Roger Lipsey. Bollingen Series, no. 89. Princeton, N.J.: Princeton University Press, 1977.

COOPER, J. C.   *Symbolism. The Universal Language.* Willingborough, England: Aquarian Press, 1982.

DANIELOU, ALAIN.   *Shiva and Dionysus.* New York: Inner Traditions, 1984.

DAUMAL, RENÉ.   *Mount Analogue.* New York: Viking Press, 1959.

DAVIS, MIKOL, and EARLE LANE.   *Rainbows of Life: The Promise of Kirlian Photography.* New York: Harper and Row, 1978.

DELANEY, GAYLE.   *Living Your Dreams.* San Francisco: Harper and Row, 1979.

DEMENT, WILLIAM.   *Some Must Watch While Some Must Sleep.* San Francisco: San Francisco Books, 1976.

DEUTSCH, ELIOT.   *Advaita Vedanta.* Honolulu: University of Hawaii Press, 1969.

DONAHOE, JAMES.   *Dream Reality.* Oakland: Birch Press, 1979.

DYCHTWALD, KEN.   *Bodymind.* Los Angeles: J. P. Tarcher, Inc., 1986.

ECKHART, MEISTER.   *Meister Eckhart.* Translated by Raymond B. Blakney. New York: Harper and Row, 1941.

EDINGER, EDWARD.   *The Creation of Consciousness. Jung's Myth for Modern Man.* Toronto: Inner City Books, 1984.

ELIADE, MIRCEA.   *The Forge and the Crucible.* New York: Harper and Row, 1962.

———.   *A History of Religious Ideas.* 2 vols. Chicago: University of Chicago Press, 1979, 1982.

――――. *Images and Symbols.* New York: Sheed and Ward, 1969.

――――. *Ordeal by Labyrinth.* Chicago: University of Chicago Press, 1982.

――――. *Shamanism: Archaic Techniques of Ecstasy.* Bollingen Series, no. 76. Princeton, N.J.: Princeton University Press, 1972.

――――. *The Two and the One.* New York: Harper and Row, 1965.

――――. *Yoga, Immortality, and Freedom,* Princeton, N.J.: Princeton University Press, 1969.

ELIOT, T. S. *Four Quartets.* New York: Harcourt Brace Jovanovich, 1968.

ELKIN, A. P. *Aboriginal Men of High Degree.* New York: St. Martin's Press, 2d ed., 1977.

THE EPIC OF GILGAMESH. Translated by N. K. Sandars. New York: Penguin Books, 1960.

EVANS-WENTZ, W. Y., ed. *The Tibetan Book of the Dead.* New York: Oxford University Press, 1960.

――――. *Tibetan Yoga and Secret Doctrines.* New York: Oxford University Press, 1958.

――――. *Tibet's Great Yogi Milarepa.* New York: Oxford University Press, 1928.

FADIMAN, JAMES, and DONALD KEWMAN. *Exploring Madness: Experirence, Theory, and Research.* Monterey, Calif.: Brooks/Cole, 1973.

FERGUSON, MARILYN. *The Aquarian Conspiracy.* Los Angeles: J. P. Tarcher, 1981.

FRANKL, VICTOR. *Man's Search for Meaning.* New York: Washington Square Press, 1963.

FREUD, SIGMUND. *Beyond the Pleasure Principle.* London: Hogarth Press, 1942.

FULLER, BUCKMINSTER. *Synergetics.* New York: Macmillan, 1975.

FURST, PETER T. *Hallucinogens and Culture.* San Francisco: Chandler and Sharp, 1976.

GARDNER, HOWARD. *Art, Mind, and Brain.* New York: Basic Books, 1982.

GARFIELD, PATRICIA. *Creative Dreaming.* New York: Ballantine, 1974.

GIMBUTAS, MARIJA. *The Goddesses and Gods of Old Europe.* Berkeley: University of California Press, 1982.

GODWIN, JOSCELYN. *Mystery Religions in the Ancient World.* San Francisco: Harper and Row, 1981.

GOLEMAN, DANIEL. *Varieties of Meditative Experience.* New York: E. P. Dutton, 1977.

GORDON, DAVID. *Therapeutic Metaphors.* Cupertino, Calif.: Meta Publications, 1978.

GORDON, W. J. J. *The Metaphorical Way of Learning and Knowing.* Synectics Education Systems. Cambridge, Mass.: Porpoise Books, 1966.

THE GOSPEL ACCORDING TO THOMAS. Edited by A. Guillamont. San Francisco: Harper and Row, 1984.

GOVINDA, LAMA ANAGARIKA. *Foundations of Tibetan Mysticism.* London: Rider and Co., 1960.

GRANT, JOAN. *Winged Pharaoh.* New York: Berkeley Publishing Co., 1969.

GREGORY OF NYSSA. *From Glory to Glory.* Translated and edited by Herbert Musurillo. Crestwood, N.Y.: St. Vladimir's Seminary Press, 1979.

GRODDECK, GEORG. *The Book of the It.* New York: International University Press, 1976.

GROF, STANISLAV. *Realms of the Human Unconscious.* New York: E. P. Dutton, 1976.

———. *Beyond the Brain: Birth, Death and Transcendence in Psychotherapy.* Albany, N.Y.: State University of New York Press, 1985.

GROF, STANISLAV, and CHRISTINA GROF. *Beyond Death.* New York: Thames and Hudson, 1980.

GROF, STANISLAV, and JOAN HALIFAX. *The Human Encounter with Death.* New York: E. P. Dutton, 1977.

GUENTHER, HERBERT V. *The Life and Teachings of Naropa.* New York: Oxford University Press, 1963.

———. *The Tantric View of Life.* Boulder, Colo.: Shambhala, 1972.

HADDICK, VERN, ed. *Transcendence and Transformation: Writings from the California Institute of Integral Studies.* New York: University Press of America, 1983.

HAICH, ELIZABETH. *Initiation.* Palo Alto, Calif.: The Seed Center, 1974.

HALIFAX, JOAN. *Shaman: The Wounded Healer.* New York: Crossroad Publishing Co., 1982.

HARNER, MICHAEL. *The Way of the Shaman.* San Francisco: Harper and Row, 1980.

HARTMANN, FRANZ. *Jacob Boehme: Life and Doctrines.* Blauvelt, N.Y.: Multimedia, 1929.

HENDERSON, JOSEPH. *Thresholds of Initiation.* Middletown, Conn.: Wesleyan Press, 1967.

HENDERSON, JOSEPH L., and MAUD OAKES. *The Wisdom of the Serpent: The Myths of Death, Rebirth and Resurrection.* New York: Collier Books, 1963.

HERZOG, EDGAR.   *Psyche and Death.* New York: G. P. Putnam, 1967.

HILGARD, ERNEST.   *Divided Consciousness.* New York: John Wiley & Sons, 1977.

HILLMAN, JAMES, and MARIE-LOUISE VON FRANZ.   *Lectures on Jung's Typology.* Dallas: Spring Publications, 1971.

HIXON, LEX.   *Coming Home: The Experience of Enlightenment in Sacred Tradition.* Garden City, N.Y.: Doubleday, Anchor Books, 1978.

HUXLEY, ALDOUS.   *The Doors of Perception.* San Francisco: Harper and Row, 1970.

————.   *Heaven and Hell.* San Francisco: Harper and Row, 1970.

————.   *The Perennial Philosophy.* New York: Harper and Row, 1970.

HUXLEY, FRANCIS.   *Dragon.* New York: Collier Books, 1979.

JAMES, WILLIAM.   *Varieties of Religious Experience.* New York: New American Library, 1958.

JANTSCH, ERICH, and CONRAD H. WADDINGTON, eds.   *Evolution and Consciousness: Human Systems in Transition.* Reading, Mass.: Addison-Wesley, 1976.

JOHN OF THE CROSS, SAINT   *The Poems of St. John of the Cross.* Translated by J. F. Nims. Chicago: University of Chicago Press, 1959.

JOHNSON, DON.   *Body.* Boston: Beacon Press, 1983.

————.   *The Protean Body.* New York: Harper and Row, 1977.

JOHNSON, RAYNOR.   *The Imprisoned Splendor.* New York: Harper and Row, 1954.

JUNG, C. G.   *The Collected Works.* Vol. 6, *Psychological Types.* Translated by R. F. C. Hull. Bollingen Series, no. 20. Princeton, N.J.: Princeton University Press, 1971.

————.   *The Collected Works.* Vol. 9, part 1, *The Archetypes and the Collective Unconscious.* Translated by R. F. C. Hull. Bollingen Series, no. 20. Princeton, N.J.: Princeton University Press, 1959.

————.   *The Collected Works.* Vol. 13, *Alchemical Studies.* Translated by R. F. C. Hull. Bollingen Series, no. 20. Princeton, N.J.: Princeton University Press, 1967.

————.   *The Collected Works.* Vol. 16, *The Practice of Psychotherapy.* Translated by R. F. C. Hull. Bollingen Series, no. 20. Princeton, N.J.: Princeton University Press, 1966.

————.   *The Collected Works.* Vol. 14, *Mysterium Conjunctionis.* Translated by R. F. C. Hull. Bollingen Series, no. 20. Princeton, N.J.: Princeton University Press, 1970.

————.   *The Collected Works.* Vol. 8, *The Structure and Dynamics of the Psyche.* Translated by R. F. C. Hull. Bollingen Series, no. 20. Princeton, N.J.: Princeton University Press, 1969.

————. *The Collected Works.* Vol. 12, *Psychology and Alchemy.* Translated by R. F. C. Hull. London: Routledge & Kegan Paul, 1953.

————. *The Psychology of the Transference* (from *CW,* vol. 16). Trans. R. F. C. Hull. Princeton, N.J.: Princeton University Press, 1969.

THE KABIR BOOK. Versions by Robert Bly. Boston: Beacon Press, 1971.

KARAGULLA, SHAFICA. *Breakthrough to Creativity.* Marina del Rey, Calif.: DeVorss, 1967.

KELEMAN, STANLEY. *Living Your Dying.* New York: Random House, 1976.

————. *Somatic Reality.* Berkeley, Calif.: Center Press, 1982.

KESEY, KEN. *One Flew Over the Cuckoo's Nest.* New York: Penguin, 1976.

KLONSKY, MILTON. *William Blake: The Seer and His Visions.* New York: Harmony Books, 1977.

KOESTLER, ARTHUR. *The Act of Creation.* London: Pan Books, 1964.

KRAMRISCH, STELLA. *The Presence of Siva.* Princeton, N.J.: Princeton University Press, 1981.

KRIPPNER, STANLEY, and DANIEL RUBIN, eds. *Galaxies of Life.* New York: Gordon, 1973.

KRISHNA, GOPI. *Kundalini: The Evolutionary Energy in Man.* Boulder, Colo.: Shambhala, 1971.

KRISHNAMURTI, JIDDU. *The Flame of Attention.* San Francisco: Harper and Row, 1984.

LABERGE, STEPHEN. *Lucid Dreaming.* Los Angeles: J. P. Tarcher, 1985.

LACARRIÈRE, JACQUES. *The Gnostics.* New York: E. P. Dutton, 1977.

LAING, R. D. *The Divided Self.* New York: Pantheon Books. 1969.

————. *The Politics of Experience.* New York: Ballantine, 1978.

LAKOFF, GEORGE, and MARK JOHNSON. *Metaphors We Live By.* Chicago: University of Chicago Press, 1980.

LARSEN, STEPHEN. *The Shaman's Doorway.* New York: Harper Colophon Books, 1976.

LAUF, DETLEF. *Secret Doctrines of the Tibetan Books of the Dead.* Boulder, Colo.: Shambhala, 1977.

LEARY, TIMOTHY. *Flashbacks.* Los Angeles: J. P. Tarcher, 1983.

LEARY, TIMOTHY, RALPH METZNER, and RICHARD ALPERT. *The Psychedelic Experience.* New York: University Press, 1964.

LEE, JOHN Y.   *Death and Beyond in Eastern Perspective.* New York: Gordon and Breach Science Publications, 1974.

LEVINE, STEPHEN.   *Who Dies.* Garden City, N.Y.: Doubleday, Anchor Books, 1982.

LIFTON, ROBERT.   *The Life of the Self.* New York: Simon and Schuster, 1976.

LOWEN, ALEXANDER.   *Bioenergetics.* New York: Penguin, 1976.

DE LUBICZ, ISHA SCHWALLER.   *Her-Bak: Egyptian Initiate.* New York: Inner Tradition International, 1978.

LUCE, GAY.   *Body Time.* New York: Pantheon Books, 1971.

MACLAINE, SHIRLEY.   *Out on a Limb.* New York: Bantam, 1983.

MAHARSHI, RAMANA.   *The Spiritual Teachings of Ramana Maharshi.* Foreword by C. G. Jung. Boulder, Colo.: Shambhala, 1972.

MANN, EDWARD.   *Orgone, Reich, and Eros.* New York: Simon and Schuster, 1974.

MARKLEY, O. W., et al.   *Changing Images of Man.* Edited by the Center for the Study of Social Policy–SRI International and O. W. Markley, Elmsford, N.Y.: Pergamon Press, 1981.

MEAD, G. R. S.   *The Doctrine of the Subtle Body in the Western Tradition.* Wheaton: Theosophical Publishing House, 1919.

METZNER, RALPH.   *Know Your Type: Maps of Identity.* Garden City, N.Y.: Doubleday, 1979.

———.   *Maps of Consciousness.* New York: Macmillan, Collier Books, 1971.

MILLER, ALICE.   *The Prisoners of Childhood.* New York: Basic Books, 1981. (Subsequently re-issued under the title *The Drama of the Gifted Child*)

MILTON, JOHN   *Samson Agonistes.* Edited by F. T. Prince. New York: Oxford University Press, 1957.

MISHRA, SHRI RAMAMURTI.   *Self Analysis and Self Knowledge.* Lakemont, Ga.: CSA Press, 1977.

MONROE, ROBERT.   *Journeys out of the Body.* Garden City, N.Y.: Doubleday, 1977.

MOODY, RAYMOND A.   *Life after Death.* Atlanta: Mockingbird Books, 1975.

MUKERJI, DHAN GOPAL.   *The Face of Silence.* London: Servire Publications, 1973.

MURPHY, MICHAEL, and RHEA WHITE.   *The Psychic Side of Sports.* Reading, Mass.: Addison-Wesley Publishing Co., 1978.

MURRAY, HENRY A.   *Endeavors in Psychology.* Edited by Edwin S. Shneidman. New York: Harper and Row, 1981.

MURTHY, T. S. ANANTHA. *Life and Teachings of Sri Sai Baba of Shirdi.* Bangalore, India: T. S. Anantha Murthy, 1976.

NEIHARDT, JOHN. *Black Elk Speaks.* Lincoln: University of Nebraska Press, 1961.

NEUMANN, ERICH. *The Origins and History of Consciousness.* Bollingen Series 42. Princeton N.J.: Princeton University Press, 1973.

THE NEW ENGLISH BIBLE. New York: Oxford University Press, 1961.

NICHOLSON, R. A. *The Mystics of Islam.* London: Routledge and Kegan Paul, 1975.

NIKHILANANDA, SWAMI. *Man in Search of Immortality.* New York: Ramakrishna-Vivekananda Center, 1968.

NORMAN, DOROTHY, ed. *The Hero: Myth/Image/Symbol.* New York: World Publishers, 1969.

OCHS, CAROL. *Behind the Sex of God: Toward a New Consciousness Transcending Matriarchy and Patriarchy.* Boston: Beacon Press, 1977.

O'FLAHERTY, WENDY. *Asceticism and Eroticism in the Mythology of Siva.* New York: Oxford University Press, 1973.

ORANGE, A. R. *On Love.* New York: Samuel Weiser, 1974.

OSIS, KARLIS. *Deathbed Observations by Physicians and Nurses.* New York: Parapsychology Foundation, 1961.

OTTO, WALTER. *Dionysus: Myth and Cult.* Translated by Robert B. Palmer. Bloomington: Indiana University Press, 1965.

OUSPENSKY, P. D. *In Search of the Miraculous.* New York: Harcourt, Brace & World, 1949.

PAGELS, ELAINE. *The Gnostic Gospels.* New York: Random House, 1979.

PARTRIDGE, ERIC. *Origins. A Short Etymological Dictionary of Modern English.* New York: Macmillan, 1958.

PELLETIER, KENNETH. *Mind as Healer, Mind as Slayer.* New York: Delta, 1977.

PERERA, SYLVIA BRINTON. *Descent to the Goddess.* Toronto: Inner City Books, 1981.

PLATO. *The Republic.* Edited by James Allen. London: Cambridge University Press, 1909.

POPUL VUH. Translated by Dennis Tedlock. New York: Simon & Schuster, 1985.

PREM, SRI KRISHNA. *The Yoga of the Bhagavat Gita.* London: Stuart and Watkins, 1969.

PRESTERA, HECTOR, and RON KURTZ. *The Body Reveals.* San Francisco: Harper and Row, 1976.

THE PRINCIPAL UPANISHADS. Edited and translated by S. Radhakrishnan. London: George Allen and Unwin, 1974.

PSYCHIATRIC DICTIONARY. Edited by Robert J. Campbell. 5th ed. New York: Oxford University Press, 1981.

RAMAKRISHNA, SRI. *The Gospel of Sri Ramakrishna.* Translated by Swami Nikhilananda. New York: Ramakrishna-Vivekananda Center, 1942.

RANK, OTTO. *Beyond Psychology.* New York: Dover Publications, 1958.

RAWSON, PHILLIP, and LASZLO LEGEZA. *Tao: An Eastern Philosophy of Time and Change.* New York: Bounty Books, 1974.

REICH, WILHELM. *Character Analysis.* Translated by Theodore P. Wolfe. New York: Farrar, Straus and Giroux, 1949.

———. *The Function of the Orgasm.* New York: Simon and Schuster, 1974.

RIG VEDA. Translated by Wendy Doniger O'Flaherty. New York: Penguin Books, 1981.

RILKE, RAINER MARIA. *Selected Poems of Rainer Maria Rilke.* Translated by Robert Bly. New York: Harper and Row, 1981.

———. *Sonnets to Orpheus.* Translated by M. D. Herter Norton. New York: W. W. Norton and Co., 1942.

RING, KENNETH. *Heading Toward Omega.* New York: William Morrow, 1984.

———. *Life at Death.* New York: Coward, McCann and Geoghegan, 1980.

ROBERTS, JANE. *The Nature of Personal Reality: A Seth Book.* Englewood Cliffs, N. J.: Prentice-Hall, 1974.

———. *The Nature of the Psyche: Its Human Expression.* Englewood Cliffs, N.J.: Prentice-Hall, 1979.

ROBINSON, JAMES M. *The Nag Hammadi Library.* San Francisco: Harper and Row, 1977.

RUMI: POET AND MYSTIC. Translated by Reynold A. Nicholson. London: Unwin Paperbacks, 1978.

RUSSELL, PETER. *The Global Brain.* Los Angeles: J. P. Tarcher, 1982.

RUSSELL, WALTER. *The Secret of Light.* New York: W. Russell, 1947.

SANNELLA, LEE. *Kundalini: Psychosis or Transcendence.* San Francisco: H. S. Dakin Co., 1976.

SATPREM. *The Mind of the Cells.* New York: Institute for Evolutionary Research, 1982.

————. *Sri Aurobindo, or the Adventure of Consciousness.* San Francisco: Harper and Row, 1968.

SCHACHT, RICHARD. *Alienation.* Garden City, N.Y.: Doubleday, Anchor Books, 1970.

THE SECRET OF THE GOLDEN FLOWER. Edited and translated by Richard Wilhelm. New York: Harcourt, Brace and World, 1931.

SENGSTAN. *Hsin Hsin Ming.* Translated by Richard B. Clarke, Buffalo: White Pine Press, 1984.

STANDARD DICTIONARY OF FOLKLORE, MYTHOLOGY, AND LEGEND. Edited by Maria Leach. New York: Funk and Wagnall, 1972.

STONE, MERLIN. *When God Was a Woman.* New York: Harcourt Brace and Jovanovich, 1976.

SUZUKI, SHUNRYU. *Zen Mind, Beginner's Mind.* Tokyo: Weatherhill, 1970.

SWEDENBORG, E. *Heaven and Hell.* Translated by Sadataro Suzuki. London: Swedenborg Society, 1908.

TAO TE CHING. Translated and introduced by D. C. Law. New York: Penguin Books, 1963.

TART, CHARLES, ed. *Altered States of Consciousness.* New York: John Wiley and Sons, 1969.

————. *Psi. Scientific Studies of the Psychic Realm.* New York: E. P. Dutton, 1977.

————. *Transpersonal Psychologies.* New York: Harper and Row, 1975.

TAYLOR, C. W., and F. BARRON, eds. *Scientific Creativity: Its Recognition and Development.* New York: Wiley, 1966.

TEILHARD DE CHARDIN, PIERRE. *The Phenomenon of Man.* San Francisco: Harper and Row, 1965.

THOMAS, LEWIS. *Late Night Thoughts on Listening to Mahler's Ninth Symphony.* New York: The Viking Press, 1980.

————. *The Lives of a Cell.* New York: Penguin Books, 1974.

THOMPSON, WILLIAM IRWIN. *The Time Falling Bodies Take to Light.* New York: St. Martin's Press, 1981.

THE TIBETAN BOOK OF THE DEAD. Translated by Francesca Freemantle and Chogyam Trungpa. Boulder, Colo.: Shambhala, 1975.

TOFFLER, ALVIN. *The Third Wave.* New York: Bantam, 1981.

TOMPKINS, PETER, and CHRISTOPHER BIRD. *The Secret Life of Plants.* New York: Harper & Row, 1973.

TREASURY OF TRADITIONAL WISDOM. Edited by Whitall Perry. New York: Simon and Schuster, 1971.

TRISMOSIN, SOLOMON. *Splendor Solis.* Translated by Jocelyn Godwin. Edinburgh: Magnum Opus Hermetic Sourceworks, 1981.

TYBERG, JUDITH M. *The Language of the Gods.* Los Angeles: East-West Cultural Center, 1970.

UNDERHILL, EVELYN. *Mysticism.* New York: New American Library, 1955.

WAITE, A. E., ed. *The Hermetic Museum.* 2 vols. 1893. Reprint. New York: Samuel Weiser, 1983.

WASSON, R. GORDON. *Soma: Divine Mushroom of Immortality.* New York: Harcourt Brace Jovanovich, n.d.

WASSON, R. GORDON, CARL A. P. RUCK, and ALBERT HOFMANN. *The Road to Eleusis: Unveiling the Secret of the Mysteries.* New York: Harcourt Brace Jovanovich, 1978.

WATKINS, MARY. *Waking Dreams.* New York: Harper & Row, 1976.

WATTS, ALAN. *Myth and Ritual in Christianity.* Boston: Beacon Press, 1968.

WHEELWRIGHT, PHILLIP. *Metaphor and Reality.* Bloomington: Indiana University Press, 1962.

WHITE, JOHN, ed. *Kundalini, Evolution, and Enlightenment.* Garden City, N.Y.: Doubleday, Anchor Books, 1979.

WHITE, JOHN, and STANLEY KRIPPNER, eds. *Future Science.* Garden City, N.Y.: Doubleday, 1973.

WHITMAN, WALT. *Leaves of Grass.* New York: Random House, 1892.

WILBER, KEN. *The Atman Project.* Wheaton, Ill.: Theosophical Publishing House, 1980.

———. *Eye to Eye.* Garden City, N.Y.: Doubleday, Anchor Books, 1983.

———. *A Sociable God.* New York: McGraw-Hill, 1983.

WOLKSTEIN, DIANE, and SAMUEL NOAH KRAMER. *Inanna: Queen of Heaven and Earth.* New York: Harper and Row, 1983.

YOGANANDA, PARAMAHANSA. *Autobiography of a Yogi.* Los Angeles: Self-Realization Fellowship, 1973.

YOUNG, ARTHUR. *The Reflexive Universe.* New York: Seymour Lawrence, 1976.

ZEN FLESH, ZEN BONES. Compiled by Paul Reps. Garden City, N.Y.: Anchor Books, Doubleday, & Co., n.d.

Index

About the Author

Ralph Metzner was born in Germany and educated in England. He obtained a B.A. in philosophy and psychology at Oxford University, and a Ph.D. in clinical psychology at Harvard University, where he also did post-doctoral research in psychopharmacology. He worked with Timothy Leary and Richard Alpert on psychedelic research, edited the *Psychedelic Review*, and co-authored *The Psychedelic Experience*. Subsequently he has practiced psychotherapy in a variety of clinical settings and pursued research in states of consciousness and their relationship to personal growth. He became a student of Agni Yoga and a teacher of meditation in the School of Actualism founded by Russell Schofield. He has also written *Maps of Consciousness,* and *Know Your Type.* Currently, he is professor of East-West psychology as well as Academic Dean at the California Institute of Integral Studies in San Francisco, where he is also in private practice as a psychotherapist.